RELIGION, POLITICS, AND PEACE

BOSTON UNIVERSITY STUDIES IN
PHILOSOPHY AND RELIGION
General Editor: Leroy S. Rouner

Volume Twenty

Volume One
Myth, Symbol, and Reality

Volume Two
Transcendence and the Sacred

Volume Three
Meaning, Truth, and God

Volume Four
Foundations of Ethics

Volume Five
Religious Pluralism

Volume Six
On Nature

Volume Seven
Knowing Religiously

Volume Eight
*Civil Religion and Political
Theology*

Volume Nine
*Human Rights and the World's
Religions*

Volume Ten
On Freedom

Volume Eleven
Celebrating Peace

Volume Twelve
On Community

Volume Thirteen
Selves, People, and Persons

Volume Fourteen
Can Virtue Be Taught?

Volume Fifteen
The Changing Face of Friendship

Volume Sixteen
In Pursuit of Happiness

Volume Seventeen
The Longing for Home

Volume Eighteen
Is There a Human Nature?

Volume Nineteen
Loneliness

Religion, Politics, and Peace

Edited by
Leroy S. Rouner

UNIVERSITY OF NOTRE DAME PRESS
Notre Dame, Indiana

"For the Children," by Gary Snyder, from *Turtle Island*. Copyright © 1974
by Gary Snyder. Reprinted by permission of New Directions Publishing Corp.

Paperback edition, ISBN 0-268-01665-8

Library of Congress Cataloging-in-Publication Data

Religion, politics, and peace / edited by Leroy S. Rouner.
     p.   cm. — (Boston University studies in philosophy and
religion ; vol. 20)
    Includes bibliographical references and index.
    ISBN 0-268-01664-X (alk. paper)
    1. Religion and politics.   2. Peace—Religious aspects.
I. Rouner, Leroy S.   II. Series.
  BL65.P7R437   1999
  291.1'77—dc21   98-48108

Manufactured in the United States of America

For Jeanne Knoerle, Sister of Providence;

Our favorite nun; our dear friend; and our constant help in time of fiscal trouble. More than once she has persuaded her colleagues at the Lilly Endowment to suppport us.

China scholar; College President; Foundation Executive; she has followed her calling in Christ in various ways, and we have been the beneficiaries of her wisdom, her faithfulness, and her care.

Contents

Preface   ix

Acknowledgments   xi

Contributors   xiii

Introduction • *Leroy S. Rouner*   1

PART I: RELIGIOUS FAITH AND POLITICAL RECONCILIATION

Political Reconciliation • *Jürgen Moltmann*   17

Politics and Forgiveness • *Jean Bethke Elshtain*   32

The Urgency of Hope • *Elie Wiesel*   48

PART II: THE POLITICS OF PLURALISM

The Voice of Religion in Political Discourse
 • *Bhikhu Parekh*   63

Peace as Politics • *Stephen Darwall*   85

Common Ground and Defensible Difference
 • *John Clayton*   104

Religious Strife and the Culture Wars
 • *Ronald F. Thiemann*   128

PART III: WORLD RELIGIONS AND PEACE

Gandhi: The Fusion of Religion and Politics   •   *John Hick*   145

Can We Keep Peace with Nature?   •   *Stephanie Kaza*   165

Religions and the Culture of Peace   •   *Raimon Panikkar*   185

Author Index   205

Subject Index   207

Preface

Boston University Studies in Philosophy and Religion is a joint project of the Boston University Institute for Philosophy and Religion and the University of Notre Dame Press. The essays in each annual volume are edited from the previous year's lecture program and invited papers of the Boston University Institute. The Director of the Institute, who is also the General Editor of these Studies, chooses a theme and invites participants to lecture at Boston University in the course of the academic year. The Editor then selects and edits the essays to be included in the volume. Dr. Barbara Darling-Smith, Assistant Director of the Institute, regularly copy edits the essays. In preparation is Volume 21, *Civility*.

The Boston University Institute for Philosophy and Religion was begun informally in 1970 under the leadership of Professor Peter Bertocci of the Department of Philosophy, with the cooperation of Dean Walter Muelder of the School of Theology, Professor James Purvis, Chair of the Department of Religion, and Professor Marx Wartofsky, Chair of the Department of Philosophy. Professor Bertocci was concerned to institutionalize one of the most creative features of Boston personalism, its interdisciplinary approach to fundamental issues of human life. When Professor Leroy S. Rouner became Director in 1975, and the Institute became a formal part of the Boston University Graduate School, every effort was made to continue that vision of an ecumenical and interdisciplinary forum.

Within the University the Institute is committed to open interchange on fundamental issues in philosophy and religious study which transcend the narrow specializations of academic curricula. We seek to counter those trends in higher education which emphasize technical expertise in a "multi-versity" and gradually transform undergraduate liberal arts education into preprofessional training.

Our programs are open to the general public and are often broadcast on WBUR-FM, Boston University's National Public Radio station. Outside the University we seek to recover the public tradition of philosophical discourse which was a lively part of American intellectual life in the early years of this century before the professionalization of both philosophy and religious reflection made these two disciplines virtually unavailable even to an educated public. We note, for example, that much of William James's work was presented originally as public lectures, and we are grateful to James's present-day successors for the significant public papers which we have been honored to publish. This commitment to a public tradition in American intellectual life has important stylistic implications. At a time when too much academic writing is incomprehensible, or irrelevant, or both, our goal is to present readable essays by acknowledged authorities on critical human issues.

Acknowledgments

We pay our authors very little and make outrageous demands, so I am, once again, enormously grateful that such a distinguished group of philosophers and theologians would be willing to participate in our program. Our deep appreciation to them all. A special word for Elie Wiesel, who lectures for us each year. This is uncommon generosity from an uncommon man. I am glad for this occasion to salute him as a gracious man of letters and a valued colleague; thank him for his friendship; and bless him on his way as one of the true prophets of our time.

Barbara Darling-Smith is the Institute's Assistant Director and, truth to tell, the one who makes it all work. She is the editor of *Can Virtue Be Taught?* and has been copy editor of nineteen volumes in this series. Without her the whole operation would come crashing down. In a world where so many have varied skills, it is almost impossible to find someone who is genuinely indispensable. Trust me; Barbara is one.

But she is not the only one who makes this series work. Ann Rice at the University of Notre Dame Press is the person who guides the manuscript through the publication process. We are always calling her at the last minute with our publication problems and she is always friendly, unfazed, and precise. And overseeing the whole process is our friend Jim Langford, Director of the University of Notre Dame Press—our colleague and friend, and one of our lecturers in an earlier volume—who, some twenty years ago, decided to take a chance on us, and thus made this series possible.

Our thanks also to the organizers of the UNESCO seminar in Barcelona, Spain, for permission to reprint an edited version of Raimon Panikkar's paper for the UNESCO Seminar in Barcelona (April 13–18, 1992).

    Funding for this year's program comes from the Lilly Endowment, Inc., the Stratford Foundation, the Graduate School of Arts and Sciences at Boston University, and several generous friends. The Institute is particularly grateful to Chris Reaske and Linda Jenkins in Boston University's Development Office for their fundraising efforts on our behalf.

Contributors

JOHN CLAYTON is Professor of Religion, Chair of the Department of Religion, and Director of the Division of Religious and Theological Studies at Boston University. He came to Boston University in 1997 from the University of Lancaster, where he served as Professor of Religious Studies and the Head of the Department of Religious Studies. He is author, editor, or coeditor of a number of books, among them *The Concept of Correlation*; *Ernst Troelsch and the Future of Theology*; *Christ, Faith, and History*; and *Religionsphilosophische Schriften/Writings in the Philosophy of Religion*, vol. 4 of *Paul Tillich: Hauptwerke/Main Writings*. He studied at Hardin-Simmons University, Baylor University, Southern Seminary, and Emmanuel College at the University of Cambridge, where he received the Ph.D.

STEPHEN DARWALL's honors include the James B. and Grace J. Nelson Faculty Fellowship in Philosophy; the University of Michigan College of Literature, Science, and the Arts Excellence in Research Award; the University of Michigan Humanities Award; the Julia Jean Lockwood Award for excellence in research; a National Endowment for the Humanities Fellowship for University Teachers, and a number of others. His Ph.D is from the University of Pittsburgh, and he received the B.A. from Yale University *magna cum laude*. Professor of Philosophy at the University of Michigan, he is author of *Philosophical Ethics: An Historical and Contemporary Introduction*; *The British Moralists and the Internal 'Ought': 1640–1740*; and *Impartial Reason*; and he has edited several books as well.

JEAN BETHKE ELSHTAIN studied at Colorado State University before going on to receive a Ph.D. from Brandeis University.

She has taught at the University of Massachusetts/Amherst and Vanderbilt University and is now the Laura Spelman Rockefeller Professor of Social and Political Ethics at the University of Chicago. She is the author of books too numerous to mention— among them *Public Man, Private Woman: Women in Social and Political Thought*, which was selected by *Choice* as one of the top academic books of 1981–82; *Women and War*, which has been translated into Italian and Japanese; *Democracy on Trial*, which was named a *New York Times* notable book; and *Augustine and the Limits of Politics*, which *The Christian Century* listed as one of the top five religion books of 1996.

JOHN HICK was born in England and educated at Edinburgh University, Oxford University, and Westminster Theological College, Cambridge University. He has held professorships and named chairs at various universities, including Cornell University, Princeton Theological Seminary, Cambridge University, Birmingham University, and the Claremont Graduate School. Books he has written include *Faith and Knowledge*, *Evil and the God of Love*, *An Interpretation of Religion*, *The Metaphor of God Incarnate*, *Problems of Religious Pluralism*, and many others. *Classical and Contemporary Readings in the Philosophy of Religion*, *The Existence of God*, *Gandhi's Significance for Today*, *The Myth of Christian Uniqueness*, and *Three Faiths, One God* are a few of the influential books he has edited.

STEPHANIE KAZA is Associate Professor of Environmental Studies at the University of Vermont. Before going to Vermont she taught at the University of California at Santa Cruz, the University of California at Berkeley, and the Graduate Theological Union in Berkeley. A long-time student of Zen Buddhism, practicing at Green Gulch Zen Center in California, she served for seven years as chair of the board of directors for the Buddhist Peace Fellowship. She has written *The Attentive Heart* and her book in progress is *Green Buddha Walking*. Her training is in Biology (B.A. from Oberlin College, Ph.D. from the University of California at Santa Cruz), Education (M.A. from Stanford University), and Feminist Theory/Theology and Ethics (M.Div from Starr King School for the Ministry).

JÜRGEN MOLTMANN is Professor of Systematic Theology *Emeritus* at the University of Tübingen, and he has also been Woodruff Visiting Professor at Emory University. His first degree, doctorate, and habilitation degree are all from the University of Göttingen. His 1967 *Theology of Hope* has become one of the most influential theological works of the post-World War II period. He is also well known for his theology of the cross developed in *The Crucified God* and for his articulations of political theology. His extensive bibliography also includes *The Church in the Power of the Spirit*, *The Future of Creation*, *Experiences of God*, *The Trinity and the Kingdom*, and *God in Creation*. Among his many honors are the Elba Literary Prize and the Gifford Lectureship.

RAIMON PANIKKAR has lived and studied in Spain, Germany, Italy, and India. He holds a Ph.D. and a D.Sc. from the University of Madrid, and a Th.D. from the Lateran University (Rome). He was on the Religious Studies faculty of the University of California at Santa Barbara for a number of years. The author of many books in a number of languages—among them *La India: Gente, Cultura, Creencias*; *Religion and Religions*; *The Unknown Christ of Hinduism*; *Kerygma und Indien: Zur heilsgeschicten Problematik der christlichen Begegung mit Indien*; *The Vedic Experience*; and *Blessed Simplicity: The Monk as Universal Archetype*—he now serves at the Center for Intercultural Studies in Barcelona.

BHIKHU PAREKH obtained his Ph.D. from the London School of Economics and is Professor of Political Theory at the University of Hull. For many years he was Deputy Chair of the British Commission for Racial Equality. He was also Vice Chancellor of the University of Baroda, India, from 1981–1984. He has taught at a number of universities, including, most recently, serving as Visiting Professor of Government at Harvard University. His books include *Hannah Arendt and the Search for a New Political Philosophy*, *Karl Marx's Theory of Ideology*, *Gandhi's Political Philosophy*, and (as editor) *Bentham's Political Thought*. He was elected the British Asian of the year in 1992.

LEROY S. ROUNER taught at the United Theological College, Bangalore, India (1961–1966) before becoming Professor of Philosophy, Religion, and Philosophical Theology and Director of the Institute for Philosophy and Religion at Boston University. He studied at Harvard College, Union Theological Seminary (New York), and Columbia University. He has edited seventeen volumes in the Boston University Studies in Philosophy and Religion series and contributed to many of them. He has also edited *Philosophy, Religion, and the Coming World Civilization: Essays in Honor of William Ernest Hocking*. He is the author of *Within Human Experience: The Philosophy of William Ernest Hocking; The Long Way Home* (a memoir); and *To Be at Home: Christianity, Civil Religion, and World Community*.

RONALD F. THIEMANN is John Lord O'Brian Professor of Divinity and Dean of the Harvard Divinity School. He has also taught at Haverford College, Villanova University, Lutheran Theological Seminary (Philadelphia), and Yale University. His M.A., M.Phil., and Ph.D. are all from Yale University, and his earlier studies were at Concordia College (Illinois), Concordia Senior College (Indiana), Concordia Seminary (Missouri), and Eberhard-Karls Universität (Tübingen). Recipient of a number of awards and fellowships—including the Martin Foss Award, the Mellon Humanities Fellowship, the Christian and Mary Lindback Foundation Award for Distinguished Teaching, the Whitehead Research Grant—he has written *Religion in American Public Life, Toward an American Public Theology: The Church in a Pluralistic Culture*, and *Revelation and Theology: The Gospel as Narrated Promise*.

ELIE WIESEL is the Andrew W. Mellon Professor in the Humanities at Boston University. He has written more than thirty-five books, including novels, essays, stories, portraits, legends, a cantata, plays, and memoirs. His numerous awards include the Prix Medicis for *Beggar in Jerusalem*, the Prix Livre Inter for *The Testament*, and the Grand Prize for Literature from the City of Paris for *The Fifth Son*. Among his other books are *Night, The Town Beyond the Wall, The Gates of the Forest, Souls on*

Fire, and *Four Hasidic Masters*. He lectures internationally and travels widely on behalf of various humanitarian causes. He has been awarded the Congressional Gold Medal of Achievement, the Medal of Liberty Award, and the 1986 Nobel Prize for Peace.

Introduction

LEROY S. ROUNER

AMERICAN POLITICAL LIFE has long honored the separation of church and state as the best way to protect religion from control by the state, and the state from control by religion. The brief early flirtation with theocracy in the Massachusetts Bay Colony was a healthy inoculation against further invasions of the theocratic virus in the American body politic. At the same time, however, religion has been a critical resource for the moral foundations without which the state crumbles. George Washington made this point in his "Farewell Address" in 1796:

> Of all the dispositions and habits which lead to political prosperity, religion and morality are indispensable supports. . . . Let it simply be asked where is the security for property, for reputation, for life, if the sense of religious obligation desert the oaths, which are the instrument of investigation in Courts of Justice.[1]

Washington had more to say on the topic, but the point need not be labored since the significance of religion for American political and economic life is everywhere evident. The Declaration of Independence appeals to God as insuring the rights of free individuals; the sworn oath of office at presidential inaugurations is done on the Bible; God is inevitably invoked on those two great festival days of American civil religion, Memorial Day and the Fourth of July. And, perhaps most tellingly for a free-enterprise nation zealous for endless economic betterment, our legal tender—from the lowly penny to the exalted hundred dollar bill—proudly announces, "In God We Trust."

From time to time, however, well-organized and lavishly funded religious groups try to impose their own political agenda on the larger community, as they have occasionally in the United States. In such

1

situations religion becomes a political mischief-maker. And when religious communities become a state theocracy, as they have in Iran and elsewhere, then the influence of religion becomes downright demonic.

This same paradox is reflected in the relation between religion and peace. Religion has probably been the single most significant cause of warfare in human history and, at the same time, the single most significant force for peace. The passion for a single Ultimate Truth which authorizes the slaughter of infidels is also, simultaneously, a passion to feed the hungry and care for the afflicted, with "leaves for the healing of the nations." The essays which follow will not untangle this paradox, even though they recognize it. For the most part, they are concerned to explore ways in which religion has both enhanced political life and served the cause of peace.

Spurred on by Stephen Carter's influential study of *The Culture of Disbelief*, there has been a growing suspicion among thoughtful people of various political persuasions that the doctrine of church-state separation has too often been used to trivialize religion in society and marginalize it in politics. Our authors, for the most part, follow Carter's lead in arguing that religion has a valid voice in the political process and sometimes even a healing role for the body politic.

Part One deals with "Religious Faith and Political Reconciliation." This section includes reflections on the personal experience of the authors. Theology and philosophy are always done in the context of one's life, and that context is an important part of the meaning of one's subsequent point of view. In urging this view on its authors the Institute has been swimming upstream against the main current of academic convention. The academy has regularly been embarrassed and suspicious of reflections lacking in "objectivity." To be sure, dangers abound when analytical thinkers become subjective, and it is not always easy to find a graceful blend of the personal and the theoretical. When successful, however, theoretical reflection gains compelling power, and personal experience finds a wider meaning.

In the background of this first section is an issue which Reinhold Niebuhr stated some years ago in *Moral Man and Immoral Society*. Niebuhr was a "Christian realist," a chastened liberal, persuaded that liberalism had been wrong in its optimistic expectation of human history and its positive evaluation of human nature. His liberalism was evident in his view that individuals were capable of a high level of morality. His chastening was evident in his view that large groups were not. The problem was the interactions among love, power, and justice. Individuals, he argued, can sometimes be moral and embody an ethic of love. But nations must be concerned with power, being primarily responsible to their own self-interest, so they can never be moral in the same way that individuals can. Nations can hope to be just, but not loving. Hence forgiveness and spiritual reconciliation—both acts of love—would be possible among individuals, in Niebuhr's view, but not among nations. Our first two essays, by Jürgen Moltmann and Jean Bethke Elshtain, challenge that view. And Elie Wiesel's reflections on the urgency of hope indirectly support them.

Moltmann was drafted into the German army in 1944, engaged in the battle for Arnhem, was taken prisoner by the English in 1945, and was a prisoner of war in England until his repatriation in 1948. In 1947 he and other POWs were invited to the first postwar, worldwide conference of the Student Christian Movement. They went "in fear and trembling," under guard, wearing either their old uniforms or their prisoners' jackets. "What were we to say to the reproaches of responsibility for German war crimes and the mass murder of Jews in the concentration camps? But we weren't confronted with reproaches at all. We were accepted and welcomed as 'brothers in Christ', and were permitted to eat and drink, sing and pray, together with Christian students from all over the world. During those nights my eyes often filled with tears."

Moltmann reports that this and subsequent experiences of acceptance were liberating for him and were the source of genuine reconciliation with English and Dutch students who had suffered much at the hands of the German army. He contrasts this experience with the "incomplete de-Nazification" in Germany after 1945. The United Protestant Church courageously published the Stuttgart Confession of Guilt. Although Moltmann finds that confession "pretty weak," it was nonetheless a bombshell which aroused much controversy with former German army officers who argued angrily that they were only "doing their duty." Meanwhile old Nazis were finding their way back into the government under Adenauer's Christian Democratic Party in "a kind of painless, unrepentant, bogus 'reeducation' of the old Nazis into new democrats."

Moltmann is persuaded, nevertheless, that the church has a healing discipline to offer to the political community. It is taken from the ancient penitential ritual of the church and involves three steps. The first is personal confession: "acceptance of the truth of what happened, the recognition of guilt which can never be made good, and private or public acknowledgment of this past as one's own." The second is "contrition of the heart," involving inward grief and a change of attitude. The third is acts of amendment which will help restore the social and political values which have been destroyed.

Jean Bethke Elshtain shares Moltmann's concern for reconciliation in her essay on "Politics and Forgiveness." She agrees with him that the theological category of "forgiveness" can and must be political. Her essay makes it clear that this position is not a revival of the old liberal optimism about the essential goodness of human nature, any more than it was for Moltmann. This is a new "Christian Realism." Politics demands a new beginning after the modern horrors of holocaust, genocide, and apartheid. Realistically, only genuine forgiveness can provide that. Her reflections come largely from her recent visit to South Africa and her interviews with members of the Truth and Reconciliation Commission.

She begins with a criticism of the presently popular "confessions" of daytime television talk shows, which she finds "tawdry" and "shameless." And in the political process, whenever she encounters the *mantras* of "let's put this thing behind us," or "let's achieve closure," she suspects "contrition chic"—"a bargain basement way to gain publicity, sympathy, and even absolution by trafficking in one's status as victim or victimizer." This, she says flatly, is bogus. For an authentic view of the matter she turns to Hannah Arendt's statement in *The Human Condition* that Jesus of Nazareth's greatest contribution to politics was the idea of forgiveness.

Moltmann's contribution to the politics of forgiveness was a recapitulation of an ancient Christian theological ritual of penitence. Elshtain's contribution is philosophical, the conception of *"political restorative justice,* a form of political forgiveness concerned with justice. This means that it is neither cheap forgiveness nor the 'dominant Western mode of retributive or punitive justice.'" It does involve a certain "forgetting," as an inevitable part of genuine forgiveness. But this happens only when the victimizer has publicly acknowledged what he or she did. "Those who violated human rights in a gross way are being denied the status of martyrs to the old order. Nor will they be maintained in prison as a symbol of the past and a burden on tax-payers. Instead, they must face a very new community that has full knowledge of what they did—when, where and how."

We conclude this section with Elie Wiesel's reflections on "The Urgency of Hope." He notes that "what is missing in today's society . . . is a message that it is not too late. That the train is not running to the abyss. That catastrophe can be averted. That hope is possible. That it has a future." This is his bond with Moltmann, whose *The Theology of Hope* came directly from his experiences as a prisoner of war. But Wiesel, too, is a realist. He recalls the hope which socialism brought to his generation before it turned into Communism and eventually destroyed the hope which it had so carefully nurtured. Wiesel's paradox is as personal as Moltmann's and Elshtain's. "That hope can be an obstacle to hope and even to survival; that it could become a source of peril and a trap laid by Death, has become clear to my generation. . . . Many communities were wiped out in Eastern Europe because they had hoped that the enemy would not dare to implement his threats, that the civilized free world would stop him, that human beings would always remain human, that God would keep His pledge and observe the terms of His covenant with His children."

It did not happen. And what can he say of hope now? "I have often wondered: why haven't we given back the Torah to the Almighty . . .?" But he has an autobiographical response to his own question. "Strangely and paradoxically enough, those of us who awoke in 1945 and realized that we were still alive, were carried by a powerful hope that must seem bizarre today. We were convinced fifty-four-odd years ago that something must now happen to the world, that so much pain, so much suffering, so much anguish would make a difference in History, and provoke a change, a mutation in the human condition, in the human self-image."

This, too, has not happened. But he once commented, almost wryly: "Some things that happened are not true; and some things are true that never happened." He is still a realist. "If anyone had told us then that, in our lifetime, there would be vicious, ugly, morally repugnant people who would have the gall to deny our past and publicly declare that our testimony is false and our victimhood invented, we would have considered such talk as unreasonable, implausible, and rather silly. But I belong to a generation that considers despair a question, not an answer." And he adds that "no hope is as powerful as a wounded hope."

Our second section deals with "The Politics of Pluralism." A major issue here is that *religion* in America no longer means that related family of faiths which Americans used to call "the Judaeo-Christian tradition," and which was, in fact, a Protestant era. Today America constitutes a more radical pluralism which includes Buddhists of several persuasions, Muslims in plenty, more and more Hindus, native American religions, and numerous devotees of various African faiths.

We begin with Bhikhu Parekh's essay on "The Role of Religion in Political Life." Parekh stands with Stephen Carter in the view that both law and politics have recently trivialized the role of religion. His argument is that we need the voice of religion if our political discourse is to avoid superficiality and become effective. While Parekh's background is Hindu, and Niebuhr was a Christian, they have a bond in that both are "chastened liberals." For Niebuhr, the target was liberal optimism about human nature and the liberal hope for human history. Parekh, on the other hand, is a critic of liberal individualism.

While not a "communitarian" in the sense which Alasdair MacIntyre has described in his *After Virtue* and *Whose Justice? Which Rationality?* Parekh is nevertheless a steady critic of liberal individualism, and he begins with an analysis of those liberal fears which would seem to disqualify religion from a role in politics: religion is concerned with otherworldly matters; it speaks of absolutes and arouses deep emotions, whereas liberal politics is based in rational discourse; and religion tends to be intolerant and aggressive in supporting its distinctive notion of the good life. But liberalism's objections to these religious characteristics have been ineffective, and a high proportion of the population in Britain and Europe still claim to believe in God. So religion still remains an important force in people's lives.

Parekh concludes that religion *cannot* be excluded from political life because "people feel strongly about the political articulation of their religious beliefs." Further, we *should not* exclude it from political life because it has an important contribution to make by providing foundational values; and the political experience is valuable for religion in that religion becomes a politically accountable institution through the processes of self-criticism and democratization. He concludes that religion should not be left to "sulk and scowl menacingly from outside the public realm" but rather it should be "subject[ed] to the latter's educational and political discipline."

Stephen Darwall's examination of "Peace as Politics" is a reexamination of what may seem to be a long-settled question. The question is why religious toleration was problematic in the first place. Why did the state feel threatened by varieties of religious thought and practice? Darwall's answer is that the early moderns saw religious difference as challenging political legitimacy by contesting the source of political authority. In short, "religious toleration seemed to license something like sedition."

Darwall's project is twofold. First, he wants to show "why religious toleration was such a problematic idea." But then he also wants to show how liberalism made religious toleration possible by removing the authority for governance from the interactions between the divine and the human, and rested it entirely in the hands of equal, autonomous, individual citizens. In other words, if the state is to claim some "divine right" for its authority, then a variety of religious views, claiming a variety of interpretations for this divine right, are a constant threat to the legitimacy of the state. If, however, the state is—as we would say today—thoroughly secularized, then religion is moved away from the center of political life, and can be encouraged to flourish on its outskirts. Darwall puts this as an issue of freedom for the moral subject. One view makes the moral subject *subjected to* the commands of God, and therefore *God's subjects.* The other view is the freedom of the moral subject to lead a life in which the subject is his or her own moral authority.

But the careful reader can almost hear Parekh, leaning over Darwall's shoulder, whispering in his ear, "But religions get cranky when they are politically marginalized. And most folk in a 'secular' society are actually 'religious.'" Darwall's response is that religions can be a force for peace by modeling tolerance through respectful dialogue. He quotes medieval Iberian philosopher Raymond Lull and his *Book of the Gentile* as an example of folk who began hoping for common belief and who ended celebrating "the intrinsic authority of the others as rational persons."

John Clayton's "Common Ground and Defensible Difference" is a challenge to those who say that religiously pluralistic cultures need some sort of common ground in order to avoid intellectual relativism and political disintegration. American Protestants, nostalgic for those days, not long past, when theirs was the defining ethos of the nation, are particularly drawn to that argument, although it is hard for them to imagine what that common ground might be, now that Protestantism has been superseded. Nor is this nostalgic yearning for common ground only an American preoccupation. Clayton has spent many years teaching in England, and the common ground idea, for him, "evokes public parks and village greens. It is an image full of warmth and reassurance, exuding a sense of community and well-being. It is an image that can inspire even the likes of former British Prime Minister John Major to eloquence in homage to village cricket, warm beer, and prim spinsters cycling to Evensong."

Clayton's view, however, is that "clarification of defensible difference, not identification of 'common ground', may be what is required to gain the cooperation of disparate religious interests in achieving pragmatically defined goals." Clearly, diverse groups need to find some way to come together. Clayton's argument is that we do this in defining specific common goals, rather than some general common ground. The argument is unabashedly pragmatic. The generalized but inoperative principles of common ground will not serve us as well as the specific, instrumental reasons for common goals.

The body of Clayton's paper is a careful comparative study of how interreligious argumentation has worked in various cultures. Unlike today's "interreligious dialogue," where Western religionists lay aside their own persuasion in order better to understand the commitments of others, Clayton outlines a feisty set-to among classical Asian religionists, where disputation settled little but led to mutual respect and became a common venture. "By this means, from different motives and disparate grounds, specific limited goals may be tactically agreed upon by culturally diverse groups who share no common historical narrative and occupy no common ground save only the fragile and threatened planet that fate has destined as our shared home."

Ronald Thiemann shares Clayton's view that the quest for "common ground" is misdirected. He begins with a criticism of Arthur Schlesinger, Jr.'s *The Disuniting of America*. He shares Schlesinger's concern about the current fragmentation of American culture along racial, ethnic, religious, and ideological lines, but he rejects "the 'melting pot' mythology." Schlesinger argues that America was, from the beginning, a self-consciously multiethnic society, and that its brilliant solution for the inherent fragility of such a society was "the creation of a brand-new national identity, carried forward by individuals who, in forsaking old loyalties and joining to make new lives, melted away ethnic differences."

Thiemann takes a deep breath and bravely calls this "bad history," arguing that "maintenance of cultural identity has always been essential to the successful integration of immigrant populations into the larger American society." His point is that America was not some "new race of men"; it was a community of "citizens who are dedicated to the fundamental values of democracy: liberty, equality, and mutual respect." In other words, America is not a culture; it is a creed. So Thiemann does not necessarily find our current "politics of the particular" a threat to our historic sense of a national identity. The stridency and passion of much contemporary debate in the so-called culture wars "may be signs of the robustness of democracy rather than indications of its decay."

So he disagrees with "communitarian" philosophers like Alasdair MacIntyre who argue that American life now pits one set of "incommensurable" values against another and suggest that our religious differences are leading us to cultural contention and discord. Following the philosopher Donald Davidson, he regards the idea of "incommensurable moral values" as a substantial overstatement; and he finds classical conceptions of Christian faith open to cultural dialogue because they do not hold to an absolutist conception of truth. He advocates a "pilgrim citizenship" which is not ethical relativism; it is "faith seeking understanding" and therefore not to be equated with apodictic or absolute certainty.

Our concluding section deals with the question of peace in three different religious contexts. The first is Gandhi's curious amalgam of Jainism's spiritual nonviolence, Advaita Vedanta's metaphysical nondualism, and Christianity's ethical love for the neighbor. The second is Stephanie Kaza's interpretation of a possible Buddhist ecology in the contemporary Western world. The third is the unique pan-religionism of Raimon Panikkar's view of world religions as servants of world peace.

We begin with John Hick's essay "Gandhi: The Fusion of Religion and Politics." Hick's essay is not, itself, autobiographical, but he notes that one can only understand Gandhi's thought in the context of his life. After dealing with the fundamentals of Gandhi's thought, especially the principle of *ahimsa* or nonviolence and the notion that Truth is God, Hick turns to an evaluation of Gandhi's legacy. In one sense it would be easy to argue that Gandhi has no legacy. Where are the advocates of *ahimsa* in India today? And having fought urbanization, modernization, and Westernization, Gandhi's India has seemingly lost the spiritual heritage which Gandhi embodied. There may be a growing political movement of Hindu nationalism in India today, but it is the kind of Hinduism which led to Gandhi's assassination, not to his vision of the new India.

Hick admits that there is much about contemporary India which "would have made Gandhi weep." Nevertheless, he argues that the core of Gandhi's teaching is still relevant today. Gandhi's credo was that "the truly noble know all men as one, and return with gladness good for evil done." Hick sees this teaching standing over us "as an ideal that continually challenges us and that proves itself when, all too rarely, it is acted upon." More specifically, he argues that *ahimsa* maintains its relevance because it is a long-term strategy. He dismisses as pointless the question about how Gandhi would have fared in Nazi Germany. Clearly he would have been quickly eliminated. But the more useful question, Hick insists, "is what would have happened if someone like him had been at work in Germany for the previous twenty years."

Gandhi's ecological concern put him far ahead of his time, and Hick notes that several contemporary philosophers of ecology have credited Gandhi's emphasis on a low-level technology in a decentralized culture as the first realistic program for a viable world economy. Hick is also intrigued with Gandhi's "feminism." Hick admits that Gandhi never entirely broke free of his culture's patriarchal assumptions, but his concern for the social status of women in society was matched by his own embodiment of virtues and attitudes of mind which are often characterized as "feminine." Finally, Hick finds Gandhi's ecumenicity a model for interreligious relations today. "And underlying all this, as an available source of inspiration for each new generation, is Gandhi's indomitable faith in the possibility of a radically better human future if only we will learn to trust the power of fearless nonviolent openness to others and to the deeper humanity, and indeed deity, within us all."

Stephanie Kaza is shaping a contemporary philosophy of ecology, and her primary resource is an interpretation of some classical Buddhist ideas and values. Her essay is distinctive in that her manner of argument is not the linear rationality of her colleagues in this volume, but rather a traditional Buddhist fourfold logic of investigation which states a thesis and then proposes four responses: 1) No; 2) Yes; 3) Both Yes and No; 4) Neither Yes nor No. Her thesis is that we can keep peace with nature, and that Buddhism provides distinctive and critical resources for this venture. "Keeping peace with nature" means simply that humans can live peacefully on this overtaxed planet in a way which sustains the viability of the natural world.

The No argument takes its cue from Ian Harris's criticism of the methods and claims of recent "green Buddhists." He argues that there is no unified tradition of environmental thought or practice in the various Buddhisms of Asia, nor is there a common understanding of what Westerners mean by *nature*. Further, he suggests that Western and nationalistic thinking has so pervaded Eastern behavior that "it is hard to find the Buddhism behind Thai or Japanese exploitation of the natural world." The Yes argument, on the other hand, finds evidence in both the philosophical congruities between Buddhist thought and environmentalism, and in numerous examples of Buddhist environmental activism in the West today.

The "Both Yes and No" argument is concerned with human fallibility and imperfection. Yes, this is part of our ideal vision of the world; No, it is not something we are actually working at. Vacillation and contradiction are part of human nature, and realism demands recognition of human ambivalence. She ends, however, with "Neither Yes nor No," and this is "the negative space behind all the others, the undefined realm, the source of unknown events, any of which could spur cultural change beyond our wildest imagination." Here the classical Buddhist notion of "nothingness" verges on an Aristotelian principle of potentiality.

Like Hick, and also like Wiesel, her hope for the future is not grounded in historical experience as much as it is in ideal possibility. Realists like Reinhold Niebuhr would say, "It is not going to happen," but Kaza has a realism of her own, pointing out that no one knows what is going to happen. Practicing with a "don't-know mind" can both protect one from despair and keep one open to the possibility of a brighter future.

Our concluding essay is from Raimon Panikkar on "Religions and the Culture of Peace." Here, especially, autobiography is critical

for philosophical understanding. The child of a Hindu and a Spanish
Catholic, Panikkar was trained at the Gregorian in Rome, has written books in seven different languages and done prodigious research in three others, and for many years lived some months of each
year emulating the life of a Brahmin in India, and the others as an
American academic, first at Harvard and later at the University of
California at Santa Barbara. His early book on *The Unknown Christ
of Hinduism* was widely influential, written from his perspective as a
Catholic philosopher, expert in Sanskrit and deeply versed in Hindu
thought. In later years, however, he has incorporated various religious
traditions into his own spiritual life. Like the nineteenth-century
Hindu teacher Sri Ramakrishna, he lives an internalized religious
ecumenicity. So he announces at the outset that his lifelong reflections
on the relation of religion to peace are both a theoretical and personal
issue for him, "being myself a Catholic priest, a Hindu believer in my
dharma, an initiated Buddhist, and a staunch secular person."

Panikkar opens his paper with the argument that world religions
have gone through three periods in the last six thousand years. The
first is monism, in which religion is a dimension of all human activities
and inseparable from human identity. The second is dualism, in which
religion becomes a distinct phenomenon, largely identified with intellectual doctrine. The third is nihilism, in which religion becomes
culturally irrelevant. None of these attitudes do justice to religion, in
Panikkar's view, and he proposes a radical transformation of religions
through a closer identification with political life. This transformation
involves both changing attitudes toward other religious communities
and a change in our understanding of the nature of religion itself.

Our attitude toward other religions must be grounded in the
kind of understanding which sees the truth as the other sees it, and
shares in the other's self-understanding. This is a phenomenology of
both love and truth. "Without love no really personal understanding
is possible." The change in the understanding of religion is a "passage
from religion to religiousness." Others might call this a transition from
the formalism of separate religious institutions to an integration of
spirituality into all aspects of ordinary human life. A culture of peace
then becomes a political possibility because culture *per se* has become
religious.

It is instructive to note both similarities and differences among
our authors. Moltmann, Elshtain, and Wiesel believe that the tran-

scendental religious themes of reconciliation and political hope are viable in contemporary politics, and—in spite of all the difficulties and limitations attending that viability—they ground that belief in personal experience. Elshtain has seen reconciliation at work in South Africa; Moltmann has seen glimpses of it in Germany and elsewhere in Europe; Wiesel may hope largely because despair is not an option for him, but the fact that he and others of his generation are still working for peace is testimony to the practical power of hope.

For Parekh, Darwall, Clayton, and Thiemann the issue is largely understanding how varieties of religious experience can coexist creatively in a political situation which has not regularly welcomed them. They are agreed that religion has a contribution to make to political life, although they are wary of claiming too much for that role. Liberals all—with various degrees of chastening—they support a secular state even as they tend to oppose the marginalization of religion in the political community.

Hick, Kaza, and Panikkar present a different view. They are visionaries and idealists. True, they make an occasional bow in the direction of the operational and the instrumental, but there are no pragmatists here. They focus less on what is than on what ought to be. Reinhold Niebuhr would remind them that we live in a sin-sick and weary world where ideals are not regularly realized, and they acknowledge that. But Kaza can go Niebuhr's realism one better: No one *really* knows the future. And while Hick and Panikkar have not personally suffered the Holocaust, they have a right to their hope, as Wiesel has a right to his.

NOTES

1. W. B. Allen, ed., *George Washington: A Collection* (Indianapolis: Liberty Classics, 1988), pp. 521–22.

PART I

Religious Faith and Political Reconciliation

Political Reconciliation

JÜRGEN MOLTMANN

WE ALL KNOW WHAT forgiveness of guilt, reconciliation, and the beginning of new community means in *personal* life, whether it be in a marriage or in the family, among relatives or neighbors. We believe that it is possible, and many of us have experienced it for ourselves. But does the same thing exist in the *political* life of nations too? Or does politics exclude anything like reconciliation, if we have to pursue politics in the form of "power politics," where the rights of the stronger are all that counts, while the weaker have to disappear? When we ask whether political reconciliation is possible, and enquire about the forms it could take, we have to ask first whether reconciliation can be transformed from personal to political life; and second we have to enquire about the nature of politics, and its humanity or inhumanity.

I shall confine myself to the political experiences I have had myself, so I am not speaking as an objective historian. I am talking as a contemporary witness who was personally affected by events, and personally involved in them, and I shall look at what were general experiences in the mirror of my own impressions. At the same time, I have checked the historical accuracy of my own impressions, so as not to say what would be wrong if it were generalized.

I am a German, and I have experienced two large-scale attempts at a new beginning in the political life of my country. The first was de-Nazification in the German Federal Republic (West Germany) after 1945. The second was de-Stalinization in what was formerly the German Democratic Republic (East Germany) after 1989.

In both cases the aim was to restore, or newly to establish, democracy and human rights after years of dictatorship, with its contempt for human beings. How do democracies deal with the perpetrators and the victims, the informers and the fellow travelers of the dictatorships they have overthrown? What happens to the guilt of

17

the murderers, and the injustice which the victims have suffered? According to which law can we condemn retrospectively what was done earlier in the lawless condition of a rule of violence? How can victims and perpetrators live together without forgetting and without retaliation?[1]

Let me begin with a story about one reconciliation experienced after the war. I should then like to go on to describe German forms of what is called *Vergangenheitsbewältigung*. This word can be translated as "coming to terms with the past"; but it is really as untranslatable as it is inexpressibly false and hypocritical. After that I shall speak about the violations of human rights in the civil war in Bosnia, and the war crimes trials at the International Court of Justice in the Hague. And finally I shall try to make a few suggestions for political reconciliation after dictatorship and civil war.

I. RECONCILIATION BEHIND BARBED WIRE

I was born in Hamburg in 1926, and was drafted into the German army in the middle of 1944. Thrust, hardly trained, into the battle for Arnhem, I was taken prisoner by the English in 1945, and in 1948 was "repatriated," as the term went at that time. In July 1947, together with some other POWs, I was invited to the first worldwide conference held by the SCM after the end of the war. The conference was held in Swanwick, in central England.[2] For us, the invitation alone was a little miracle, for we had been enemies, and we wore either our old uniforms or prisoners' jackets with numbers on the back. We were taken to this conference under guard, and went "in fear and trembling." What were we to say to the reproaches of responsibility for German war crimes and the mass murder of Jews in the concentration camps? But we weren't confronted with reproaches at all. We were accepted and welcomed as "brothers in Christ," and were permitted to eat and drink, sing and pray, together with Christian students from all over the world. During those nights my eyes often filled with tears.

Then a group of Dutch students came and asked to speak to us officially. Again I was frightened, for as a soldier I had been thrown into action on the fringe of the battle for the Arnhem bridge. But the Dutch explained to us that the bridge on which they were crossing to us was Christ. Without Christ they wouldn't be able to talk to us at all. They told about the terror of the German Gestapo, about the loss of their relatives and their Jewish friends in German concentration camps, and about the destruction of their homes by the SS. We too, they told us, could tread this bridge which Christ had built from them to us, and could acknowledge the guilt of our people and ask for reconciliation. At the end we all embraced.

For me that was an hour of liberation. The photographs of Belsen and Auschwitz which had been put up in our camp had cast me into a profound depression. Now I felt as if newborn. From that moment on I was able to live with the unbearable guilt of my people, without denying anything and without being destroyed by it. This unforgettable gesture of reconciliation on the part of the Dutch students had set me in the truth, and at the same time opened up the prospect of a new life in freedom. I went back to my prisoner-of-war camp from that SCM conference without caring how much longer the imprisonment was going to last. I had been freed from another imprisonment. This experience taught me, first, that only complete truth can make us free; and, second, that the readiness for reconciliation, which stretches out a hand to the other, gives us the strength to look the full truth in the face, without extenuating it and without destroying ourselves, and enables us to shoulder the responsibility for guilt.

II. THE INCOMPLETE DE-NAZIFICATION AFTER 1945—RECONCILIATION WITH POLAND (1972)

When I returned from my prisoner-of-war camp in 1948, the German Federal Republic was already caught up in the process of "reconstruction." By that I don't just mean the rebuilding of the German cities out of their rubble. Nor do I only mean the integration of twelve million refugees and displaced persons from the eastern parts of Germany. I am also talking about the reconstruction of social and political institutions in this devastated country. What had happened between 1945 and 1948? The Nuremberg Trials had taken place, according to laws given retrospective force. The chief offenders had been executed. The others were in prison. But it was the Allies, not the Germans themselves, who had put the Nazi murderers on trial and declared them guilty. In 1949 we acquired the *Grundgesetz,* the

Basic Law or constitution of the German Federal Republic. It had been formulated by German democrats. But democracy hadn't been fought for and won by the German people, in the face of the Nazi dictatorship. It had been conferred on us as a gift by the victorious powers. We Germans had not been capable of it.

In 1945 the United Protestant Church in Germany, in what was then a highly courageous act, published the Stuttgart Confession of Guilt, in which it talked, if in admittedly general terms, about the "infinite suffering" caused to the peoples "through our fault," and accused itself of "not having believed more firmly, loved more passionately, and hoped more greatly."[3] In retrospect, this confession of guilt made by the church on behalf of the whole German people may seem to us pretty weak, in the first place because it doesn't mention the Jews, against whom Hitler's whole annihilating madness had been turned; and in the second place because Hitler's "willing helpers" in the Christian church are not mentioned either. But in spite of that, the confession burst like a bombshell. I remember a public discussion with Martin Niemoller at Göttingen University in 1948, when he was howled down by furious former officers, who claimed only to have done their duty, and to be completely guiltless. In postwar Germany it was far from opportune to talk about war guilt—either guilt *for* the war, or guilt *during* the war.

Before Germany could make any serious attempt to clean up its act by itself, to repent of the Nazi dictatorship and make a fresh start, the political situation in the world as a whole changed. It was in Germany (latterly only divided into two) that the East-West conflict began. In 1950 the Korean War started, and America needed as ally a reliable German Federal Republic, rearmed and a member of NATO. In 1950 the SS criminals who had been sentenced to imprisonment were released. This was evidently meant to be a present for the Germans. Under Chancellor Konrad Adenauer, the restoration of civil and military institutions in the German Federal Republic began. Former Nazis were no longer tracked down. From 1951 onwards, Article 131 of the Basic Law permitted them to return to their old offices and positions.[4] This was the beginning of the remarkable trick of a seeming "political reconciliation" after the Hitler dictatorship: the Christian Democratic Union especially (but not the CDU alone) admitted members of the Nazi party into its own party ranks, and saw to it that they were given posts and pensions. Adenauer's closest adviser was Herr Globke, the inglorious legal commentator on the Nuremberg racial laws, under which the Jews in Germany were dispossessed, persecuted, and put under arrest. The first well-known commentary on the democratic Basic Law was written by Professor Maunz of Munich, who was not merely a former Nazi, but who even after the war went on writing Nazified newspaper commentaries for the *Deutsche Nationalzeitung*. Everywhere, the old Nazis, in their fresh guise as new Christian Democrats, found their way back to their former offices. It was only the conspicuous war criminals who were excluded. What the CDU did under Adenauer (but not just the CDU) was a kind of painless, unrepentant, bogus "reeducation" of the old Nazis into new democrats.

As an argument *in favor of* this reconciliation without reform it might be said that the formation of a neo-Nazi or radical right-wing party was thereby very effectively prevented. As an argument *against* it, we have to say that it introduced plenty of old nationalist and Fascist notions into the CDU—but not into the CDU alone. Firmly ensconced in the alliance of the "free" Western world, the German Federal Republic, as we then discovered, was denationalized but not de-Nazified. It was not until fifteen years later, in 1966, at the insistence of enraged students, that the German universities cleaned themselves up and got rid of old Nazi scholars, scientists, and ideologists. It then emerged that in Tübingen old proponents of racist ideology occupied chairs in biology, that in Aachen a high-up SS officer under a false name was Rector of the University of Technology, and so on. Most of the people chiefly incriminated were already retired, however, and were enjoying their good pensions.

The self-purification of the universities was belated; but unlike the universities, the German legal machinery never addressed its own past in the unjust rulings of the Third Reich at all.[5] "After all, what was once law cannot be unlawful now," maintained the naval judge Filbinger who, even after the war had ended, continued to sentence German soldiers in Norway to death for desertion, and who for years was president of the state of Baden-Württemberg.

The Jewish victims of the Holocaust were "compensated" by way of billions paid as reparations to the state of Israel. The courts should have dealt with the real criminals, writes Albert Friedlander. But although over 90,000 cases were investigated, only 6,478 persons were found guilty. 82,467 trials ended without any sentence being passed.[6] Even today the perpetrators are still out of reach, because the Federal Republic's archives haven't been opened, except in the case of the Investigating Agency for Crime in Ludwigsburg. Even today the return of expropriated Jewish property, sold on the cheap to good Germans in 1938, is still pending, fifty-four years after the end of the war. Even today, Jewish survivors of the concentration camps now living in the countries of eastern Europe are still waiting for compensation from Germany. This will no doubt happen only after the last survivors are dead.

At the time of the East-West conflict, the integration of the Federal Republic into the West went forward unspectacularly and without any major problems. But a new policy of expiation and reconciliation towards the peoples of Eastern Europe and Russia was effectively prevented by the Associations of Displaced Persons and People Deprived of their Rights (*Verbände der Heimatvertriebenen und Entrechteten*). It must be said that twelve million Germans had been driven from the eastern territories to the west. The recognition of the Oder-Neisse Line between the German Democratic Republic and Poland (which was now pushed further west) was a particularly sore point. Here the United Protestant Church in Germany made the first move in 1965 with an Eastern Memorandum which, together with the painful acceptance of that new frontier, expressed a plea for reconciliation and a readiness for new community. At that time leading West German politicians said: "The church must lead the way. If we do so, we shan't be reelected." The church did lead the way, and lost members, but gained credibility. The Catholic Church followed later along the road that had thus been paved. Today Poland is on the brink of entry into the European Community.

The symbolic conclusion of this German policy of reconciliation towards Poland came in 1972, on the famous occasion when the German Federal Chancellor Willy Brandt fell on his knees in front of the memorial to the Warsaw Ghetto. He was not just kneeling before the victims of the German rule of violence. He was expressing humility before God, and to the survivors repentance and the readiness for a new beginning. As a socialist, Brandt had been forced to leave Germany as early as 1933, and he had fought against the Nazis in Norway. So he was in a position to kneel before the victims as a representative of the murderers and their children. His political opponents mocked this gesture, and fought against his policy of reconciliation as a "policy of renunciation."

Let me say a word about the political perpetrators and their victims. As early as 1967, the psychoanalysts Alexander and Margarete Mitscherlich testified to an "inability to mourn"[7] among the concentration camp murderers and their SS henchmen. It must unfortunately be said in general that among the perpetrators there was, and still is, no sense of guilt. They no doubt accepted that what they had done in the mass murders was reprehensible. But the continually reiterated excuse was that they were simply forced to do the "dirty work," and were therefore more to be pitied than punished. The men of the shameful Hamburg Police Battalion 101 had no need to undertake the shooting of Jews in the Ukraine. Any of them could have refused, and nothing would have happened to them. But almost without exception they performed their "painful duty" as they were told to do.[8] Acceptance of guilt seems to destroy the last little bit of self-confidence, to strip the soul naked, and to be an invitation to punishment. Rather live a lie than appear mean and paltry in the light of truth. Hardly a ray of truth pierced through this armor of untouchable unconcern among those involved. For that reason—that is the effect—the perpetrators always have only short memories. In court too, their "lapses of memory" were phenomenal. But the victims always have long memories, for suffering carves deep wounds. Time never heals them. So if they are to enter into the truth of what they have done, the perpetrators who have lost their memories need the memories of the victims, so that they may come face to face with themselves. In Germany we need the concentration camp memorials and the Holocaust museums, not just in order to be reminded of the victims and those they left behind, but so that those who live in the long shadows of the perpetrators can enter into the truth and become free.

III. GERMANY'S REUNIFICATION WITHOUT RECONCILIATION AFTER 1989

In the autumn of 1989 the possibility of a peaceful reunification loomed on the horizon in divided Germany. The military power of the

Soviet Union had destroyed the economic power of the Eastern bloc. Mikhail Gorbachev tried with *glasnost* and *perestroika* to bring about an internal socialist reform, but foundered on the growing nationalism and separatism of the peoples who were united and repressed in the Soviet Union. After the war in Afghanistan had been lost, the central committee of the Communist Party of the Soviet Union indicated that it was prepared to withdraw Russian military presence from eastern Europe. President George Bush was able to convince the former allies England and France (against the will of Margaret Thatcher and Francois Mitterand) that a united Germany no longer presented any threat to Europe. In East Germany the civil rights groups and the peace movement had gained in persuasiveness since 1986. From 1981 onwards, very small peace groups had met every Monday evening in the Nikolaikirche in Leipzig, to pray for peace; and in the autumn of 1989 thousands of people joined them and, at the end of the prayers, formed huge protest processions through Leipzig's city center. Eventually 300,000 people protested with prayers and candles against the police and the army tanks which had been brought up. The Russians prevented a "Chinese solution" of the kind enforced in Tiananmen Square in Beijing shortly before. On November 9, Schabowski, the SED Party Secretary in East Berlin, in passing or accidentally, stated that the Berlin Wall would be opened for visits in both directions. Thousands of people thereupon streamed to the Wall and pulled it down. The police and the government stood by, helpless. The following year Germany was "reunited." It is a noteworthy fact that this was the first successful and *peaceful* revolution in Germany. Some people called it "the Protestant revolution."[9] The party dictatorship in East Germany collapsed. The federalist democracy in West Germany had won. But with this the problems of reconciliation had only begun.

The "reunification" of Germany wasn't a reunification of two equal, hitherto divided, parts, with the same rights. It was merely the affiliation of East Germany to West Germany under conditions imposed by Bonn—an *Anschluss,* to pick up the word used for Austria's affiliation to Germany in 1938. First of all the West German currency—the Deutsch mark—was introduced, and after that democracy. The privatization of socialized industry and agriculture followed under the agency of the *Treuhandanstalt*, the trust body that was made responsible. And that was the beginning of completely new difficulties.

When the Soviet Union crumbled, and Germany was reunited, the Comecon, the economic community of the Eastern bloc, disintegrated too. East German industry was no longer able to supply goods to other East European countries, and it was unable to compete in the West. East Germany was largely deindustrialized. The build-up of competitive concerns and a modern infrastructure swallowed up millions in Western capital and brought only modest results. All of a sudden the population dropped out of the full employment it had enjoyed under socialism, into capitalist unemployment: today the unemployment rate is 20 percent on average, in some regions 50 percent.

The drift of young people to the West began. The people in what are now called "the new federal states" had twelve years of Nazi dictatorship and forty years of Communist dictatorship behind them. Now they had to get used to an unfamiliar democratic capitalist culture. It is true that the SED state was a party dictatorship, but as long as its children were obedient, it also looked after them. They were lapped in social security from the cradle to the grave, and that was a substitute for personal liberty. This social security was now replaced by the liberty of the market economy. Before, everyone was his or her neighbor's watchdog. Now neighbors became competitors for work and property. Now everyone had to look out for himself or herself. For the mass of the people who were now unemployed, this was more than they could handle, and that is true today more than ever, nine years after reunification. The physical Wall in Berlin has fallen, but the mental and cultural Wall in heads and hearts is still there, and for some people higher than it ever was.[10] "Reunification" became an affiliation, an *Anschluss;* and the *Anschluss* of the East to the West brought no inward reconciliation.[11]

Reconciliation was also hindered by the open question of what was to be done in united Germany with the mass of SED party members, the people who had wielded power in the GDR, as well as the members—and also the informers—of the state security system which had hitherto been omnipresent. A general amnesty? Acceptance, in the way that former Nazis were accepted in 1951 under the new Article 131 of the Basic Law? Banishment from their offices? Withdrawal of their pensions? Punishment of the lawbreakers?

The "joint German solution" was first of all to throw open the archives of the state security service, so that everyone could discover in the files of the Gauck Authority who had been an "informal collaborator," a spy and informer for the state security. Government offenders who were guilty according to the laws of the GDR had to stand trial. Party members employed by the state—and professors are also state employees in Germany—were left alone, but were not taken over into the new government service. They were simply "removed." No one who could be shown to have had a discernible proximity to the "unjust state" was taken over or newly appointed. The head of state, Honecker, was allowed to emigrate to Chile. The head of the state security service, Mielke, had to stand trial on the grounds of earlier crimes, committed before 1933. Today he is living in Berlin, with a small pension.

On the political and legal levels, the wrongs of the dictatorship were condemned according to the constitutional criteria of democracy. There were no retrospective laws and no general amnesty. Shots fired to kill at the Wall, unjust verdicts, and crimes of violence were punished; support for the dictatorship, on the other hand, wasn't punished by the courts, but merely socially.

What became a severe human and social problem was the opening of the state security archives by the Gauck Authority. East German politicians, professors, pastors, even bishops—simply friends and neighbors too—were exposed by the dozen as "informal collaborators" of the STASI, the state security service.[12] This octopus had had its thousand tentacles, ears, and eyes everywhere. The atmosphere in public life under the socialist dictatorship in East Germany had been almost totally poisoned, and after the archives had been opened this remained so, more than ever. Of the seven professors on the theological faculty of the Humboldt University in Berlin, five were "informal collaborators" and had had to spy on each other and send in reports on one another. But none of them knew about the others. In 1990 all of them had to leave the university.

Again we are brought up against the question of a reconciliation between the perpetrators and the victims, and a new community between them. And again, the first question is the "truth" question. During the last eight years there has hardly been a single case where informers of the state security service sought out their victims, declared themselves for what they were, and asked for forgiveness. For many people today—those professors of theology included—it is evidently easier to live with the lie, and justify the guilt, than to face up to the truth and ask for reconciliation. Not even in the Christian

churches have there been to any extent admissions of guilt and recon-
ciliations.

IV. THE POLICY ON HUMAN RIGHTS IN EUROPE

The inward dissolution of the socialist party dictatorships was
brought about by the civil rights movements—in Czechoslovakia by
Charter 77, in Poland by *Solidarnocs,* and in East Germany by civil
rights groups. Their approach was both legal and loyal. They set up no
political opposition to the Communist party, nor were they infiltrators
from Western countries. They demanded legitimate civil rights, in
accordance with the United Nations Universal Declaration of Human
Rights of 1948—for with their entry into the United Nations, all those
socialist states had signed that declaration. The legitimacy of the
groups was strengthened by the "Helsinki Final Act" (or Helsinki
Accords), which concluded the 1975 Conference on Security and Cooperation in Europe (CSCE). With that, a phase of effective human
rights policies began in Europe. Irrespective of the differences between the various political, economic, and social systems, the European countries in East and West wanted to work together on humanitarian, cultural, and international levels. But with this the socialist
states recognized the human rights of their people, so that they could
be charged with violations of human rights by the civil rights movements at home and by the CSCE from outside. "The dictatorship
of the proletariat" (Lenin's phrase), which their party dictatorships
claimed to be, found its limits and, with them, its end in the human
rights of the people.

No human being is just the sustainer of the rights and duties of
his or her people, country, and social system. Everyone is also the
sustainer of any human rights which can lawfully be claimed. This
truth was certainly disputed during those years by the Confucian edu-
cative dictatorships in Asia—for example, in Korea and Singapore.
The Korean military dictatorships denied human rights to their own
people because they were "Western values," not Asiatic ones. But the
Christian and trades union civil rights movements in Korea (to which
I was very close at that time) said: "So are we just Koreans and Asians,
and not also and primarily *human beings* with inalienable human
rights?" And in Korea they overthrew the military dictatorship and

actually put the dictators on trial. In Europe, in the war in Bosnia, we have seen violations of human rights of undreamt-of personal cruelty, especially directed against women. But the International Court of Justice in The Hague has brought charges against the war criminals whenever they can be caught, convicting them according to law. In this way human rights are enforced as civil rights. To bring charges about violations of human rights in countries belonging to the UN is certainly "interference in the internal affairs" of these individual countries; but by acknowledging the Universal Declaration of Human Rights of 1948, and the International Covenants on Human Rights of 1966, the individual countries have *de jure* surrendered their sovereign rights over their people to the international community of states. Governments can no longer do whatever they like with the people they govern.

V. POLITICAL EXPIATION AND RECONCILIATION

When political power is legitimated and restricted by universal human rights, no longer through the alleged "power of the strongest," then political reconciliation is possible even after human rights have been violated. The open acknowledgment of guilt and an inward turning away from the ideologies of violence, the forgiveness of guilt, and the beginning of a new shared and just life: all this becomes the sign of new humane politics. How is it possible? I believe we can transfer basic elements of the church's practice of repentance and forgiveness into the policies whereby democracies come to term with the crimes committed under dictatorships, with the violations of human rights and the consequences.

According to the church's ancient penitential ritual, there are three steps that lead to a turn from the guilt of the past into the light of a free future:

1.   *Confessio oris,* "personal confession." This is acceptance of the truth of what has happened, the recognition of guilt which can never be made good, and private or public acknowledgment of this past as one's own.
2.   *Contritio cordis,* "the contrition of the heart" and the preparedness to turn away from the ideas and compulsions which led to the crimes, and to turn back to the humanity of human rights.

The first of these elements—the inward contrition—is called in German *Trauerarbeit,* "the work of grief." The second is called *Gesinnungswandel,* "a change of heart or attitude." Both are important if the conversion is not to remain merely superficial. In the case of politically motivated crimes, this involves and requires open criticism and renunciation of the ideologies and religious delusions which rob people of their natural inhibitions about killing and cruelty. I am thinking of Fascist and Communist ideologies, but also of the ideologies of "national security" in Latin America, and Islamic extremism in Algeria.

3. *Satisfactio operum.* These were acts of "satisfaction" or amendment made through the performance of good works, so that the offender might again be in good standing with God. Today it means such indemnification of the victims and their families as is still possible. It was this spirit which after the war inspired a group called Aktion Sühnezeichen in which, as "tokens of expiation," young Germans rebuilt something which their fathers had destroyed in Poland or Russia, or helped in the build-up of Israel.

The acceptance and acknowledgment of guilt, the work of grief, and a change of heart and attitude: these are first steps to the justice which aims to right wrongs. These are the possibilities open to us, personally and collectively, as a way of emerging from a guilt-laden past into a liberated future.

This penitential practice as a whole is *determined* by the forgiveness of guilt and the hope for reconciliation. But it is only through this penitential practice that forgiveness of guilt and hope for reconciliation can be *implemented.* The two things condition each other mutually: without a thought of forgiveness for guilt, none of us can acknowledge our guilt without glossing it over, or destroying ourselves. Without hope for reconciliation and a new common life, no one can kneel down before the memorial to his or her victims. But forgiveness of guilt and the offer of reconciliation remain superficial and are misused unless they lead along the path of repentance and expiation.

Are forgiveness and reconciliation only possible between individuals, not between peoples?

We have seen from the suppressions of the truth in Germany after 1945 and 1989 that justice, which must be exercised by the courts, must not be passed over. Amnesty without expiation leads to forgetting, and forgetting kills a second time. Yet the retaliating justice of penal law doesn't in itself lead to a new common future, and ultimately doesn't help the victims, or the perpetrators either.

Perhaps the Truth and Reconciliation Commissions in South Africa have found a way leading from personal to political life, and a path linking justice for the victims with possible conversion for the perpetrators. That would be of vital interest, not just for South Africa, but for us in Europe too.

NOTES

1. Brian Frost, *The Politics of Peace* (London, 1991); Donald Shriver, *An Ethics for Enemies: Forgiveness in Politics* (New York, 1995); Geiko Müller-Fahrenholz, *The Art of Forgiveness: Theological Reflections on Healing and Reconciliation* (Geneva, 1997).

2. See my account "Wrestling with God," in *The Source of Life*, trans. Margaret Kohl (London, 1997), pp. 1–9, and—from the other side—Pamela Howe Taylor, *Enemies Become Friends: A True Story of German Prisoners of War* (Sussex, 1997).

3. Martin Greschat, *Die Schuld der Kirche: Dokumente und Reflexionen zur Stuttgarter Schulderklärung vom 18/19 Oktober 1945* (Munich, 1982).

4. *Das Grundgesetz* (Basic Law), Article 131: "Rechtsverhältnisse früherer Angehöriger des öffentlichen Dienstes."

5. Ingo Müller, *Furchtbare Juristen: Die unbewältigte Vergangenheit unserer Justiz* (Munich, 1989).

6. Albert Friedlander, *Riders Towards the Dawn* (London, 1993).

7. Alexander and Margarete Mitscherlich, *The Inability to Mourn*, trans. B. R. Placzek (New York: 1975).

8. In this respect Daniel Goldhagen is right; see his *Hitler's Willing Executioners* (London, 1996).

9. Gerhard Rein, *Die protestantische Revolution 1987–1990: Ein deutsches Lesebuch* (Berlin, 1990); Jörg Swoboda, *Die Revolution der Kerzen: Christen in den Umwälzungen der DDR* (Wuppertal and Kassel, 1990).

10. Heino Falcke, *Die unvollendete Befreiung: Die Kirchen, die Umwälzung in der DDR und die Vereinigung Deutschland* (Ökumenische Existence heute, no. 9, Munich, 1991).

11. Ehrhart Neubert, *Vergebung oder Weisswascherei: Zur Aufarbeitung der Stasiprobleme in den Kirchen* (Freiburg, 1993); Richard Schröder,

Deutschland schwierig Vaterland: Für eine neue politische Kultur (Freiburg, 1993).

12. Hans-Joachim Maaz, *Der Gefühlsstau: Ein Psychogramm der DDR* (Berlin, 1990); Hans-Joachim Maaz, *Das gestürzte Volk oder die verunglückte Einheit* (Berlin, 1991).

Politics and Forgiveness

JEAN BETHKE ELSHTAIN

WE ARE AWASH in confession these days. There is the low form on daytime television talk shows and the slightly higher form in bookstores. Rectitude has given way to "contrition chic," as one wag called it, meaning a bargain basement way to gain publicity, sympathy, and even absolution by trafficking in one's status as victim or victimizer. This confessional mode now extends to entire nations, where separating powerful and authentic acts and expressions of regret from empty gestures becomes even more difficult than it is on the level of individuals, one to another.

Given the tawdry, shameless nature of so much of our popular culture, and the way in which it cheapens notions of forgiveness ("let's put this behind us," "let's achieve closure") it would be tempting to end the matter right here and to dismiss all acts of public contrition as bogus. But what is required, if one aims for a more thoughtful approach, is to distinguish between instances of contrition chic and more serious acts of public or political forgiveness. What sorts of deeds warrant the solemn drama of forgiveness between nations or groups, in contrast to those easier gestures undertaken in a diluted and debased confessional mode?

When Hannah Arendt called forgiveness the greatest contribution of Jesus of Nazareth to politics, she surely did not have in mind an individual figure crying: "Can you forgive me?" And, obviously, the spectacle that unfolds on daytime television in America was far from her mind, a spectacle she would have denounced as vulgar and beneath contempt. Rather, she was gesturing towards a way—the *only* way, she claims in her great book, *The Human Condition*—for repetitive cycles of vengeance to be broken. The only way for the often deadly playing out of horrible deeds done and equally horrible vengeance or payback sought is to be disrupted by an unexpected act that opens up space for something new to begin. This way alters the horizon of expectations so that bloody deeds will *not* haunt generation upon generation, dooming sons and daughters to repeat the sins of fathers and mothers.[1]

Although individual acts of forgiveness—one human being to another—most often take place outside the full glare of publicity, there are others that are noteworthy for embodying a radical alternative to contrition chic. One thinks here of Pope John Paul II, who, having barely survived an assassin's bullets, uttered his first public words from his hospital bed to the violent shooter now described as "my brother, whom I have sincerely forgiven." These words preceded John Paul's extraordinary visit to his brother and would-be-killer in jail once he was up and about. There is a *gravitas* manifest in this narrative that is altogether lacking in American quasi-therapeutic, talk-show-like confessions that are most often blatantly self-exculpatory rather than the way one professes a demanding faith—Christianity, in this instance, the faith within which forgiveness is a constitutive dimension. Those for whom forgiveness is central and solemn engage in what theologian L. Gregory Jones calls the "craft" of forgiveness in his recent book, *Embodying Forgiveness: A Theological Analysis.* Pope John Paul II was practicing this craft and, in so doing, displaying to the world the ways in which forgiveness is not primarily about a singular confessional moment but about an enactment within a particular way of life which is shaped, not by a foggy sentimentalism, but by certain hard-won and difficult truths.[2]

Within the frame of such broad-based events, often driven by desperate political purpose, individuals who are shaped by the practice of forgiveness should try to practice what they believe or preach. But an individual cannot (or such moments will be exceedingly rare), by himself or herself, stem the rushing tide of violence. Are there, then, forms of authentic *political* forgiveness? Who forgives whom and for what? Remember: forgiveness is not a one-way street. It implies a relationship or some transitive dimension. Forgiveness in general is not primarily about self-exculpation in any case, *pace* pop culture distortion, but about the creation of a new relationship or order of things or the restoration of an order of things or a relationship that has been broken or torn by violence, cruelty, indifference.

Forgiveness is also something quite different from aloofness or detachment—just not giving a damn—also mistakenly presented nowadays as a form of forgiveness. What is at stake, then, is a tougher discipline by far than are public acts of easy repentance and "forgiveness" as a kind of willed amnesia. It is too easy to get cynical when one contrasts the Rev. Jimmy Swaggart sobbing on television or the whole Watergate crew lapsing into multiple acts of contrition with John Paul's forgiveness of a violent shooter. How does one sift such matters? Political forgiveness must have a public dimension, for politics itself is public speech of a certain kind. And when people sincerely try to make amends it would be churlish to withhold from them any possibility that what they say, or do, might make any difference in the future. Perhaps one key to our discussion lies here. The public repentance of a political figure—an act related to forgiveness, certainly— cannot simply be a matter of words. Words and deeds cannot be disentangled. By their acts ye shall know them. Again, this is far easier to conjure with and even to *see* on the level of individual transformation than anything like forgiveness between nation-states or warring political parties or factions. Here the sheer weight and density of history seems at times intractable: how can one "get past" a particularly horrible series of events? Doesn't one have to punish people before one can move on? Forgiveness of a strongly political or public sort presumes communities, places, histories of a tangible, concrete sort. Real issues are involved and the stakes are often high. Entire peoples are now often crying to heaven against specific injustices and horrors.

When Arendt lamented the ways in which events take on a cyclical and repetitive quality, it was a particular version of history she surely had in her sights as a target. People are very fond of citing Santayana's claim that those who don't know their history are doomed to repeat it. But perhaps the reverse is more likely, namely, that those who know their history too well are doomed to repetition. Perhaps a certain amount of *knowing forgetting* is necessary in order to elude the rut of repetition.[3] If a people's collective horizon is limited to the reencoding of past glories or horrors, the past eviscerates any possibility of future transformation. By *knowing forgetting,* then, I have in mind a way to release present-day actors from the full burden of the past in order that they not be weighed down by it utterly.[4] Forgetting, in this case, does not mean one falls into radical present-mindedness and the delusion that the past counts for nothing; rather, one assesses and judges just what the past does count for in the present, and how much the past should frame, shape, even determine present events. As Lawrence Cahoone has pointed out, too much past overwhelms the future. But too little past empties the future, or the selves "we carry into the future. Beings without memory would have no need for retribution, but no identity either."[5]

Too often these days, when forgiveness is mentioned it gets translated into a kind of bland nonjudgmentalism: "There but for the grace of God go I," translated erroneously as "I have no right to say anything at all about anybody else's behavior and words." But if this is the tack one takes, forgiveness is altogether unnecessary. There can never be anything to forgive if no real wrong has been suffered; no real sin committed; no evil deed perpetrated; no record of historic injustices mounted. There are certain tendencies in modern liberal culture that push us to move precisely to the route of cheap grace in these matters. We are all invited to "validate" one another incessantly but never to offer correction and reproof, on the level of individual relationships and in the wider social and political arena. One thinks here of, for example, the whole "self-esteem" movement dedicated, as it is, to the principle that any criticism and any insistence that certain norms or standards be upheld is rejected as a form of harsh judgmentalism. Only bland affirmations that help us to put everything "behind us" will do. But those practicing the craft of forgiveness recognize in such affirmations a flight from the hard work of forgiveness rather than stirring examples of it. And forgiveness in public or political life also involves the painful recognition of the *limits to forgiveness* if what one seeks is full expiation, a full accounting, total justice, or a kind of annihilation of the past. There are wrongs suffered that can never be put right. Indeed, this recognition is itself a central feature of an overall structure of political forgiveness, for it opens up space for a person or a people to partially unburden themselves from the hold the past has on them.

Here is a concrete, if hypothetical, example of what I have in mind, beginning with the individual political level. Then we will move to tougher cases. Suppose that a young woman first becomes aware of the history of female inequality and all the many affronts and structures of encoded inequities to which women were subjected in the past, including the history of her own culture. A feminist consciousness dawns. How does this past weigh upon her? If the past is read as *nothing but* a story of "women's oppression," she too easily takes on the identity of present-day victim, as if no forces have been involved in shaping her other than the concatenated effects of male dominance and perfidy. She sees the world solely through the lens of victimhood, a particular temptation in a culture that specializes in creating stock victims and in which claims to victimization carry special resonance rhetorically.[6] This invites, in turn, a politics of resentment and grievance seeking, even retribution for past wrongs, that often gets called "justice."

But there is another possibility. Aware of these past wrongs, the young woman in question becomes a champion of fairness and equity, understanding, as she does, that politically there are things that can be done to forestall future repetition of past wrongs from which women suffered. She also refuses to read the past as a doleful tale of "nothing but," as if no women were villains or heroes; no men anything other than villains. The past is not forgotten but is kept alive as a tradition that must be continually engaged. She understands that her twenty-year-old male contemporary did not "do it," did not bring a previous structure of dominance and power into being. But she is also alert to the need to assess and to judge his actions from the standpoint of current standards of fairness. This imposes a burden on her, too, the burden of accountability incumbent upon all free agents. Is forgiveness involved in this latter scenario? Of a sort, in the sense that the young woman relinquishes part of the burden of the past, or a highly skewed version of that past, not allowing it to define her within the vortex of fear, loathing, resentment, victim identity. This, then, is a form of *knowing forgetting.*

There are many examples one could not turn to. How does a culture fully expiate for the Shoah? For slavery? Wrongs that cannot wholly be righted must, nonetheless, be acknowledged, and part of that acknowledgment will consist in a knowing and explicit articulation of the terrible fact that full expiation is impossible.[7] This is *not* forgetting as a type of collective amnesia; rather, it is an acknowledgment of the full scope of a given horror and the inability of a subsequent generation or generations, not themselves directly responsible for that horror, to put things right. *The events stand.* Acknowledgment of these events is required by those most directly implicated and even those not so directly implicated who, perhaps, stood by and did nothing.

Remembrance of violent deeds goes forward in all its fullness and detail. A recounting of events serves as an ongoing judgment of those most responsible tied, at the same time, to a tragic recognition that some wrongs cannot be righted. This must have been what Arendt had in mind, at least in part. In her controversial book *Eichmann in Jerusalem,* she justified the hanging of Adolf Eichmann because he had perpetrated terrible crimes against humanity "on the body of the Jewish people," but she did so in full recognition of the fact that no scale of justice had thereby been put right and that hanging every known Nazi war criminal could not do that.[8] Reversion to a strict *lex talionis* in cases of genocide, if one interprets that requirement as a strict tit-for-tat, would be hideous, implicating victims in perpetrating precisely the sorts of deeds that caused them so much suffering.

Ironically, then, *knowing forgetting* as one feature of a form of political forgiveness may be most apt, not only philosophically but politically, where truly horrific abuses are concerned. Thus, Arendt knew that young Germans, infants in the Hitler years or born subsequently, could not be held accountable in any direct way for what had occurred earlier. But they were obliged to remember in order that they could be free to act in other ways. This is *knowing forgetting:* recollection of the past, yes, but not being so wholly defined by it that one's *only* option is to be either executioner or victim (in Albert Camus's memorable phrase) rather than an accountable human agent.

Here are a few recent concrete examples of the dynamic I have in mind. They take place in the most difficult of all arenas for the dynamic of forgiveness and *knowing forgetting* to play out, namely, the realm of relations between peoples and states. But if forgiveness is to have real political weightiness as one feature of what it means to try to attain both justice and decent order and peace, it must be tested in many arenas. My first example is drawn from the bloody ground of Northern Ireland and its centuries-old troubled relationship with Great Britain. As everyone surely knows, Irish Catholics in Northern Ireland have long been a tormented people, condemned to second-class citizenship in what they perceive to be part of their land. But Irish Catholics, relatively powerless in the overall balance of what international relations thinkers call "strategic forces," have also been tormenters, as the history of IRA terrorism and death-dealing to British soldiers and to Northern Ireland Protestants attests.

It is, therefore, significant that one clear feature presaging the peace accord voted on in 1998 was the mutual proffering of forgiveness sparked by a number of leading prelates from the Irish Catholic community, most notably Cardinal Cahal Daly of Armagh, Northern Ireland. On January 22, 1995, he publicly asked forgiveness from the people of Britain in a homily delivered in Canterbury Cathedral, England—the home, as all readers surely know, of the head primate of the Church of England, the Archbishop of Canterbury. Cardinal Daly's words on that occasion are worth pondering, especially with an eye to the vision of a horizon of justice and decent reciprocity imbedded therein:

> We Irish are sometimes said to be obsessively concerned with memories of the past. It is salutary, however, to recall that the faults we attribute to others can be a projection of faults within ourselves which we have not had the courage to confront. . . . What is certainly true is that we all need a *healing of memories* [emphasis mine]. Healing of memories demands recognition of our own need for forgiveness; it requires repentance. The original biblical term for repentance, *metanoia*, is a strong word indicating the need for radical conversion, change of attitude, change of outlook, change of stance; and all this is costly and can be painful. The old word *contrition* expresses it well. . . . This healing, this conversion, this reciprocal giving and accepting of forgiveness are essential elements in the healing of relationships between our two islands and between our divided communities in Northern Ireland. . . . On this occasion . . . I wish to ask forgiveness from the people of this land for the wrongs and hurts inflicted by Irish people upon the people of this country on many occasions during that shared history, and particularly in the past twenty-five years. I believe that this reciprocal recognition of the need to forgive and to be forgiven is a necessary condition for proper Christian, and human, and indeed *political relationships* [emphasis mine] between our two islands in the future.[9]

The Cardinal continued with words about starting "something new" and about how frightful it would be to "slide back into violence," an always present possibility. What he was saying and doing, Daly added, was avowedly political in the sense of drawing out of the Gospel "conclusions which are relevant to our daily living as individuals and as a society. . . ." Reciprocal forgiveness and reconciliation was also offered by the Anglican primate of Ireland as well as the Archbishop of Canterbury himself. A question: Is this form of forgiveness, to the extent that it is accessible and enactable, available only to communicants of the Christian faith? The Cardinal suggests not when he addresses "human" and "political" relationships more generally. For some, this is a hopelessly idealist stance out of touch with tough realities. But the riposte would surely be that it is precisely tough realities that invite this stance—indeed, that suggest it as a necessary part of a process of negotiation, reconciliation, starting something new, moving away from strictly retributive notions of justice to more hopeful possibilities.

Here is a second example of a delicate balancing act involving *knowing forgetting* or a relinquishment of the full burden of the past in order to sketch an altered horizon of expectation for the future. I rely here on press reports of Pope John Paul II's visit to the Baltic States in September 1993.[10] The situation in Lithuania was particularly delicate for John Paul because ardent Polish nationalists had been at work stirring up memories of past mistreatment (or alleged mistreatment) of the Polish minority—some 300,000 strong—in Lithuania. Thus, according to coverage in the British journal *The Tablet*, the Pope had to be "careful not to offend Lithuanian sensibilities," he being not only the primate of the Roman Catholic Church but, importantly, a Pole associated with Polish aspirations to self-determination. (It is worth reminding the reader that much of current Lithuania was once part of Poland and that the Lithuanian capital, Vilnius, is Poland's "Wilno," dear to the hearts of Poles everywhere, in part because it is the home of Adam Mickiewicz, the greatest Polish poet.)

But John Paul, while acknowledging the love Poles have for that particular place, used the Lithuanian name "Vilnius" and not the Polish name "Wilno" throughout his pastoral visit, including the one time he spoke Polish—when he delivered mass in the main Polish-language church in Vilnius. For the rest of his visit, "the Pope spoke . . . Lithuanian which he had learnt for the occasion" and "this made a tremendously positive impression on the Lithuanians." The Polish citizens of Lithuania were not so pleased, "but coming from the Pope they had to accept it. The Pope exhorted the Poles to identify fully with Lithuania, and not to dwell on the past—by which he meant not to endlessly recall the time when Vilnius was part of Poland." This account shows the ways in which ethical space, stripped of irredentist and chauvinistic aspirations, can be created or expanded, making possible a more capacious form of civic identification. It is, in effect, a call to cease rubbing salt in one's own collective wound; a call for a form of remembering that does not fuel animus; a call for communal forgiveness.

A second story: during World War II, thousands of ethnic Germans were expelled from Czechoslovakia. Their property was seized. Many were murdered. All were turned into refugees. This is a story of the famous (and infamous) Sudentenland, once home to nearly three million Germans, as well as 65,000 Jews and 800,000 Czechs. The German population was by far the largest. First, the Germans, when they annexed the Sudentenland, sent the Jewish population into exile. Next, according to a report in the *Wall Street Journal*, "Czechs eliminated Germans. Eduard Benes, the pre-Communist post-war president, decreed their expulsion in 1945. At Potsdam, the Allies approved. As Germans fled toward Bavaria, Czechs took revenge. They murdered 40,000 Germans; many died at the end of a rope." This episode was long buried in the Communist deep-freeze. But since 1989, "the expulsion has become a national nettle. . . . Czechs know that every Sudenten German wasn't guilty of Hitler's crimes."[11] Although President Vaclav Havel condemned the expulsion, then-Prime Minister Vaslav Klaus (this was in 1994) wanted to keep the episode closed. In the meantime, Jewish and German victims of expulsion began seeking the return of their family homes on a case-by-case basis, especially those who resided in or near the belle-epoque spa area of Karlovy Vary (Karlsbad). The policy the Czechs agreed to permits Jewish families with claims to regain their houses, but German families cannot. The German descendants, of course, do not understand why their troubles count for nothing: for them a primordial feature of justice was violated and has yet to be put right. One is quoted as saying, "My only crime was that for 800 years my ancestors lived in that place." German descendants want repeal of the 1945 expulsion decree and many say they want to return to their "homeland" and to villages long emptied—ethnically cleansed—of their kind.

But this won't happen. It isn't clear that it should happen. Why? Because recognition of a wrong does not carry along with it a clear-cut remedy and does not mean that the old wrongs can, at present, be righted to any significant extent if what is sought is compensatory justice or restoration of a *status quo ante*. Perhaps, then, there is nothing left for the expropriated people of German descent to do but to go on with their lives, knowing that what happened to them has at long last been recognized, for President Havel admitted that they had suffered a great injustice. This is hard to take, of course, but it may be the only way to forestall quaffing the bitter brew of injustice suffered and recompense sought even unto future generations. The Havelian gesture seems right: we Czechs, although we were victims, also knew sin.

There is a follow-up to this initial story about the Sudentenland that details the ways in which Germany agreed to apologize for its invasion of the former Czechoslovakia and the Czechs, in turn, "express regret for the postwar expulsion of millions of Sudenten Germans." The Germans apologized for Nazi "policies of violence" and the Czechs expressed regret that their expulsions "caused suffering and injustice to innocent people." But, of course, things are not thereby made right in the eyes of those who suffered most, and an organization of Sudenten Germans took strong exception to the agreement because it provided them "with neither a claim to compensation nor a right to return to expropriated properties." In addition, according to press reports, many ordinary Czechs were incensed because they oppose any apology to any groups of Germans anywhere for anything given the story of the Nazi occupation.[12]

One appreciates why the mutual gestures here involved are either too little or too much depending on the angle of vision from which one is viewing them. But still, these small steps, each of which acknowledges violation of "elementary, humanitarian principles" should not be sneezed at altogether. Full reparation and compensation and return is not in the cards, not in this case and not in the vast majority of similar cases. But acknowledgment and recognition of injustice is possible and forthcoming as a minimal expectation whereby a rudimentary requirement of justice becomes a constitutive feature of a larger pattern of political forgiveness. Maybe what this tells us is that there is a *political version of forgiveness* that must—if not all of the time certainly most of the time—step back from expectations of full reconciliation and certainly from absolution. There are no sacraments, no blessings, no benedictions in politics. Thinking politically, one might ask what sorts of deeds warrant the solemn drama of forgiveness of a sort related to, yet different from, those acts that constitute a personal redemption narrative.

Nothing here is a permit to refrain from action where action is possible to prevent an egregious collective wrong from being committed. In daily life with those we love, the process of forgiveness is an enactment that is part of the daily fabric of our existence: it makes the quotidian liveable. But in the affairs of what used to be called "men and states," these enactments are not and cannot be so ordinary and so direct. But that does not forestall *knowing forgetting,* with its complex interplay of justice and forgiveness altogether: official recognition of mutual wrongs; some form of separation, perhaps; even state-level apologies. The scales are somewhat righted. A quest for such fragile achievements within our imperfect earthly state is what the politics of forgiveness is all about.

This brings us directly to one of the most dramatic cases before our eyes over the past several years, namely, the South African Truth and Reconciliation Commission. Created by an act of the post-apartheid democratic parliament in 1995, the objectives of the commission are nothing less than to help set in motion and to secure a new political culture in South Africa. The work of the commission has been divided into three distinct but related parts: a full accounting of "gross violations" of human rights defined as the killing, abduction, torture, or severe ill-treatment of any person; or any attempt, conspiracy, incitement, instigation, command or procurement to commit an act which emanated from conflicts of the past by any person acting with a political motive; consideration of amnesty appeals; possible reparative measures. Nearly all of these activities have taken place in full view of the public.

During a trip to Africa in August 1997, I met with the Research Office of the TRC in Cape Town and with its director, Charles Villa-Vicencio. What I learned departed rather markedly from much of what I had assumed about the TRC, given press reports. For example, the TRC does not require that a perpetrator openly repent or apologize, although most if not all do this and such manifestation of regret is a consideration for any amnesty request. Minimally, what is demanded is that full disclosure of politically motivated crimes be proffered. The emphasis is on victims, not victimizers, for the commissioners recognize just how important truth—recounting the basic facts—is to those who have suffered wrongs under cover of darkness or, perhaps even more horribly, in the full light of day under state sponsorship.

What happened—when, where, how—is crucially important to survivors. Not to know is a horrible thing. And, of course, only the per-

petrators have access to certain facts, as most often there are no innocent eyewitnesses to dirty deed-doing if the victims themselves do not
live to tell the tale. So the TRC has been given the specific task of getting as "complete a picture as possible" of the "nature, causes, and
extent of gross human rights violations during the period 1960–1993;
restoring the human and civil dignity of victims by giving them an opportunity to relate their own accounts of the violations of which they
are victims; facilitating the granting of amnesty to those giving full
disclosure of politically motivated crimes during this period . . . and
making recommendations to Parliament on reparation and rehabilitation measures to be taken, including measures to prevent the future
commission of human rights violations."[13]

And why undertake this? Why go down this path rather than
some other? Writes Charles Villa-Vicencio, National Director of
Research for the TRC, "It is important that we all treat one another
in the best possible manner—that even if we are not fully reconciled
to one another, we do not kill one another."[14] And truth, he insists, is
a form of *public* cognition, central to and indeed constitutive of this
very possibility. This is a dynamic process and it must be public;
it cannot take the form of *sotto voce* murmurings and private *mea
culpas*. The fact that people were murdered, maimed, and brutalized
for their political views or the color of their skin must be acknowledged. Disclosure is an essential "antidote to any attempt by apartheid revisionists to portray apartheid as no more than a desirable
policy that went askew." In fact, apartheid was a regime that required
and legitimated violence—violence was no anomaly; it was the way
things were done.

Those who violated human rights in a gross way are being denied
the status of martyrs to the old order. Nor will they be maintained
in prison as a symbol of the past and a burden on taxpayers. Instead,
they must face a very new community that has full knowledge of what
they did—when, where, and how. Villa-Vicencio again: "An authentic
historical record of human rights abuse" is vital because it serves "as a
basis for assisting future generations to defend democracy and the
rule of law in the face of any future attempt at authoritarian rule."
This is a complex business that deploys certain theological steps to political ends and purposes: acknowledgment, contrition, preparedness
to make restitution, the extending and receiving of forgiveness as a
form of ongoing reconciliation.[15]

Small wonder even such extraordinarily sophisticated observers as Timothy Garton Ash are capable of getting things wrong. Ash, to whom we are forever indebted for his definitive works on the 1989 European revolutions, sees the "reconciliation" aspect of the TRC as, if "taken to extreme," a "deeply illiberal idea. As Isaiah Berlin has taught us, liberalism means living with unresolvable conflicts of values and goals, and South Africa has those in plenty. . . . Would it not be more realistic to define a more modest goal: peaceful coexistence, cooperation, tolerance?"[16] Ash here dramatically misunderstands the meaning of reconciliation, which does not at all imply some harmonizing of interests and beliefs, nor require blurring the edges of controversies. Instead, it means bringing matters into a frame within which conflicts can be adjudicated short of bloodshed. To the extent that Archbishop Tutu may urge upon people public acts of personal reconciliation when they may not be prepared for such gestures, the process becomes problematic. But overall the idea is, as one South African scholar put it to me, to "make possible a future. Reconciliation is the work of many life-times." In other words, I take reconciliation as a political concept to mean that one no longer begins with a deadly *a priori* that a sizeable chunk of one's fellow countrymen and -women are outsiders and enemies. Rather, we are all enclosed within a single socio-political frame and enfolded within a politico-ethical horizon. This is a difficult point and easily misconstrued.

Still, many, like Ash, will continue to ask: What about justice? Here the South Africans believe they are making a contribution in challenging the most prevalent models of justice that reign among us. What they are aiming for, they insist, is *political restorative justice,* a form of political forgiveness concerned with justice. This means it is neither cheap forgiveness nor the "dominant Western mode of retributive or punitive justice." Restorative justice aims for a future which generates no new victims of the sorts of systematic misdeeds and criminality that blighted the past. Political restorative justice, they argue, addresses the legitimate concerns of victims and survivors while seeking to reintegrate perpetrators into the community. This, they insist, is an alternative *both* to contrition chic with its sentimentalized gloss that papers over a huge indifference *and* to the horror of wrongs suffered and vengeance sought generation after generation, a *lex talionis* shorn of mercy.

The TRC is quite prepared to admit that their creative view of justice is in part a compromise, but not of a sordid sort; rather, of a sort that makes politics itself possible. In a sense certain quite legitimate demands of justice, including forms of just punishment, are foresworn in order that they might be reinstated in an order grounded in justice rather than injustice. Ironically, the moral rehabilitation of the political world requires, at the outset, that certain features of a just world or of just punishment be evacuated temporarily in the interest of a restorative project.[17] Full reparation, compensation, and just punishment is never possible when one confronts large-scale horrors, a point made to me many times over by several members of the Argentine Mothers of the Disappeared who insisted, over and over again: we want justice, not vengeance, and we know that not all the guilty ones can be punished. "That is utopian," Renee de Epelbaum told me, "and we are not utopians. We are political realists who seek justice."

The TRC Commissioners are concerned with legitimating a new and fragile democratic regime and having sufficient time to build up a culture of human rights and constitutional guarantees. So they have come up with a political form of forgiveness as an alternative form of justice, aiming for nothing less than bestowing on future generations a vision of justice that challenges many of the models with which we have long been familiar. Reconstruction and restoration, they insist, is "an inherent but often neglected part of judicial theory." In the words of Archbishop Tutu: "We speak about restorative rather than retributive justice. It is not the case that the perpetrators get off scot free. They have to stand in the full glare of their city and say I did this and this and this. . . . Having to come clean in public has a very heavy cost. While reparation is not compensation, one of the things that has happened is that people who were treated like rubbish now have a story that the whole country acknowledges. Victims have been given an official forum where they have told their story. That is something whose value we can never compute."[18]

The cycle of violence, they argue, must be broken. And they point to evidence that suggests that retributive justice, especially in a framework that simply reverses the tables of who is victimizer, who victim, can never do this. Part of what is involved in restorative justice is a dramatic transformation in the horizon of expectations. Also, when a regime falls punitive measures may harden old political attitudes and keep alive morbid convictions rather than softening them. In other words, mandatory retribution can well undermine the very democratic processes on which the rule of law is based. This does not mean one takes leave of punishment entirely, but it does mean that one recognizes one must change the framework of expectation in order that future punishment can be part of an overall structure of justice. Punishment should never be an end in itself but only a "last resort" means to an end. So the real challenge confronted by the South Africans, and by anyone who enters this realm of political-ethical debate, is to determine where and when punishment and retribution might fit as part of a decent, restorative, hopeful political project. The stakes are huge for South Africa and for our fragile globe as we enter the next century. The most difficult task of all, the TRC reminds us in the most dramatic way possible, is to remember and to forget—not forget in the sense of collective amnesia but in an altogether different way: as a release from the full weight and burden of the past.

NOTES

1. Hannah Arendt, *The Human Condition* (Chicago: University of Chicago Press, 1958).

2. See Gerhard Forde, "On Being a Theologian of the Cross," *Christian Century*, 22 October 1997, pp. 947–49, for a discussion of why a theology of the cross is not about sentimentalism but about sin, redemption, punishment, reconciliation, God's justice, and so on.

3. As will become clear as the discussion continues, knowing forgetting is also a type of remembering. I thank Lawrence Cahoone of Boston University for his emphasis on this point.

4. Patricia Cook, in her forthcoming book, *The Philosophy of Forgetting: An Inquiry through Plato's Dialogues,* notes that the Greeks offered at least twelve different meanings of forgetting. Dietrich Bonhoeffer, in his *Letters and Papers from Prison*, speaks of the capacity to forget as a gift of grace—again, not to be dominated by the past, by musings on what-should-have-been.

5. Lawrence Cahoone, "Commentary on Jean Bethke Elshtain," response delivered at Boston University on November 5, 1997, p. 3.

6. A friend told me recently of an experiment in which a group of American teenagers were asked to separate themselves according to whether

they thought they were "powerless" or had some "power." The result? Everybody wanted to be "powerless." That, clearly, is the identity of choice these days and it blunts our ability to *see* real victims, with their concrete, not abstract or ideological, claims, when they stand before us.

7. On this score, see the French Bishops' Declaration of Repentance issued September 30, 1997, near a former Jewish deportation camp in a Paris suburb. The full text of the declaration appears in *Origins* 27, no. 18 (16 October 1997): 301–5. See also L. Gregory Jones, "True Confessions," *Christian Century*, 19–26 November 1997, p. 1090.

8. Hannah Arendt, *Eichmann in Jerusalem* (New York: Penguin Books, 1964).

9. Cahal Daly, "Breakdown of the Cease-Fire," *Origins* 25, no. 35 (22 February 1996): 585–88.

10. Anatol Lieven, "The Pope's Balancing Act," *The Tablet,* 18 September 1993, pp. 1208–9.

11. All citations on this story are from "Czech Republic Fields Demands of Germans, Jews, for Lost Homes," *The Wall Street Journal,* 15 July 1995, pp. 1, 6.

12. Citations about the follow-up are drawn from Alan Crowell, "Germans and Czechs Agree to Part on Wartime Abuses," *The New York Times,* 12 December 1996, p. A12.

13. Wilhelm Verwoerd, "Justice after Apartheid? Reflections on the South African Truth and Reconciliation Commission," paper delivered at the Fifth International Conference on Ethics and Development, Madras, India, January 2–9, 1997, p. 3.

14. Charles Villa-Vicencio, "Truth and Reconciliation: In Tension and Unity," Occasional Paper of TRC, p. 2.

15. Ibid., p. 4.

16. Timothy Garton Ash, "True Confessions," *New York Review of Books,* 17 July 1997, pp. 33–38.

17. For this insight, I thank Lawrence Cahoone.

18. Frank Ferrari, "Forgiving the Unforgivable: An Interview with Archbishop Desmond Tutu," *Commonweal,* 12 September 1997, pp. 13–18.

The Urgency of Hope

ELIE WIESEL

MANY LEGENDS ARE told in Talmudic literature about King Solomon's wisdom, riches, and extraordinary gifts. He had a special ring made for himself—a ring endowed with occult powers. When he was melancholy, simply wearing the ring was enough to make his sadness vanish. And when he felt overcome with joy, it was enough for him to wear the ring and his sadness returned.

A strange legend it is for it makes one doubt the king's celebrated wisdom. We understand why a man succumbing to melancholy may need a ring to vanquish it. But why should a happy man choose to chase away his happiness?

The answer is that a happy man has everything he needs initially except . . . hope. In other words, a man who has everything, hopes for nothing. And hope is an essential part of the human condition. Just as the body cannot live without dreams, the mind or the soul cannot endure without hope. Hope has its own architecture, its own trajectory. The whole idea of redemption is rooted in the principle of anticipation, of expectation. What is messianism if not hope brought to its incandescent climax? It teaches us that God, for the believer, is the embodiment of hope; but even He is waiting for redemption. Even the Creator of the universe needs hope.

For the religious person, hope is a divine gift. Born in the most obscure realm of one's being, it blossoms only at the paradoxical moment when its absence is stronger than its presence. Hope against hope means I hope because I have no choice—because I am hopeless.

For the nonbeliever, hope represents an affirmation of one's right to impose meaning on creation and one's triumph in the name of reason. Despair is human, and so is its antidote. The secular person's mind has power, a power equal to the religious person's soul.

In pragmatic terms, hope is part of our everyday life. I go to sleep hoping to wake up in the morning. I go to work hoping to be

48

useful—and appreciated. I meet a stranger on the road hoping to make him or her into an ally, a friend. I get married hoping to have children who will improve their world. I begin a book hoping to finish it, then to publish it, and to be understood by my readers, if not by all the critics. On a purely ethical level, a generous and creative relation to "the other" implies hope in his or her future. Who knows, his or her offspring of tomorrow may bring solace and happiness to society hundreds of years from now.

The death of hope is the death of all generous impulses in me; it is the death of the inner person in the person. Thus hope emerges as a presence that accompanies and envelops my challenge and my comfort, my question and its answer, my desire and its fulfillment. The death of hope is for me the end of possibilities. The death of hope is the death of change, of renewal; of redemption too. In ancient Greece, tragedies were linked to if not caused by the notion that a hero's fate had been sealed. Prometheus' punishment was preordained, as was Hector's death. In mythology, it was always "too late" for death to be vanquished or the gods to be appeased. Antigone chose death over fear because of her hopelessness. Socrates preferred death to exile for the same reason. Seneca understood that the future of the Roman Empire was hopeless when he realized that the morality of the vanquished was superior to that of the victor.

Is there hope in Scripture? Adam and Eve *had* to leave paradise: it was a choice on their part. There was everything in it except hope. Abraham left his homeland because God had promised him hope in the Land of Canaan. The Israelites were deprived of hope in Egypt. That's why they followed Moses into the desert. The scouts were punished because they deprived them of hope.

What about Talmudic literature? Its legends are bursting with hope which is embodied in the character and personality of the Messiah. It is the ultimate hope. All creatures will be wise, all curses removed from them. There will be no sin and no punishment, no suffering and no death. Neither ignorance nor hate will debase society. God will no longer be a Judge; He will be only a Father. And Satan will remain forever in chains, a prisoner of his own evil ambitions.

However, messianic redemption is to be preceded by apocalyptic eschatology. "At that time," says a Mishna, "arrogance will grow . . . as will drunkenness. . . . Legal authority will be dominated by apostasy with no one around to object. . . . The Community house will turn into

a bordello. . . . The wisdom of scholars and writers will be repudiated. . . . Sin-fearing people will inspire disgust with Truth being
absent. . . . Old people will stand up in the presence of youngsters. . . ."

"At that time," said a Hasidic Master, "summer will be without
heat, winter without frost, the wise will have forgotten their wisdom,
and the pious their fervor."

Another Master expressed a similar idea in different imagery:
"At that time, one will no longer distinguish light from what negates
light, twilight from dawn, silence from speech, and speech from its
content." A third Rebbe said: "At that time there will no longer be any
relation between man and his face, desire and its object, metaphor
and its meaning. And people will begin hating themselves rather than
their fellow men and women."

But then—at "Akhrit hayamim," at the end of time—humankind will be saved, redeemed. Eschatology itself is endowed with
hope to which it is intrinsically linked.

But "Akhrit hayamim" is not the enemy of hope. The enemy of
hope is "Tohu vabohu," chaos.

What is missing in today's society, as we near the end of a century of unprecedented violence, is a message that it is not too late.
That the train is not running to the abyss. That catastrophe can be
averted. That hope is possible. That it has a future. This is felt especially by young people. Last year and this year, lecturing in Europe
and in our own country, most of the students' questions dealt with
this topic. More than anything, they wanted from the lecturer a sense
of promise, an orientation of hope.

For there are young men and women everywhere who claim to
be part of a despairing "X generation." It inherited too many broken
taboos, false idols, and corrupt ideals. All theories fell apart, many
victories were reduced to dust. Granted, some good things happened
in the last five decades. The defeat of Nazism, the fall of Communism.
The end of colonialism in Africa and Asia. The renaissance of Israel as
a nation in its ancestral land. Nelson Mandela's victory over apartheid,
André Sakharov's valiant struggle for human rights. But racism is still
alive, as is anti-Semitism. The idea of a European community is gaining ground: France and Germany, Poland and Russia may never again
wage war against one another. But there are other wars still being
fought—civil wars, ethnic wars, religious wars. Ugly assassinations of

innocent citizens, revolting slaughters of helpless children in Algeria. The bloodbaths in Egypt. The Bosnian chapter has not been closed. Or that of Kashmir, or Cyprus. The cease-fire in Ireland is fragile at best. In the Middle East, cowardly terrorist attacks still prevent peace from being realized. Anti-Semites desecrate cemeteries in Europe and also in this country. Fanaticism is on the rise everywhere, in the world of politics as well as in that of religion. Will sanity ever prevail? No wonder that youngsters become cynical, showing distrust towards authority. What are they to think of appointed or elected politicians whose indictments for corruption make headlines in Europe? If, eternities ago, one read about "governments in exile," today one could easily read about "governments in prison." And so cynicism gains the ground deserted by hope.

Closer to home, take the students in Boston University, on whose faculty I am so truly proud to belong. Students come here in search not only of knowledge and a career but also of hope—of reasons to hope. They want to believe that education is a noble enterprise, that communication is possible, that we are not alone, that words and images can come alive, that History is moving forward, that culture is an instrument of progress, that victory without shame is possible, that Truth without compromise is attainable.

But how far is a psychologist allowed to penetrate the consciousness, the psyche, and the memory of a patient without violating his or her right to privacy? In scientific discovery, are there limits—for instance, in genetic experiments—which one may not cross, not even for the sake of hope? And how are we to avoid turning one person's hope into another person's despair? And one people's happiness into another's distress?

Must one reach the bottom of despair to obtain a splash of hope? Our perception of despairing people may, at times, be wrong. Terminal cancer patients can cling to hope with more strength than their healthy relatives. Can any one of us measure the magnitude of hope a condemned prisoner experiences one minute before his or her execution? For them, a minute has the weight of eternity.

Hope necessarily implies an act of faith, faith in God—if one is a believer—that He cares, that He listens, that He remains present in human history. If one is an agnostic, hope implies faith in humankind, and in the humanity of our fellow human beings—-that human beings can be free and generous, and capable of glorious achievements, persons worthy of the faith placed in them by their parents, teachers, friends.

Is faith enough? Is faith possible—always? Faith in whom? In God's goodness?

> Two friends are about to cross a dangerous river infected with crocodiles. One is frightened. The other is not. "Why be afraid? God is merciful," he said. "Yes," answered his friend. "But what if God chooses today to be merciful to the crocodiles?"

More than faith, hope implies a projection into the future. But Paul Valery, the great French poet, already warned us that the future isn't what it used to be. Perhaps the same could be said of hope.

Let us analyze one example: the twentieth century gave birth to an immense political endeavor—socialism which eventually turned into Communism—which for many decades shaped history and attitudes towards it.

It began as a gigantic social awakening of the masses, issuing a powerful call for compassion, freedom, brotherhood, and truth; its covenant contained all the good words. It promised to bring bread for the hungry, stability for the uprooted, pride for the humbled. In other words, it offered hope to the hopeless.

Its appeal to idealistic young intellectuals in the early decades of the century was understandable. Fed up with war, social injustice, misery, bigotry, and anti-Semitism, they saw in its lofty yet concrete program more than a set of solutions to economic problems. They found in it a new sense of History, a new meaning for political ambitions. Their dream was metaphysical; its aim was to change the world by improving the lives of its traditional victims: the poor peasants, the hungry workers, the oppressed—and the Jews. Many of the Communist agitators were Jews. Lew Davidowics Trotzky in Russia and Rosa Luxemburg in Germany were among the best known. There were others, many others. Some came from the world of the Yeshiva. For them, Communism responded to moral outrage. Having lost patience while waiting for the Messiah, they decided to implement his promise without him. They lived to regret it. The Communist experience proved to be a gigantic laboratory in deceit, brutality, cruelty, and mass murder. If Communism emerged from a desperate need for hope, it ended up betraying it.

But what made it possible for a movement such as Communism, born from collective hunger for human dignity and hope, to become a vehicle of oppression, imprisonment, and murder? At what point do revolutions begin to devour their children?

That hope can be an obstacle to hope and even to survival, that it could become a source of peril and a trap laid by Death, has become clear to my generation, though in a different way. How did Francis Bacon put it? "Hope is a good breakfast—but a bad supper. . . ." Hope was used and misused by the enemy against our people during the darkest period of its long tormented history.

Many, too many, communities were wiped out in Eastern Europe because they had hoped that the enemy would not dare to implement his threats, that the civilized free world would stop him, that human beings would always remain human, that God would keep His pledge and observe the terms of His covenant with His children.

With each step irrevocably leading to the Final Solution, the successive waves of victims would be reassured that the previous one was the last. Berlin's war against the Jews was waged by murderers in uniform, assisted by experts in psychological warfare who excelled in luring their victims into false confidence. And their system worked. The Jews too often believed the enemy's propaganda. At first, it was so much easier to believe that the Germans meant to take only the Jews in Germany because they were assimilated, and later that only the Jews in Poland were threatened because they were not. The same tactic was used with Jews in Greece, Italy, Belgium, France, the Netherlands—everywhere in occupied Europe. When a ghetto was liquidated, others were told that it was the last in the program. The last quarter. The last street. The last transport. It was always said to be the last. And of course it never was.

Those who learned how to be immune to hope fared better. Many German Jews who refused to trust Hitler's assurances emigrated to new homes in Palestine, Great Britain, and the United States. Later, as the criminal regime of blood and ashes spread to other countries, and emigration became more difficult if not impossible, youngsters fled to the forest and joined the partisans, disregarding the German promises that they risked nothing staying with their families. Those who gave credence to German promises ended up in Treblinka, Belzec, Ponàr, Majdanek, and Auschwitz.

Their hope was dangerous and indeed terminal because it was based on delusion and falsehood. Because it originated with the enemy who used it as a ploy, a mask. Does this mean that there are well-tested blueprints and rules for hope? For instance, if offered by friends it is always good, whereas if it is handed to us by the enemy it is always evil? But then how is one to wait for the distant friend's intervention, when the enemy's sword is so near and its effect immediate, and the harrowing fear so agonizing?

Hope may at times be a consequence of fear, or a remedy for fear. They are uniquely related. As Spinoza said: "Fear cannot be without hope nor hope without fear." And how did Milton put it? "So, farewell hope, and with hope, farewell fear."

Both were wrong. There can be fear without hope. And the loss of hope does not necessarily imply a newly sworn allegiance to evil. Must the loss of hope lead to the loss of faith? There were times when Jews lost hope in the future, yet maintained almost intact their faith in God.

But not in His goodness. Jeremiah and Daniel refused to praise it. Read Jeremiah's Lamentations and you will hear with quasi-disbelief his accusatory words to the Almighty who, like an enemy, struck down His people: "Haragta velo khamalta, you have killed without mercy. Tavakhta velo khamalta, you have slaughtered without mercy." He does not merely say that God had allowed the enemy to kill and slaughter Jews. He was more outspoken, more direct. He said: "You, God, have killed and murdered your children." In Talmudic times, disciples of Rabbi Ishmael, with somewhat more restraint, cried out: "Mi kamokha baélim adoshem, who among the gods can be like You, al tikré élim [they do not say "gods" but ilémim which means "mute"]; who can be as mute as You are, oh God. Sheroe beelbon banav veshotek—for He sees the humiliation of His children, and keeps silent!"

In Hasidic literature, voices of pain and revolt were heard on behalf of Jewish victims of endless tragedies. I particularly cherish the great Rabbi Lévi-Itzhak of Berditchev who pleaded with a broken heart to the God of Israel, at times threatening him that "if You refuse to hear our prayers, I shall refuse to go on saying them. . . ." And also: "Know that if Your reign does not bring grace and compassion [lo teshev al kissakha beemet], Your throne will not be a throne of truth. . . ." And, once, before the Moussaf service on Yom Kippur, he exclaimed: "Today is Judgment Day. David proclaims it in his Psalms. Today all Your creatures stand before You so that You may pass sentence. But I, Lévi-Itzhak, son of Sarah of Berditchev, I say and I proclaim that it is You who will be judged today by those who suffer for you, who die for you and for the sanctification of your Name. . . ."

Has the Berditchiver Tzaddik lost faith? No. He has lost hope. So much so that for a whole year, he, the extrovert, the activist, the man who always had a good word, a word of consolation and encouragement for those who needed it, fell into deep melancholy. Other great Masters endured similar experiences. They seemed to have lost their élan, their capacity for joy. They too lost hope. But, after a while, somehow they succeeded in recapturing it.

Reflecting on the destiny of the people of Israel, so gloriously and tragically tested by God, filled with so much agony and oppression, I often wondered: why haven't we given back the Torah to the Almighty—as the Yiddish poet Yacov Glatstein suggested in his poem about the Holocaust? "We received the Torah at Sinai and gave it back at Majdanek," he said. Why, in the course of centuries, has there been no gathering of our great spiritual leaders to discuss such a possibility? Just imagine, in the time of the Crusades, of the Khmelnicki pogroms, what if those scholars and teachers had come out with a Manifesto that would present a logical challenge to their Creator: "Master of the World, God of Abraham, Isaac, and Jacob, You have chosen us as custodians of your Torah which we tried to study and implement in spite of the hardship and suffering we had to endure. But now we are tired, exhausted. We can no longer absorb so much pain. We cannot continue like this. If you, in Your eternal wisdom, prefer to have a world without Jews, so be it! We shall then be the last Jews on earth, if that's what You really want!"

Actually, it happened—once. After the destruction of the Temple in Jerusalem, at least one community advocated total abstinence and absolute asceticism. The name P'rushim—or Pharisees—was given to them because "sheparshu minshotéhem" ("they separated from their wives") so as not to have any more children. It was their way of saying to God: "For us, it's enough! Without the Temple we cannot go on living like husbands and wives." They too had given up hope.

But they were admonished by the Sages who told them: "Will you stop eating meat because sacrifices are no longer offered in Jerusalem? And wine because the priests no longer use it for their rituals? Will you stop eating bread and drinking water because bread and water were also in the Temple's services?" Faced with such rigorous logic, the husbands returned to their wives.

Since Abraham we are commanded to believe that hope is an essential part of life and faith. Why was the Book of Job accepted in the canon only after lengthy debates? Because it sounded too pessimistic. If at the end the scale tipped in its favor, it was mainly due to its happy end.

Certain books of the apocalypse—such as Ben Sira, Baroukh daleth, Hanokh alef and bét—were rejected in spite of their great literary quality. Why? Because they offer no hope to the reader.

A tale of hope against hope or faith against faith is told about Rabbi Yishmael and his martyrdom. At one point, during his torment, he began to weep. A heavenly voice was then heard, saying: "Yishmael, Yishmael, if you shed one more tear, I shall restore the entire universe to its primary state of chaos." So Rabbi Yishmael stopped crying.

But why did he? Why didn't the old Master turn to the Almighty and say: "If this is the way the world will continue—ruled by violence and fear, torture and death—I don't mind allowing or even forcing you to start all over again! Yes, from the beginning!" He could have said that. He had all the reasons in the world to lose hope for society and all faith in History! Why then did he stop weeping? Because God told him to do so. Except for the son of Abouya, the notorious Akhér, no Sage and no Hasidic Master has repudiated the Creator of the universe or lost faith in His divine truth.

Still, what about their hope? Hope for what, in the name of whom? The response is always to be found in messianic redemption. It is a constant theme in Talmudic literature. Ultimately, the Messiah represents the existential hope of humanity. Whether he is a person or a metaphor—some sources speak more about messianic times than about the Messiah himself—he remains a living promise, an eternal hope to be fulfilled. And shared.

Earlier I mentioned chaos being the enemy of hope. It is, in God's eyes, the ultimate punishment.

What is chaos? A nebulous situation in which all frontiers have vanished. Good and evil, beauty and ugliness, substance and frivolity, the sacred and the profane, anticipation and memory, hope and despair—nothing distinguishes them anymore. In other words: chaos is indifference on a cosmic scale.

The opposite of hope is indifference. But there came a time, centuries later, when there was much indifference in the world.

In human terms, hope seemed unattainable and almost unnatural. Think of our people in the walled-in ghettos. We read about them in personal diaries and in well-documented chronicles. Marriages were celebrated over there. One day before being deported in cattle-cars to death camps, young men and women would swear eternal love to one another. Women gave birth to children; circumcisions were performed. Underground schools were opened for children to study sciences, mathematics, the Bible, Jewish history and literature. What in the world did they hope to achieve with their diplomas? Did they really think they would help them get into prestigious universities?

While the outside world was indifferent to their fate, the ghetto inhabitants, paradoxically, clung to hope. Some may call such hope absurd—but, strangely enough, it was not false. For such is the nature of the human condition. One hour before dying, teachers teach and students learn from them essential lessons about the human's fate and the meaning of his or her passage on earth. One reads a novel and dies before coming to its dénouement? One plants a tree and is taken away the next day? Such is human destiny that all tales are interrupted. The last word is not ours. But the one before the last, which is ours, sounds as if there can never be an end to the tale. Again such is the human mystery that every significant moment contains its share of immortality.

Those who learned this awesome lesson best are survivors of catastrophes in general and the "Shérit Hapléta," the "Saving remnant" of the Holocaust, in particular.

Where did they draw the strength, where did they find the courage to start a new life again? Marry again? Have children and build new homes for them? Read about the men and women who dwelled in displaced persons camps and you will be astonished. They had lost everything that reminded them of their past, and yet they built schools and theaters, engaged in a variety of cultural and financial activities. You could hear them sing Zionist songs on weekdays or Shabbat songs on the Sabbath, argue about Jewish politics, tell jokes and laugh, and make others laugh, and invent all kinds of crazy projects for a future grounded in hope, in hope above all, in spite of everything. Hadn't they learned the facts of life yet? Had they forgotten yesterday's despair? How did they manage to overcome their justifiable suspicion and anger so as to trust another person, especially a non-Jew? Having seen their former hopes ridiculed, profaned, and murdered, how did they manage to invent new ones?

Is it that they had no choice? No, they had a choice. They could have opted for nihilism and hedonism. They could have said: "Look, we have paid our dues. Hope is a word, nothing else. And words mean nothing to us. Now all we want is to enjoy wine and laughter. That is the true essence of life." Who would have dared to contradict them? Why didn't they say that? Why did they, in fact, say something else, just the opposite? Because they realized that having survived tragedy, it was their singular duty to do something with their experiences. So they invented hope in order to pass it on to others.

How did they manage to achieve it?

I belong to a generation for whom it was tempting to renounce hope—too tempting. Unless one feels able to hope that something can be done with one's knowledge, with one's experience, with one's memories, one is crushed by feeling useless in a world from which one was expelled.

Strangely and paradoxically enough, those of us who awoke in 1945 and realized that we were alive, were carried by a powerful hope that must seem bizarre today.

We were convinced fifty-four-odd years ago that something must now happen to the world, that so much pain, so much suffering, so much anguish would make a difference in History, and provoke a change, a mutation in the human condition, in the human self-image. We were convinced then that the world had learned essential lessons from its mistakes and aberrations. Lessons about the power of evil and the innumerable dimensions of despair. Lessons about solitude and silence, hunger and humiliation. Lessons about the perils of indifference and the limits of persecution in times of prejudice, bigotry, and hatred. Some of us have said it many times: had anyone told us then that we would feel compelled, in our lifetime, to fight anti-Semitism, we would not have believed it. We thought that anti-Semitism died in the fires of Auschwitz. We were wrong. Jews perished there; their enemies are still alive and active.

If anyone had told us then that, in our lifetime, there would be vicious, ugly, morally repugnant people who would have the gall to deny our past and publicly declare that our testimony is false and our victimhood invented, we would have considered such talk as unreasonable, implausible, and rather silly.

But I belong to a tradition that considers despair a question, not an answer. There is "quest" in question and it keeps us motivated. "No heart is as whole as a broken heart," said Rabbi Nahman of Bratzlav. May we paraphrase it and say that no hope is as powerful as a wounded hope.

In conclusion—a few words about hope and prayer.

What is hope? It is a transcendental act which accompanies us in all our endeavors, thus allowing us to go beyond our limits and project ourselves into an uncertain future where dream and desire have the force of memory. Thus one may say that the human being is defined by his or her hope, not only by one's capacity for hope but also by one's will to impose it on destiny. Where, under which sky, would we be if we were forever deserted by hope? We would no longer sense the fragrance of dawn or the nocturnal breath coming from an open window. We would be rendered superfluous, a withered branch left behind by the wind. Nothing would be of interest because no goal would await us. Hope being the key to freedom and fulfillment, without it life itself would be a prison. For hope is a gift that a wounded memory can bestow upon itself.

As for prayer—our liturgy consists of innumerable prayers. There are prayers for every possible situation. There is one for eating bread and another for eating cake, one for fruits and another for wine, one when you meet a king and another when you greet a scholar, one when you hear thunder and one when you see lightning, and still another when you notice a rainbow, one when you are happy and one when you are not. . . . However, there is no prayer for martyrdom. The martyr may recite the usual credo, "Shma Israel . . . Hear O Israel, God is our God, God is one" which pious Jews recite three times a day. But there is no special prayer for the martyr as he or she is about to be beheaded or burnt at the stake.

The reason? Divine help may arrive at the very last moment—and the prayer, already uttered, would be wasted.

In other words, until the last breath there is hope.

But then, isn't hope the human's noblest prayer?

A great Hasidic Master, Rebbe Tzvi-Hersh of Ziditchïv, said to his friend Rebbe Yoseph Meir of Sepinke: "While our Master, the Holy Seer of Lublin, was alive, we his disciples would simply gather around him in a circle, our hands on our friend's shoulders, and we would ascend unto the highest spheres. But today we are afraid. Today even our dreams are changed."

Well—today some of our dreams often turn into nightmares.

Where is hope? I do not know. Perhaps, to some of us, there is none—there cannot be.

And yet, and yet. In Pandora's special box, at the bottom, right under the calamities, there is hope. To gain access to it, must one first go through all the calamities? The knowledge that it is there, that it exists somewhere, may be sufficient. Following Albert Camus, we ought to imagine Sisyphus happy. Created in the image of Him who has no image, it is incumbent upon our contemporaries to invoke and create hope where there is none—and to do so with words when they suggest longing for compassion, with song when it is imbued with fervor, and with silence when all else has failed.

In other words: only human beings can move me to despair. But only they can help me vanquish it—and call it hope.

PART II

The Politics of Pluralism

The Voice of Religion in Political Discourse

BHIKHU PAREKH

IT IS COMMONLY argued that religion and politics are wholly different activities and that religion not only has nothing or little of value
to contribute to political life but is a source of much mischief. It is
concerned with the otherworldly destiny of the human soul, based on
faith, approaches human life in terms of nonnegotiable absolutes,
arouses strong and often irrational passions, pursues its vision of the
good even at the risk of civil disorder, demands blind conformity, and
so forth. Political community could not be more different. It is concerned with secular or worldly interests, requires moderation and compromise, is based on rational debate and discussion, prizes civil peace
above all else, seeks an inherently tentative consensus, and so forth.
Since religion is incompatible with many of the basic preconditions of
political life and has a deeply antipolitical thrust, it should be kept out
of political life as far as is humanly possible. Although this view is a
characteristic feature of modernity and widely shared, it was first developed and has been vigorously championed by liberals. For convenience I shall therefore call it a liberal view.

Since liberals consider religion irrelevant to and on balance a
pernicious influence in political life, they argue that it should be confined to the private realm and not allowed to intrude into political life.
This means two things. First, the civil authority or the state should
be secular in the sense that it should not enforce or formally endorse
a religion, take official notice of it, or be guided by religious consider-
ations in its treatment of its citizens and formulating its laws and policies; and it should in general treat religion as a politically irrelevant
category. Second, although religion might matter to people, it should
only regulate their personal lives and not shape their judgments and
conduct as citizens. Citizenship is a political status and requires that
citizens should abstract away or bracket out their religious beliefs and

conduct their common affairs in terms of public or collectively sharable secular reasons. For some liberals, citizens should think in terms
of and be motivated by secular reasons alone;[1] others appreciate that
they cannot avoid being guided by their religious beliefs in forming
their political opinions but insist that they should at least publicly
defend the latter in terms of secular reasons alone.

The liberal separation of religion and politics is predicated on
four assumptions.

(1) Religion and politics pertain to very different areas of
human life. One is concerned with the destiny of the human soul and
its otherworldly interests, and the other with secular human interests.
The two can and should be neatly separated.

(2) Citizenship involves abstracting away religious beliefs and
being guided wholly by secular and collectively sharable reasons.

(3) Religion has nothing or little of value to contribute to political life.

(4) Religion is often a source of mischief in political life and is
subversive of some of its basic preconditions.

I suggest that (1) is only partially true, (2) is true but not in the
sense intended by liberals, (3) is false, and (4) is true. Since (4) is un-
problematic, I shall concentrate on the other three liberal assumptions and discuss each in turn.

I

The first liberal assumption implies that worldly and otherworldly interests can be easily separated and that political life is only
concerned with the former. Neither assertion is self-evident, and each
is disputed by many. However, I shall not enter into that controversy
here. Even if we accepted both these assertions, religion and politics
cannot be separated in the manner the liberal proposes.

Secular matters are of as much concern to religion as to the state
and are not the latter's monopoly. They can be defined and pursued in
several different ways, and religion represents one distinct perspective on them. Life and property are clearly secular matters. But they
raise such questions as when life begins and ends, whether human life
should enjoy absolute priority over animal life, what respect for it
entails, and whether and when the agent or society may justifiably ter-

minate it, as well as why property should be protected, within what limits, what is to be done when it damages human lives, and so on. Every religion has a view on and is actively interested in these and related questions. Matters of global justice, universal human rights, legitimacy of war, whether a country has obligations to outsiders and how they limit its pursuit of its national interests, and the human relation to nature are all secular but, again, religion has much to say about them.

Secular interests have an inseparable distributive dimension, and that too is of vital concern to religion. However unworldly its orientation might be, every religion has a moral core with its inevitable social and political implications. If I am expected to be my "brother's keeper" or to love my neighbor as I love myself, or if I believe that every human being is made in the image of God, it is a matter of deep concern to me how my fellow humans live and are treated by others including the state. To be religious is to make and be guided by certain moral and spiritual commitments and to define the meaning and purpose of one's life in terms of them. This does not mean that religious persons are necessarily committed to social and political activism, for they may consider this a distraction and leave the fate of fellow humans to God. They might just as consistently define their commitments in an activist manner and believe that, even if they avoid secular entanglements, they cannot remain wholly indifferent to their fellow humans.

Even as and precisely because the otherworldly concerns of religion have an inescapable worldly dimension, the state's secular concerns require it to take an active interest in religious practices and even beliefs. The state is vitally concerned with its own security, maintenance of public order, preservation of human life, the well-being of its citizens, etc., and religion impinges on all these. A religion might advocate rebellion against all secular authorities, mass suicide as a form of release from the valley of fears, hatred of other religions, murder of infants, or dangerous drugs, or its practices might pose threats to public health, morals, and peace or make unacceptable demands on public resources, or its internal organization might involve gross maltreatment of its members or inhuman punishment of dissenters. The state cannot remain indifferent to any of these. Even if it decides not to intervene actively in the internal life of a religious community, it would want to use noncoercive measures to discourage patently unacceptable beliefs and practices. If secularism means that the state should scrupulously stay clear of religious beliefs and practices, no state is or can afford to be secular.

II

The second liberal assumption—that participation in political life involves abstracting away or "rising above" one's religious beliefs and being guided exclusively by secular reason—is open to several objections. Contrary to liberal belief, secular reasons are not politically neutral or commonly shared. Since they come easily to and express the worldview of secular but not religious persons, they privilege the former and discriminate against the latter. Secular citizens are able to lead whole and integrated lives whereas religious citizens, who are asked to forget their deepest beliefs, are subjected to moral incoherence and self-alienation. Furthermore, since they hold certain beliefs dear and even define themselves in terms of these, it is difficult to see how they can be required to abstract them away without compromising their moral integrity or realistically expected to do so successfully. This is not to say that they are constituted by their beliefs and cannot suspend them for political purposes, but rather that such self-abstraction devalues what gives meaning to their lives, deprives them of a moral compass, and imposes an invidious form of moral self-policing.

Even if we can show that we are morally entitled to ask religious people to think or at least to defend their views publicly in secular terms, it is difficult to see how we can do so in a democracy in which they might and generally do constitute a majority. There is no way to stop them from acting on their religious beliefs, and any such attempt will only turn them against the political system that denies public expression to what they deeply cherish. The liberal demand is predicated on the assumption that society already is or would over time become wholly or substantially secular and that religion would either cease to matter to people or do so only marginally. The reality is quite different.

Consider the recent findings of the *European values study*, first carried out in 1981 and repeated in 1990.[2] 72% of Europeans believe in God (73% in 1981), 61% in the soul (57% in 1981), 63% define themselves as religious persons (62% in 1981), 52% consider God important in their lives (51% in 1981), 44% believe in life after death (43% in 1981), 48% draw comfort or strength from religion (48% in 1981), and 60% of them need moments of prayer (57% in 1981). Only 4.4% (4% in 1981) were confirmed atheists. Britain is generally considered more secular than the rest of Europe, but here too the figures are only marginally different. 71% of Britons believe in God, 64% in soul, 54% define themselves as religious, 44% consider God important in their lives, 44% believe in life after death, 44% draw comfort or strength from religion, and 53% need moments of prayer. In the U.S. the figures are even higher. Nearly 80% of its people believe in God, and rather surprisingly so do 39.3% of scientists, which is only a fraction less than the figure of 41.8% recorded in 1916. 72% of the Americans believe in the healing power of personal prayer, 56% consider religion to be very important in their lives, 40% go to church once a week or more, and 45% regularly give money to their church.[3]

Obviously we should not exaggerate the significance of these figures. The ideas of God, worship, and prayer mean different things to different people, and do not have the same meaning and force today that they had in earlier ages. For example, those who claim to believe in God also say that they do not generally expect Him to intervene in human affairs as their forebears did, that they pray for personal peace rather than in the hope of an immediate reward, and that their views of the other world do not cast a long shadow over their affairs in this one. This does not mean that their religiosity is shallow and inauthentic but rather that it is different in nature and mediated and moderated by a secular worldview. The only point we can confidently make on the basis of these figures is that religion still remains an important force in people's lives and that the kind of inexorable and comprehensive secularization predicted and hoped for by liberal writers has not occurred even in the advanced Western societies.

Religion is not only very much alive but refuses to remain confined to the private realm. Ninety per cent of U.S. Congresspersons claim to consult their religious beliefs before voting on important issues. Although the figure in other Western countries is smaller, it is not negligible. Many activists in the Green movement, antiracist organizations, campaigns for the rights of native peoples, antipoverty struggles, peace and disarmament movements, campaigns for human rights and global justice, and so forth, also claim to derive inspiration from their religious beliefs. Deeply regretting the privatization of Christianity and the concomitant separation of religious and political concerns, 2700 evangelical Christians from 150 countries met in Lausanne in 1974 to explore how best they could give their religious beliefs a suitable political expression. In a series of publications they applied the central values of Christianity to contemporary social, economic, and political issues, and developed interesting bodies of ideas on such issues as global justice, the minimum wage, world poverty, ethical investment, illegitimacy of interest on certain types of loans, the ethical consumer, and the market. Even the relatively unworldly fundamentalist Christians have begun to rethink their position. Jerry Falwell, a fundamentalist American Christian, had argued in 1965 that true Christians had nothing to do with politics.

> We have few ties to this earth. . . . We pay our taxes, cast our votes, . . . obey the laws of the land, and do other things demanded of us by the society in which we live. But at the same time we are cognizant that our only purpose on this earth is to know Christ and to make Him known. Believing in the Bible as I do, I would find it impossible to . . . begin doing anything else—including fighting communism or participating in civil rights reforms.[4]

By 1980, when he wrote *Listen America,* his approach had changed. He now wants Christians to become politically engaged and "turn America around." This involves campaigning for the usual right-wing moral agenda but also for such things as equality for all Americans, an attack on world poverty, and a struggle against social injustice. As he says: "We must insist that equal education and employment opportunities are available to all Americans regardless of race, sex, religion or creed. Fundamentalists have been woefully negligent in addressing this issue. We can no longer be silent on this matter."[5]

The Second Vatican Council offered a similar reassessment of the social and political role of the Catholic Church. To be sure, the Catholic Church had always emphasized social and economic issues, but it now began to do so in a much more active and forthright manner. In its two important documents, *Dignitatis Humane* and *Gaudium et Spes,* it argued that campaigning for peace and justice and participation in the struggle to change the world were not morally optional but constitutive features of the Church's divine mission to redeem the human race. The Church was to discern "the signs of the times" and relate its eternal truths to the central economic and political issues of our age. Thanks to the lead given by Vatican II, Catholic churches all over the world have felt encouraged to intervene actively in the public life of their countries, of which the American Bishops' Pastoral Letters of 1983 and 1986, speaking out respectively against nuclear weapons and unrestrained capitalism, are good examples.

The social and political involvement of religion should not surprise us. Religious people generally seek wholeness in their lives and do not think it possible or desirable to separate their private and political concerns. This is why many of them participated in antislavery, anticolonial, temperance, anticapitalist, anti-Communist, and other movements. One new factor has emerged to reinforce this trend in our times, namely, a feeling of moral and political vacuum and the renewed search for a sense of meaning and purpose. Many of the secular ideologies such as Communism and even liberalism that have hitherto been the vehicles of radical transformative aspirations have lost much of their appeal or momentum, and there is an increasing demand for new ways of thought. Material satisfaction which has hitherto taken up most of people's energies is today at least a reality for many in the West, and people now aspire toward something different and more fulfilling. The earlier faith in the ability of science to solve the mystery of the universe or even to provide solutions to social and economic problems has declined, so much so that it is the scientists who are now seeking a rapprochement with religion.

The increasing emergence of the global civil society has created a space for global action and has proved particularly attractive to universalist religions who now no longer feel constrained by the need to demonstrate their loyalty to the nation-state. There is also a greater appreciation that the good life cannot be lived at the personal level unless the collective life is appropriately restructured and that religion should make its appropriate contribution towards the latter. The experiences of the Nazi and Communist regimes have highlighted the ease with which political and civil institutions capitulate before determined groups, and have caused many to wonder if the churches may not have a vital role to play in sustaining free societies. Alongside and partly in response to the sense of moral and political vacuum, major religions have themselves begun to reassess their social and political role along the lines described earlier.

III

The third liberal assumption, that religion has nothing of value to contribute to political life, is profoundly mistaken. Historically speaking religion has been a source of many an emancipatory movement. Antislavery, *anti-laissez faire* capitalist, antifascist, and other movements were often led by religious leaders or those with deep religious commitments. This is also the case with more recent movements such as India's struggle for independence under Gandhi, the 1960s civil rights campaigns in the United States, antiracist movements in Britain, France, Germany, the Netherlands, and elsewhere, campaigns for global justice and nuclear disarmament, and protests against the Gulf War, especially in the United States. This is not to say that secular people did not or do not play a crucial role in these and other movements, or that religion has not for centuries justified slavery, capitalism, wars, crusades and, more recently, the cold war. Yet though religion has been a force for evil, it has also been a force for good, generating a kind of energy, commitment, passion, and willingness to suffer that sometimes have been lacking in wholly secular motivations. Nothing in human life is an unmixed good, not even liberty and equality, and we ought not to judge the historical role of religion in a one-sided manner.

Religion also provides a valuable counterweight to the state, nurturing sensibilities and values the latter ignores or suppresses. Just as we need opposition parties to check the government of the day, we need powerful non-state institutions to check the state. The state has traditionally claimed to monopolize morality, regarding its interests as being of the highest importance and deserving of the greatest sacrifices. This attitude needs constant questioning, and religion is ideally equipped to provide an alternative source of morality and allegiance and to continue to remind us that a human being is more than a citizen. This is, again, not to deny the obvious fact that religion has often supported aggressive nationalism and horrendous wars, but to say that it also has a universalist and humanitarian dimension which can be used to criticize, embarrass, and contain its nationalist propensities.

Modern social and political life encourages a quasi-utilitarian attitude to morality. When the main concern is to get on in life and to pursue pleasure and promote self-interest, rigors of moral life are felt as burdens, leading to a tendency to cut moral corners, bend moral principles to the requirements of personal convenience, and legitimize these acts with moral sophistry. Here again, religion at its best has much to contribute. It stresses the quality of the human soul and forces people to pause and examine the kind of human beings they have become. It insists, too, on fundamental values and demands that should not be compromised, at least not without compelling reasons. When the Roman Catholic Church insists on the sanctity of human life and rules out all forms of abortion, it is clearly being absolutist, unworldly, unrealistic, and oppressive. However, it also serves the vital function of affirming an important value, nagging our consciences, requiring us to reflect publicly and critically on our moral practices, and forcing us to consider issues we would happily prefer to suppress or ignore. We might, and in this and other matters should, challenge and even reject the Church's views, but this does not detract from the fact that its voice deserves to be heard with respect.

From its very beginning the modern state has been abstracted from society and has tended to become bureaucratic and remote. While this has enabled it to rise above social, ethnic, religious, and other divisions as well as to institutionalize such great values as equality before the law, liberty, and common citizenship, it has also been a source of many of its weaknesses. Although its administrative and moral reach is wider than that of its earlier counterparts, it is also shallower and more tenuous. The state remains external to society and its interventions are necessarily crude and arouse deep fears. As a result it is inherently incapable of nurturing the moral life of the community and fostering such valuable qualities as moral self-discipline, a sense of personal responsibility, family values, love of the good which alone gives depth and energy to moral life, the spirit of mutual concern, and a sense of social obligation. The resulting moral vacuum needs to be filled or the communal life suffers and the state itself becomes either hollow or excessively overbearing and authoritarian. Along with the family, schools, voluntary associations, and other social institutions, religion plays an important part in sustaining the deeper springs of morality. That a large number of human beings consciously or unconsciously derive their moral values and love of the good from religion reinforces its role in public life.

Religion also performs several other important public functions. It rejects the claims of the state and the economy to be governed by their own narrow values, and subordinates them to wider moral concerns. It stresses the unity of the human species and challenges the tendency to limit morality to the territorial boundaries of the state. It raises issues politicians are often too timid or opportunistic to debate, and broadens the public agenda. As an institution of premodern origin encompassing several historical epochs, it nurtures a wide range of moral and cultural sensibilities and dispositions. In so doing it provides a counterpoint to the haughty self-assurance of the rationalist modernity, brings to political life the accumulated insights and wisdom of rich historical traditions, and reminds us of human finitude. It also challenges the privatization and relativization of morality to which liberal societies are particularly prone and insists, even if at times misguidedly, on the objective and universal dimension of morality.

Although religion can make a valuable contribution to political life, it can also be a pernicious influence, as liberals rightly highlight. It is often absolutist, self-righteous, arrogant, dogmatic, and impatient of compromise. It arouses powerful and sometimes irrational impulses and can easily destabilize society, cause political havoc, and create a veritable hell on earth. Since it is generally of ancient origin, it is sometimes deeply conservative, hidebound, insensitive to changes in the social climate and people's moral aspirations, and harbors a deep antifemale bias. It often breeds intolerance of other religions as well as of internal dissent, and has a propensity towards violence. And despite its primary concern with the otherworldly destiny of the human soul, it has often struck up most disgraceful alliances with the established secular authorities and subserved their interests.

IV

In the earlier sections I criticized the liberal view of the political role of religion. I argued that religion has a legitimate interest in secular affairs and cannot be excluded from their conduct, and that conversely the state has a legitimate interest in religious practices and even beliefs which cannot therefore be placed outside its purview. Religiously minded citizens cannot be asked to abstract away their deeply held beliefs because this is unfair to them, runs the risk of alienating them from and even turning them into the enemies of the political system, and is undemocratic. And while religion can be a force for evil, it can also be a force for good in political life. In the light of our criticism we need to reconsider the liberal separation of religion and political life; we must ask instead how we can assign religion its legitimate place in political life and benefit from its contribution, while guarding against its obvious dangers by subjecting it to the constraints and discipline of political life.

V

Since religious persons think in religious terms and seek wholeness in their lives, they should as citizens be free to speak in a religious language and justify their views and criticize those of others from a religious perspective. Respect for our fellow citizens requires that we should respect and within reasonable limits accommodate their characteristic modes of self-constitution and self-expression. The principle of equality of citizenship also points in the same direction, for the secular language is not politically neutral, and to require all citizens to speak it discriminates against those for whom it is at best a poorly mastered second language. Besides, religion is best able to contribute its insights and enrich political debate when it is allowed to speak in its authentic idioms.

Liberals feel uneasy with this for two reasons. First, it goes against their view of citizenship. And second, they cannot understand how a sensible political debate is possible if the participants speak in different conceptual languages. In the liberal view citizenship is an autonomous and self-contained status governed by a body of distinctly political values and concerns. This view is open to several objections. As we saw, it disadvantages and discriminates against nonsecular citizens and might even disenfranchise some of them. It also fragments the individual, divides up his or her life into several autonomous areas, and militates against the search for wholeness and integrity. We would strongly object if someone argued that the economic life should only be governed by the economic values of profitability, productivity, and efficiency, and that the *homo economicus* is subject to no other constraints. The liberal view of citizenship is a political counterpart of this, and just as flawed. Furthermore, it arbitrarily defines certain values as political, and does not explain why liberty and equality are political values but solidarity, community, compassion, and mutual concern are not. It also takes a static view of the political realm and insulates it against the fertilizing influence of new ideas and sensibilities.

Rather than see citizenship as representing the whole of a part of the individual as liberals do, we should see it as a partial expression of the whole of an individual. Not the so-called political part but the whole of an individual enters the political realm. Citizenship is not a detachable aspect but a mode of being in the political realm with its built-in empirical and normative constraints. When one enters the political realm one encounters equals whom one may not treat as instruments of one's will. They have views one must respect, interests one must accommodate, differences with oneself that one must resolve by discussion. Political life also has a coercive dimension and is equipped to realize only that aspect of the good which is amenable to coercion. Political values do not constitute an autonomous world of their own; rather they are those moral values that are at any given time deemed to be politically relevant, realizable, and worthwhile, and naturally they are subject to periodic redefinition. Citizens need not therefore strip themselves of their religious, moral, and other beliefs as a precondition of entering the political realm; they may bring all of these with them, as indeed they cannot help doing, provided that they respect its constraints and define, debate, and defend their views in a politically appropriate manner.

As for the liberal anxiety that no political debate, let alone a sensible one, is possible if different groups of citizens speak in different languages, it is highly exaggerated. Political debate in every modern society is multilingual in character and would remain so even if no one spoke in a religious language. Conservatives, liberals, Marxists, fascists, racists, and others speak in very different languages. The fact that these languages are all secular does not mean that their differences are not deep or that their speakers always understand each other. Indeed several secular ideologies, such as some varieties of Marxism, conservatism, and even liberalism have a quasi-religious orientation and form, and conversely formally religious languages sometimes have a secular content, so that the dividing line between a secular and a religious language is sometimes difficult to draw. If our political life can cope with a variety of secular languages, as indeed it has done for centuries, there is no reason why it cannot accommodate a religious language as well.

Liberals often take a highly unrealistic view of political debate, and think of it as taking place in a face-to-face national forum between transparent participants who advance and weigh up rational arguments and decide on the basis of what convinces most or all of them. This is why they insist that the participants should speak in a single language, appeal to a single set of values, and be fully intelligible to each other. The political debate is rarely like this. It is fragmented, takes place in multiple forums in each of which it takes a distinct form, and is suitably filtered and reformulated as it moves from one forum to the next. It is never articulated in terms of arguments alone, and involves appeals to emotions, ideals, unspoken sympathies and antipathies, disparate values, and an inherently messy collective self-understanding. Insofar as political debate includes arguments, they are never homogeneous in nature and involve passages of varying degrees of incomprehension. Not every argument needs or calls for a response either, for it is sometimes only meant to indicate where the speaker is coming from, how she wishes to position herself, and how strongly she feels about a given issue.

When some groups of citizens speak in a religious language, we can and do in fact respond in various ways. When Martin Luther King demanded racial equality on the ground that all human beings are children of God, his demand was readily conceded by most Americans who recognized it as their constitutionally enjoined value. Its religious basis did not become a subject of political debate and was politically relevant only because it indicated why racial equality mattered to King and should in his view matter to his fellow citizens as well and because it helped him mobilize like-minded people behind it. As John Rawls argues, King's religious language reinforced and revitalized a much cherished American political value, and therein lay its political relevance and importance.[6]

A different and difficult situation arises when the values or practices advocated on religious grounds do not enjoy widespread consensus. The grounds themselves then become subjects of public debate, and the religion concerned exposes itself to public scrutiny with all its attendant advantages and disadvantages. This is what happened when a large body of Christians led by the Catholic Church demanded a total ban on abortion on the ground that since human life is God-given and sacred, we are never justified in terminating an innocent life. The fact that the argument is religious in nature does not mean that it is inaccessible to secular citizens or that they cannot critically engage with it. It can be and was in fact debated at two levels, internal and external.

We could argue, as many did and do, that the Catholic position is internally inconsistent and misrepresents the central doctrines of the Church. The Church is theologically committed to valuing not life *per se* but the human person, and the fetus at least until a certain age is not a person as traditionally defined by Aquinas and several other theologians of the Church itself. We could also argue that since the Church leaves many a contentious economic and political issue to individual conscience, it is wrong to make such a rigid exception in the case of abortion, and that since it allows just wars in which innocent lives are taken, it is wrong not to think in terms of just abortions. We could also show that the Church's view is heavily influenced by the doctrine of the natural right to life and is at odds with the traditional doctrine of the natural law on which it relies in other areas, and that its current stand is of relatively recent origin and out of step with its earlier approach. Such an internal critique goes a long way towards answering the Catholic argument, and has the additional advantage of triggering off an internal debate and opening up the diversity of views among the Catholics themselves.

We might also criticize the Church's stand on external grounds. We could show that while it is free to ban abortion among its followers, it has no legal or moral right to use the machinery of the state to impose a ban on others, and that its attempt to do so violates the central principle of the very constitutional democracy that gives it the freedom to propagate its views. We could also argue that if the Church thinks it right to impose its deepest beliefs on others, liberals are equally justified in imposing their fundamental belief in equality of the sexes on the Church and requiring it to ordain women priests, appoint women cardinals, and periodically elect women popes. We might follow a different route and contend that since many communities do not welcome children born out of wedlock or have no means to support them, the Church must either provide a nationwide support system or refrain from making irresponsible and impossible demands. We could reinforce the point by showing that unwanted children lack love, carry emotional scars, etc., and that banning abortion damages human dignity as much as and to an even greater degree than allowing it.

The point of this discussion is not to offer a conclusive refutation of the Church's view but to show that religious language in politics creates no more difficulties than the usual variety of secular languages, and that it can be debated by secular citizens in internal and external terms. It might be argued that many secular citizens know little about their own religion, let alone others, and cannot and should not be expected to engage in an informed debate with religious persons. The argument is well taken but overstated. When a large body of citizens think and argue in religious terms, it is part of the training for common citizenship that future citizens should grow up with some knowledge of their society's major religious traditions. As I argue later, there is a strong academic and political case for teaching religion in schools.

Furthermore, political participation is a process of mutual education. Just as religious citizens learn to appreciate the complexity and relative autonomy of political life, close interaction with them gives their secular counterparts the rich opportunity to widen their intellectual and moral horizons, learn new ways of looking at familiar issues, and gain a moderate degree of multilingual competence. It is true that they cannot have an intimate knowledge of different religious traditions, but that need not matter. After all, most citizens understand little of the highly complex economic issues either, yet they have to pass a judgment on the government's economic competence and policies. They listen to experts, try to make some sense of their arguments, and rely on their common sense to form a view. Something similar occurs in the case of a religiously based political demand. It is likely to be critically discussed within the religious communities themselves and to throw up arguments, a variety of views, and information upon which outsiders can rely to form their judgment. If a religious argument is wholly incomprehensible or appears bizarre to other citizens, they are entitled to ignore it. If religious persons wish to persuade others, they must speak in a manner to which the latter can imaginatively relate and respond.

Just as we should allow religious citizens to speak in a religious language, we should also find other ways of valuing their presence and encouraging their contribution to collective life. The state could give them a charitable status as it generally does in all liberal societies, contribute towards their upkeep as it does in Germany, Sweden, the Netherlands, Britain, and elsewhere, encourage them to undertake philanthropic and welfare activities, and so forth. It might be argued that public funds should not be used to support sectional interests. If that were so, no public authority would be justified in supporting or giving a charitable status to museums, art galleries, universities, and operas, spending public funds to rescue mountain climbers or those lost in dangerous expeditions, or providing designated areas to anglers and ramblers. We rightly want it to support these activities because they are valuable, are shared by sizable sections of citizens, and add to the richness of collective life. Religion belongs to this category.

We might also explore ways of drawing religious communities into the mainstream of political life. We might set up or encourage a national interreligious forum, or advisory council, or some such mechanism for consulting them on a regular basis. Such arrangements serve several purposes. They show that the political community values religious opinions and sensibilities, and give the religious communities a moral and emotional stake in the maintenance of free societies. They enrich the quality of public debate by bringing to bear on public issues perspectives that are otherwise likely to be ignored. They bring together different religious groups, promote mutual understanding, and build up a climate of trust and goodwill among them. By requiring them to test their religious beliefs and values against the intractable and complex reality of political life, such arrangements also introduce a measure of realism and responsibility and open up spaces of freedom and debate within each of them.

There is also a good case for teaching religion in schools on both educational and political grounds. One of the principal aims of education is to familiarize children with and to get them to appreciate the great achievements of the human spirit, and religion is one of these. Like literature and the arts, religion represents a profound exploration of the human condition, and to deny children access to it is both to impoverish them morally and emotionally and to cut them off from the ways of thought and life of a large part of humankind. A society's major religions also generally shape its history, social structure, and self-understanding, and to remain ignorant of them is to lack a coherent understanding of the latter.

There are also good political reasons for teaching religion. If schools do not teach it, children will come to depend wholly on their families and religious organizations, which only expose them to their own religion and that too from a narrow sectarian standpoint. Besides, once we recognize religion as one of the several respectable languages of political life, it is essential that citizens should feel comfortable with and be moderately literate in it. They should be able to appreciate how a religious person thinks and reasons and why he feels strongly about certain issues, as well as acquire at least some knowledge of their society's major religious traditions. Such shared religious knowledge and sensibility forms one of the important constituents of common citizenship, and is as essential to intelligent citizenship as the familiarity with their society's history, geography, and constitutional and political arrangements. Part of the reason why religion arouses strong passions in the United States has perhaps to do with the fact that it is not taught in schools as an academic subject. The religious people pick up their religion from sectarian churches, and the nonreligious, having never been systematically exposed to it, find it alien and troubling. Dogmatism of one reinforces and is in turn reinforced by the nervous hostility of the other, and the quality of the public debate is one of the first casualties.

How to teach religion in school raises difficult questions, but these are not unanswerable. The teaching of history, civics, literature, and social studies too was once a highly contentious issue, and there is now a broad consensus on how best to approach it. Once we agree that the reasons for teaching religion are broadly those sketched above, it is clear that it should be taught in more or less the same way as these subjects. The job of the school is not to challenge or subvert its pupils' religious beliefs as militant secularists and nervous liberals argue, nor to reinforce them as the orthodox argue, but to discuss them in a comparative, analytical, and respectful manner. It should teach its pupils how the major religions originated, interacted, developed in history, shaped and were shaped by the cultural climate of the wider society, came to be interpreted in a certain manner, threw up doctrinal divisions, and became subjects of internal disputes. Such an approach sensitizes pupils to the very different ways in which religions deal with shared human experiences, and enables them to hold and examine their own beliefs in a responsible manner. Families and religious communities that wish to indoctrinate children in their respective traditions should be free to do so, but the school is not the place for that. It is not concerned with one religion but several and aims at religious education rather than religious training, initiation, or indoctrination. There are, no doubt, areas such as the teaching of creationism where disputes are likely to arise, but these can be tackled without compromising the school's academic integrity. There is no reason why creationism, for example, should not be taught as long as the school presents it as one view among many, shows why some subscribe to it and others don't, and teaches evolutionary and other theories as well.

VI

While welcoming religion to political life, we should also guard against the havoc it can easily create. In its own interest as well as that of the wider political community, it must willingly accept or be made to accept the limits of its public role as defined by the constraints of political life.

By its very nature religion is both worldly and otherworldly, concerned with secular interests as well as the destiny of the human soul. Its relation to political life is therefore necessarily partial and limited. While remaining actively interested in the general quality of collective life, it should retain critical distance from it and scrupulously avoid getting sucked into day-to-day politics with all its partisanship, intrigues, and dubious alliances. This means a number of things. Governing a political community requires skills, dispositions, motivations, ambitions, and qualities of temperament that are quite different from those required and cultivated by religion. A religion must therefore resist the temptation to capture political power and run the state, for it would then most certainly risk losing its integrity and making a mess of political life. Too close an alliance or identification with the government of the day or the institutions of the state exposes it to similar dangers, and must also be avoided.

Political issues are often exceedingly complex, requiring detailed knowledge of the subject in question, judgment, an intuitive understanding of the available range of possibilities, etc., which only a total immersion in political life can provide. A religion that pontificates or mounts a campaign on every conceivable issue or pretends to possess the key to the ideal state or economy not only acts irresponsibly but also loses its credibility and moral authority. Religion is society's conscience and moral sentinel, a guardian of its moral values. Its primary objective should be to keep an eye on the general quality of collective life, to alert fellow citizens to its disturbing trends, and to summon them to their basic values and ideals; and the best way to attain that objective is to persuade, to inspire, to criticize, and occasionally to agitate. When a religion loses sight of this central objective in pursuit of cheap popularity, power, political influence, or sectarian secular interests, it betrays both itself and the political community.

A society generally includes people belonging to several religions as well as to none. Just as one religious community feels strongly about its beliefs, so do others, and just as one of them is tempted to shape the society in its own image, so are they. If one of them were to impose its beliefs on others, it would not only provoke disorder but also violate their moral integrity. A culturally plural society should be based on mutual respect, toleration, democratic debate, and the spirit of compromise. Since a religious group that seeks to organize society on its own terms declares its inability to accept others as equals and to respect their integrity, it forfeits its claim to their tolerance and goodwill. We welcome religion into the public realm because it represents a distinct and valuable point of view whose participation in the deliberative process enhances the quality of the political debate and the legitimacy and authority of the decisions reached. A religion that seeks to monopolize the public realm and refuses to engage in an open-minded dialogue with other points of view impoverishes the quality of the public debate, diminishes the representative character of the public realm, and defeats the very grounds for welcoming. The civil authority may under certain circumstances legitimately restrict its freedom and, in exceptional cases, even ban it.

There is a pervasive tendency among religious people to claim to be in possession of divinely vouchsafed infallible and final truths which they are not at liberty to compromise and which others must always respect. This is a wholly false reading of religion. Every religion is a joint creation of God and human beings. Its origin and inspiration are divine but human beings determine its meaning and content. The divine will is revealed to a human being who, however inspired, has human limitations, and is communicated in a human language with all its obvious limitations. The founder's life and deeds are recorded by fallible human beings from their different perspectives. In Christianity the four Gospels give somewhat different accounts of Jesus' life. In Islam scholars had to decide what *hadiths* are genuine, as there are many different accounts of what the Prophet said. Bukhari, the most respected scholar, selected as genuine only just over seven thousand out of a total of about six hundred thousand.

As for the sacred text itself, it is human beings who must decide what does and does not belong to it. It is composed in a particular historical period and its original meaning is not always recoverable. It is dense and complex and full of parables, allegories, elusive metaphors, and cryptic aphorisms, which can be interpreted in several different ways. Its moral principles are necessarily general and abstract and need to be interpreted and adopted to changing circumstances. In the Qur'an only the seventy-odd verses out of six thousand deal with personal law, and can be read in several different ways as the disputes over polygamy, divorce, and inheritance of property demonstrate. The New Testament has even less to say on moral and social practices, with the result that its views on such subjects as homosexuality, private property, women priests, and inter-gender relations are often ambiguous.

The authorized guardians of the sacred text too are fallible human beings, tied up with the prevailing structures of power in complex ways and operating under interpretative and political constraints. They are under constant pressure to accommodate conflicting interests and to adjust the traditional religious beliefs and practices to cultural, technological, economic, and other changes. In short, as we successively move from God to God's human vehicle, the text, the tradition, its recognized guardians, and finally the individual believer, there is increasing human mediation with its inescapable fallibility, corruption, and the intrusion of conscious and unconscious biases.

Since every religion is a human construction based, no doubt, on divine inspiration, its adherents cannot hide behind God's authority, and must accept responsibility for what they say and do in its name.[7] It is never enough for them to say that they must do such and such a thing because God or the Bible or the Qur'an says so. The divine will is a matter of human definition and interpretation, and requires them to show why they interpret their religion in one way rather than another and why they think that their interpretation entails a particular form of behavior. Religion does involve faith but is not a matter of faith alone, which is why the two should not be equated. It also necessarily involves personal judgment, choice, and decision, and hence reason and personal responsibility. Religiously minded citizens are not therefore excused from a rational discussion of their politically relevant beliefs and practices. While others need to appreciate that religious beliefs are not like scientific beliefs and require a more contextual and sensitive form of reasoning, they may legitimately challenge and even refuse to respect them if they appear bizarre, evil, pernicious, or are not backed up by good reasons. Political life recognizes no infallible truths, only those that carry conviction with the bulk of citizens.

VII

We should never expect religion to be respectable and compliant, for its basic concerns are quite different from and even in tension with those of political life. It will always remain a little awkward, difficult to accommodate, often speaking in an irritating and occasionally incomprehensible language. Rather than regret this, we should see it as religion's attempt to be true to itself and retain its critical distance from the homogenizing dominant culture. To be awkward and a source of creative tension, however, is quite different from being subversive, overbearing, intolerant, or demanding to play the game of politics by its own rules. When that happens, religion corrupts both itself and the political life and needs to be checked in the interest of both. Richard John Neuhaus remarked a few years ago, "When I hear the term 'Christian America,' I see the barbed wire." He was right, for any alliance between religion and the state poses a grave threat to human freedom and dignity. However, the best way to avoid his nightmare is not to let religion sulk and scowl menacingly from outside the public realm but to welcome and subject it to the latter's educational and political discipline.

NOTES

1. Robert Audi, "The Separation of Church and State and the Obligation of Citizenship," *Philosophy and Public Affairs* 18 (Summer 1989): 284–90.
2. N. Timms, *Family and Citizenship: Values in Contemporary Britain* (Dartmouth: Aldershot, 1992).

3. R. Inglehart, *Cultural Shift* (Princeton, N.J.: Princeton University Press, 1990); *Religion Watch* 11, no. 10; "U.S. Scientists Retain Belief in God, Survey Discovers," *The Guardian*, 3 April 1993.

4. Cited in Jose Casanova, *Public Religions in the Modern World* (Chicago: University of Chicago Press, 1994), p. 148.

5. Ibid., p. 157.

6. John Rawls, *Political Liberalism* (New York: Columbia University Press, 1993), p. 250.

7. For a fuller discussion see Bhikhu Parekh, "The Concept of Fundamentalism," in *The End of "Isms"?*, ed. Alexandras Shtromas (London: Blackwell, 1994).

Peace as Politics

STEPHEN DARWALL

THOMAS HOBBES FAMOUSLY defined peace as the absence, not just of actual battle, but of the known willingness to battle. Just as "foul weather, lieth not in a shower or two of rain; but in an inclination thereto of many days together, so," Hobbes writes, "the nature of war, consisteth not in actual fighting; but in the known disposition thereto, during all the time there is no assurance to the contrary."[1] Hobbes's purpose with this definition was to argue that individuals without common political authority are unavoidably in a state of war. Lacking a sovereign with the authority to demand obedience, individuals lack sufficient assurance of others' peaceful intentions to make it sensible for them to do anything but "seek and use all helps and advantages of war" (14.4). This is common knowledge, moreover. Everyone knows (and knows that they know) that everyone is sensibly disposed to war. And this just *is* a state of war.

But what creates sufficient uncertainty about others' peaceful intentions to warrant the willingness to do battle? After all, war carries significant costs of its own. Unless I have some reason to believe that others think they have something to gain at such a cost, or to believe that they believe that I think I do, then nothing in my relative ignorance of their actual intentions seems to warrant preemptive hostility.

Hobbes lists three "principal causes of quarrel": competition, diffidence, and glory (13.6). Diffidence can't cause conflict by itself, however. It can only multiply the effects of the other two. Only if something else puts us at odds will mutual vulnerability be a cause of quarrel. Otherwise, it may simply draw us more closely together.

"Competition" is for possessible goods and the power over them. Men "invade for gain" to "make themselves masters of other men's persons, wives, children, and cattle" (13.7). And "glory" is reputation, honor, or esteem—expressions of value from others. "Every man looketh that his companion should value him, at the same rate he sets upon himself" (13.5), and when others dishonor him by not doing so, "endeavours to extort a greater value from his contemners, by damage; and from others, by the example" (13.5).

As significant as these are, there is another cause of conflict that was especially salient to Hobbes as he wrote in the midst of the English Civil War, namely, religious difference and discord. Hobbes devotes fully half of *Leviathan* to religion, and Part III is concerned with how to organize a Christian Commonwealth so as to remove what Hobbes calls "the most frequent pretext of sedition and civil war": the "difficulty . . . of obeying at once both God and man" (43.1).

Hobbes's solution in *Leviathan* to the problem presented by Civil War England is to mount an internal argument from within a religious framework that is common to the major contending parties. Starting from elements of Christian doctrine that he argues are most firmly supported by scripture and reliable evidence, Hobbes argues that these dictate obedience to the sovereign, even if he is not a Christian. And if he is a Christian, they dictate acknowledging him as head of the church in the territory he rules. In effect, Hobbes tries to achieve what Rawls calls an "overlapping consensus" from within the major going religious doctrines on two propositions: first, that subjects owe obedience to the sovereign "in all things not repugnant to the laws of God" (31.1); and second, that there is never a reasonable basis for concluding that the laws of God and the sovereign conflict.

Hobbes's arguments could hardly have been expected to carry conviction, even in his own time. Even had they been accepted widely by Protestants, and they weren't, they left Roman Catholics, not to mention Jews, out of account. Of course, Hobbes wasn't unusual in these forms of exclusion. Intolerance was far more common than religious toleration in seventeenth-century Europe, both in theory and in practice. And these days, Hobbes's idea of achieving an overlapping religious consensus on the absolute political and religious authority of established sovereigns seems simply a nonstarter. If there is a going project in political philosophy, it seems closer to Rawlsian political liberalism, the hope of finding an overlapping consensus within, at least, reasonable religious and comprehensive moral views for a *political* conception, prominent within which is an ideal of religious toleration.

I want to reflect on this phenomenon from various perspectives. In some ways, the idea of religious toleration has become so familiar to us that we are apt to wonder what all the fuss was (or is) about. What threat could be posed to the state by allowing citizens to engage in religious rituals of their own choosing? To understand why religious toleration could have seemed so deeply problematic to the early moderns, we must appreciate how religious differences were seen by them to pose fundamentally political challenges. I shall argue that, in many cases, religious dissent was perceived to contest political legitimacy, by contesting the very source of political authority. The issue was not simply whether to allow others to lead lives that would preclude their salvation, as one saw it, or even whether to allow others to engage in practices that, by one's own lights, were morally wrong. Rather, religious toleration seemed to license something like sedition.

Partly, then, I will be concerned to understand why religious toleration was such a problematic idea. But I also want to understand what can, and I think should, be so deeply attractive about this idea to us today. If toleration of religious difference is most problematic when religious views are seen essentially to concern relations of divine and earthly *governance,* then, perhaps unsurprisingly, the toleration of religious difference makes most sense when political authority is held to derive from some source other than divine will. Here my theme will be that religious toleration's value is best accounted for within a democratic liberalism that holds political legitimacy to derive from the equal authority and dignity of all citizens as independent, autonomous persons. Toleration is most problematic when the dignity of human beings and human institutions is seen to derive from their place in a structure of command and when religious disagreements are viewed as contesting the character of that structure. And it is best justified when human beings are seen to have an authority and dignity in themselves that is independent of any being's will, even God's. So viewed, practices of religious toleration express respect for this very value.

To put the point another way, this transition in attitudes towards religious toleration amounted to a transition between two different views of the moral subject.[2] On one view, to be a moral subject is to be subject *to* a structure of command that is ultimately grounded in divine authority. The crucial fact about moral subjects, on this view, is *subjection.* We are *God's subjects.* On the other view, moral subjecthood means, not being *subject to* externally imposed command but the capacity self-consciously to lead and be the *subject of* a life, and the authority or standing one has by virtue of that capacity. On the first view, human dignity is conditional and extrinsic, since it depends entirely on our standing in God's chain of command. On the second, human dignity is unconditional and intrinsic, since it depends entirely on features that are inherent in the moral person herself.

I should make it clear that I shall be discussing religious toleration, considered in itself. There are familiar enough processes of in-group/out-group formation, and religious differences can easily be markers in such a process. When intolerance results in this way, however, it may have nothing to do with religious difference *per se*. Religion may mark some relevant "otherness" without posing a challenge in itself. Or it may be related to other markers, such as race, nationality, ethnicity, class, and so on. In cases like these, intolerance may have nothing *intrinsically* to do with religion.

Similarly, intolerance of religious difference may result from a history of grievance, real or imagined, such as perceived disrespect for sacred places, as for example in the recent conflict between Muslims, Hindus, and Sikhs in India. But here again, the source of intolerance seems not to be any threat posed by religious difference *per se*. That people are intolerant for *these* reasons would not make the idea of religious toleration inherently problematic for them.

My interest will be in how religious difference could have been seen to pose a challenge to political order *in itself*—a challenge so threatening, indeed, that the idea of religious toleration could seem inherently problematic almost to the point of paradox. And my claim, again, will be that in sixteenth- and seventeenth-century Europe religious differences were seen essentially to contest moral and political authority.

As a final preliminary, I should say something about what I mean by "religious toleration." We can distinguish broadly between individual-regarding and group-regarding conceptions. On an individual-regarding conception, religious toleration consists in an ensemble of claims or rights of individuals, such as freedom of conscience and worship, the freedom to hold office and participate in political debate regardless of religious association, and so on. On a group-regarding conception, on the other hand, religious toleration consists in the politically recognized standing or claims of different *religions* (that is, religious groups) to conduct worship, organize institutions such as marriage and the family, and so on. An example of the former would be the ways that religion and the separation of church and state are treated in American constitutional law. Examples of the latter would include the "millet system" of the Ottoman empire, under which Jews, Muslims, Greek Orthodox, and Armenian Christians were recognized as autonomous political subunits, and similar arrangements in Imperial Rome.[3]

I will be discussing toleration as it relates to a changing conception of the dignity of individuals, so my focus will be on the individual-regarding conception. So understood, religious toleration protects, not the rights of religious groups, but the rights of individuals with respect to religion. Importantly, it protects not just the rights of individuals to enter into religious practice, but also their rights to exit. And equally importantly, it protects their rights not to engage in religious practices at all. As I will be considering it, religious toleration protects atheists no less than religious minorities.

I. SUBMISSION, AUTHORITY, AND RESPECT

My theme will be authority, so I shall begin by distinguishing different attitudes that relate to authority. Consider, first, the difference between *submission* to authority and *respect* for it. Submission involves the acknowledgment of *de facto* authority—that one will be ruled, will not challenge rule, and so on. Think, for example, of the way a defeated male elephant seal defers to the dominant male, or the way a beaten dog shows its neck. What is most important for our purposes is that submission expresses no view or attitude about *de jure* authority. We need not suppose that elephant seals have or express any attitude concerning the warrant or justification for the alpha male's dominance. Moreover, one can submit to rule one thinks unjustified. Certain kinds of behavior simply count as acknowledging *de facto* rule.

Compare this with *respect*. Unlike submission, behavior constitutes respect only if it involves or expresses a normative attitude toward that by which one is ruled or governed *de facto*. Respect for authority presents itself as being *as of de jure* or *normative* authority. Its internal object is the *dignity* of, say, the sovereign's office or his right to rule. Thus whereas submission is entirely external, respect involves the subject's internal *acceptance* of the sovereign's authority. And this means that although the subject is governed by the sovereign *de facto*, there is a sense in which she also governs herself, since she is not submitting to something she does not herself accept.

One way this can happen is if the subject accepts a norm that gives authority to the sovereign. This is how things are meant to work in Hobbes's system. *Leviathan*'s subjects do not merely submit to the sovereign's rule; they respect it by expressing their acceptance of a norm ("that men perform their covenants made" [15.1]) that grounds the sovereign's *right* to rule.

Acceptance of authority-grounding norms is not, however, the only way that someone can be seen to have authority. Consider the emotion of *awe*. There is very little in the psychological literature on awe, but the O.E.D. gives two current meanings: first, "from its use in reference to the Divine Being this passes gradually into: Dread mingled with veneration, reverential or respectful fear; the attitude of a mind subdued to profound reverence in the presence of supreme authority . . . ," and second, "the feeling of solemn and reverential wonder, tinged with latent fear, inspired by what is terribly sublime and majestic in nature."[4] Both are reminiscent of the "fear mingled with reverence" that Pufendorf says we feel when we appreciate God's power to reward and punish together with His "just reasons" for doing so.[5] But awe is not restricted to what we justly fear. The Indo-European roots of *awe* lead to words for east and the sun. Think of coming through the darkest night, say, on a boat on an uncertain sea, and looking east to glimpse the rays of the sun as it begins to rise. One might feel awe as, looking at the sun, one sees and feels its beneficial power to warm and renew life. "Let there be light!" Sun worship is no coincidence.

Awe presents itself as being *as of superior authority*. Its intentional object is power seen as superior and as appropriately or legitimately so. Awe thus differs from simple fear, or from the feeling of being subdued or overcome, in that we feel awe when in the presence of something whose powers we see as normative for us. We see what we are in awe of as something to take guidance from or be ruled by, something to respect, in this sense.

According to Hobbes, the benefits of political society depend upon a sovereign who can keep citizens "in awe" (17.1). Hobbesian citizens covenant to submit to the sovereign, and they accept a norm requiring them to keep their covenants. But it is possible to see someone or something as having superior authority without accepting any such norm. We need not think, for example, that sun worship involves the acceptance of a norm that grounds the sun's authority. In this case, the feeling or emotion of awe in the sun's presence at particularly impressive moments seems to do the work, not some norm about the right to rule. The idea is not that this experience is somehow self-validating, just that the feeling's phenomenological presentation is as of the sun's dignity or sacredness. Only if we take this feeling at face value and credit its appearance will we believe that the sun actually has authority.

Submission and awe are essentially tied to *superior* authority. However, one can regard someone as having authority without seeing that authority as superior, without seeing her as someone one should submit to or by whom one should be ruled. One may see her *as an equal*, as having an authority or dignity that is no different from one's own. For example, one may accept a norm of the equal dignity of persons according to which any person has claim to certain forms of treatment, including to treatment *as an equal*. As with awe, however, there are ways of seeing, regarding, or treating someone as having equal authority or standing that do not easily reduce to the acceptance of any norm that grants them this status. Indeed, if a norm requires not just equal treatment, but treatment *as an equal*, the norm will require treatment that itself expresses such a regard.

Seeing someone as an equal, like seeing someone as a superior, involves regarding them as having a certain dignity or authority. The difference, of course, is that the former involves seeing them as having a superior or higher dignity, and the latter involves seeing them as having an authority that is no different from one's own. Both are instances, therefore, of *respect*, the emotion or attitude whose object is something seen as having dignity or authority. Awe is an instance of what we might call *respect for a superior*. And the sort of reciprocal respect we have just been discussing is what we might call *mutual respect* or *respect for an equal*.

We know these forms of regard well enough when we see them and, of course, when we see their contraries. It doesn't take a moral theorist or a psychologist to feel condescended to, patronized, or accepted as an equal. A simple example: You are discussing a text with a student, a text that you have read and talked about a thousand times. The student advances an interpretive hypothesis that strikes you as a nonstarter. You *know* this text. You've been over it so many times that you are sure the student's interpretation can't possibly be right. The student, however, convinces you that there is another way to read a crucial passage, and that, once you do that, other passages have to be read in a new light. Slowly, a wholly fresh view of the text emerges, something very like what the student initially proposed. You make it evident that you see what the student is talking about and that, whether you accept this interpretation or not, you have come to accept the student as an interpreter, as having the standing to interpret the text in whatever way seems most sensible on the basis of evidence equally available to each of you. By the end of the conversation, at least, something like mutual respect has emerged. By taking the student's suggestions seriously, being willing to be initiated into her view of the text, acknowledging it as reasonable, and so on, one is seeing and treating the student as (that is, expressing respect for her as) an equal.

Here is another example. Suppose you are a parent who, complacent in your authority, have become overbearing and self-righteous in the direction of your emerging adolescent. For a while, your child has just been taking it, but this time you've gone too far, and your child upbraids you, saying something like, "You treat me as if I were an irresponsible boob. But the fact is that I'm just like you, and you don't like it. You're no more responsible about these things than I am, and you're a hypocrite to pretend otherwise. You wouldn't stand for me treating you the way you treat me." You might be brought up short by such a remonstrance, blood rushing to your face as you recognize the justice of your child's charge.

In feeling shame, you also feel respect for your child.[6] Your shame consists in recognizing yourself through the eyes of your child. And to do that you have to acknowledge the (epistemic) authority of your child's view. You have to see him as having sufficient judgment to evaluate you, as someone whose view of you is to be taken seriously. Moreover, in recognizing the justice of his *making* this charge, you must also see your child as having the standing to remonstrate against you. This is different from the epistemic authority you recognize when you credit his evaluation. In recognizing his standing to demand respect, you see him as someone who is, in this respect, no different than you are. You experience respect for him as an equal.

We have, then, a distinction between submitting to authority and respecting it. And we have a distinction between respect for superior authority and respect for an equal. I can now put my claim in these terms. So long as politics is grounded in submission to and respect for superior authority, religious difference must be seen inevitably to contest political authority in a way that makes religious toleration inherently problematic. On the other hand, the best justification for religious toleration is that it is essential to a political order that expresses respect for citizens as equals.

II. RELIGIOUS AND POLITICAL AUTHORITY IN EARLY MODERN EUROPE

Philosophers who write on toleration frequently refer to what they call the "paradox of toleration." The idea is that it is apparently a conceptual truth that we can tolerate only what we have some objection to, what we think bad. If we are indifferent to or approve something, then the question of whether to tolerate it doesn't even arise. But then how can toleration be anything but a necessary evil? How can we think it intrinsically good to allow what is, as we think, bad?

As puzzling as toleration can seem in general, I want to suggest that in early modern Europe *religious* toleration seemed even more problematic. The reason is suggested by Hobbes's remark that "the most frequent pretext of sedition and civil war" is the difficulty of "obeying at once both God and man" (43.1). Religious differences were seen to create divided loyalties, at best, between political and religious sovereignty. And at worst, they appeared to challenge the sovereign's very claim to authority *de jure*. How, then, could religious toleration be even a necessary evil, much less something intrinsically valuable? How could political authority be required to warrant its own destruction?

In arguing that religious difference contested political authority, I don't mean to suggest that this was the only source of religious intolerance. Aquinas had claimed, for example, that persecuting heresy was justified on the grounds that it threatened to corrupt the faithful. And, in addition to concerns about corruption and pollution, there was also, of course, the worry that the faithful might be attracted away.

None of these, however, speak to the concern that Hobbes raises, namely, that religious difference might put people at odds about the very authority of the state.

The most obvious source of this idea was *theological voluntarism*, specifically, Luther's and Calvin's claims that all moral and political authority derives from God's *command*. All "secular law," Luther wrote, exists only "as a result of God's will and ordinance."[7] This passage comes from "On Secular Authority," in which Luther argues for restricting political authority over religion, indeed, on the grounds of the importance of individual faith and conscience. But Luther was apparently less concerned about the general issue than about Catholic suppression of Protestants in particular. When it came to the authority of Protestant princes, he later argued, they are not only permitted, but obligated, to suppress public "abominations" like the Catholic mass, which idolatrously insult divine authority. For our present purposes, however, the main point is Luther's voluntarism, his view that all legal and political authority derives from divine command. As Luther put it in his reply to Erasmus, there could be a moral standard independent of God's will only if there were "another Creator over" God![8] And we can find this same line of thought in Calvin as well as in such seventeenth-century Protestant political philosophers as Pufendorf and Locke.

Voluntarism of the Luther/Calvin variety was far from the Catholic mainstream, of course. But even here there were voluntarist elements—for example, in the thought of Suarez.[9] And while Aquinas and his followers were not voluntarists, there were important issues on the relation between religious and political authority where they might as well have been. Thus Aquinas held that although believers have a defeasible political obligation to obey even unbelieving sovereigns, "this right of dominion or authority can be justly done away with by the sentence or ordination of the Church, which has the authority of God, since unbelievers in virtue of their unbelief deserve to forfeit their power over the faithful."[10]

This was no idle threat for early modern Europeans. In 1570, Pius V pronounced that Elizabeth's rule was invalid on the grounds that the pope had the right to depose heretical kings. And some English Catholics maintained that, although the faithful should obey the Queen's edicts on civil matters, a military coup launched from abroad could validly execute the Pope's sentence. From the perspective of es-

tablished Anglican authority, there seemed an all-too-easy identification between Roman Catholicism and treason. If the threat posed
to established power by Protestant sects was any individual's religious
right or obligation to assess the sovereign's relation to divine authority,
that posed by Roman Catholicism to Protestant states was a similar
right claimed by a powerful body with powerful allies—the Holy See
and Catholic states.

If all political authority is rooted in God's will and if religious
disputes extend to differences in belief about what God wills, then
there will be an obvious sense in which religious difference will seem
to contest political authority, at least potentially. This potentiality
may not be realized, of course. Different religious groups may agree
about God's will as it relates to politics. But nothing guarantees this.
And whenever a group sees itself to have a religious duty to disobey
the sovereign—for example, by participating in prohibited forms of
worship—they will have reason to question the sovereign's authority
de jure. At the least, they will see a conflict of obligations between
obedience to God and obedience to the sovereign. And they may
come to see this conflict as undermining the sovereign's authority.

In effect, what we get when political authority is implicated
in religious belief in this way is something like a Hobbesian state of
nature all over again. Even when sovereign power exists *de facto,* if
people believe that its authority *de jure* is conditional on God's will
and if they disagree about God's will on relevant matters, or even just
believe that they *might* disagree on them, then the resulting situation
has much of the same uncertainty that makes the use of preemptive
force rational in a state of nature. Not surprisingly, then, contending
religious groups may take themselves to have reason to engage in
similar forms of potentially destabilizing preemption. Of course, numbers may not make this reasonable. Unlike the state of nature, where
everyone has roughly equal power, established and disestablished religious groups may have vastly differing power. This can add to toleration's risks for established groups, since they know that it can lead to
an improvement in disestablished groups' relative power, which the
latter can then use to execute God's will as they see it.

A particularly interesting example of the way religious difference
was seen to contest political authority was the case of the Dutch Republic, which, from its founding in the late sixteenth century, showed a
highly unusual measure of religious toleration. Article 13 of the Union

of Utrecht, which served as a kind of constitution, proclaimed that "each individual enjoys freedom of religion and no one is persecuted or questioned about his religion."[11] However, the Dutch drew a sharp line between private and public religion. Although the state was prepared to tolerate Catholic and even Jewish religious practice, it did so only so long as these were conducted in buildings that bore no external religious marks. These "hidden churches" (*schuilkerken*) could be quite splendid and ornate inside, without, however, any public religious aspect. What underlay this distinction? Partly, no doubt, it was the worry that publicly expressed religious differences were likelier to spread. Thus Calvin declared that government must prevent "idolatries, sacrileges against the name of God, blasphemies against his truth, and other scandals to religion from emerging into the light of day and spreading among the people."[12] But note even here that Calvin's worry seems less about spreading different belief than about expanding sacrilege and blasphemy, that is, the spread of a certain kind of insult and disrespect of God's divine authority (for example, of the sort that Protestants believed to be involved in the Catholic Mass) that would accompany public toleration. Consider in this context the following passage from Luther:

> When an impudent rascal blasphemes, curses or insults God in the middle of the street, the authority who allows such an act and does not punish it severely, shares before God in that sin. If cursing and swearing are forbidden in a country, it is still more right here that the lay lords should prohibit and punish, because such blasphemy and such insults to God are as evident and public in the Mass as when a rascal blasphemes in the street.[13]

Luther's worry is that if the authority is seen to tolerate an insult to God's authority, as it must understand different "worship" to be, then it will be complicit; it will "share in the sin" of the insult, and so undermine its own authority, since this can only come from God.

This lands us in identity politics with a vengeance (if you will pardon the pun). In a world in which dignity and moral identity are gauged by *subjection*, by the relation human individuals and institutions have to superior divine authority, an attack on God must be understood as an attack on the source of one's own dignity and, hence, as a personal insult which, if not avenged, risks dishonor and devaluation to oneself, as it does to anything whose dignity derives from God's.

This helps explain, I think, the violence and cruelty that can characterize religious persecution and intolerance in such a world. If individuals are seen to have no dignity in themselves, but only in relation to superior authority, then perceived attacks on that authority will also be seen as personal attacks and thus as a form of violence. Once we see things this way, we are in more of a Lockean than a Hobbesian state of nature; that is, a world in which injuries are seen as *violations* to be resented and retributed rather than things simply to be avoided for the sake of self-preservation. Moreover, violent retribution will seem to have a kind of self-authorizing character. It will be seen, not just as what is called for by the authority that has been called in question, but as helping to reestablish that very authority. As Muhammad Arkoun remarks about *jihad*, "physical violence used in the Holy War . . . is not only perceived as legitimate, it is also *sacred and sacralizing*."[14] It is as though the very act of retaliatory, subjugating violence shows—indeed, *makes it the case*—that God speaks through me and not through you.

III. RELIGIOUS TOLERATION AND THE DIGNITY OF THE PERSON

It is a commonplace that the cycle of religious wars in sixteenth- and seventeenth-century Europe led over time to various forms of religious toleration as a *modus vivendi*. There was nothing necessary about this result. As recent experience in Lebanon might confirm, religious civil wars may only cement antagonisms as people look to their own traditions of faith for comfort in times of grief and loss and seek, from that perspective, to apportion blame and responsibility.[15] But, if nothing else, the European wars of religion showed that where there is a significantly powerful plurality of religious belief and practice, the costs of maintaining a conception of divinely ordained political authority together with political institutions that sanction only one religion will be very high. As it turned out, they proved unacceptably high.

It is one thing, however, to accept regimes of toleration strategically, as a means to end violent conflict. It is quite another to think that religious toleration is intrinsically valuable, that there is a justification for it that wouldn't evaporate if one were able successfully to suppress other religions.

I have argued that the distinctive form that the problem of religious toleration took in early modern Europe was due to the idea that being a moral subject is essentially a matter of *subjection*. To properly appreciate the value of religious toleration, I shall now claim, we must see it from the perspective of a very different conception of the moral subject, namely, as having an authority that derives, not from subjection to a superior power, but from the capacity for moral *subjectivity*, that is, the capacity to lead and take responsibility for one's own life. From this point of view, what is salient about religious toleration is its centrality to political institutions that express *respect* for the dignity any individual has in herself, independently of her religious belief and practice—respect for citizens as equals.

Notice how this justification differs from another that is also rooted in the value of autonomy. One might argue, as some liberals do, following Mill, that autonomy is an essential component of a valuable human life. A justification of religious toleration along these lines would argue that practices of toleration are instrumentally valuable because they cause or promote greater personal autonomy and, therefore, more beneficial lives. The justification I am pointing to, however, sees the capacity for autonomy, not simply as essential to a beneficial life, but as the source of the distinctive dignity of moral personality. From this point of view, it is what grounds an authority that can be respected or violated rather than a component of a valuable life that can be promoted or hindered. A justification of religious toleration along these lines, therefore, is that it expresses respect for the dignity of individuals as autonomous moral persons. Such a justification takes no stand on the role of autonomy in a valuable human life. Indeed, it can be accepted by those who reject the Millian thesis and think that autonomy breeds anomie or that it undermines valuable commitments of the sort that are involved in a life of religious faith. The point is rather that each individual has the *authority* to lead her own life and that practices of religious toleration express respect for this intrinsic dignity.

But how might people be brought to accept a justification of this kind? It would seem that in order to accept the idea that individuals have a dignity that is independent of religious belief and practice, and, in particular, that is independent of their relation to divinely authoritative will, people would already have to accept religious toleration in some form. In this last section, I want to provide some illus-

trations of how it is possible to move from practices of toleration as a
modus vivendi to a way of regarding and valuing persons—respecting
their intrinsic authority or dignity—that can then provide a principled
justification for those very practices.

Consider, for example, Voltaire's remark that in the London Exchange, "the Jew, the Mohammedan, and the Christian deal with one
another as if they were of the same religion, and give the name of
infidel only to those who go bankrupt."[16] Mutual advantage leads
religious enemies to participate as equals in economic transactions,
dissolving insult and contempt, even if only for purposes of exchange.
This is not yet mutual respect, of course. So far, mutual relations may
be entirely strategic and instrumental, each regarding the other
purely as sources of supply and demand. However, even participants
in economic exchange do not regard each other purely instrumentally,
since the very possibility of markets depends on mutually accepted
norms that govern them. These norms define what is acceptable and
what is unacceptable treatment of others in exchange, ruling out force
and fraud and enshrining rights of buyers and sellers. Insofar as participants accept these norms, they accept a conception of the equal
moral standing that individuals have in economic exchange, of how
they can and cannot be treated. When they engage in exchange on
this assumption, they express respect for others as equal transagents
under this conception. There will be no sharp line, moreover, between
participation in exchange and participation in an ongoing normative
discussion and critique of exchange, both of particular transactions
and of the norms that govern them. And the same forces that lead individuals to bracket religious loyalties in exchange will lead them also
to bracket them in this normative critique. The upshot is a set of practices that define a community of equal respect in which individuals
have an equal dignity defined by the norms of exchange and equal authority to make claims in light of them.

What leads "the Jew, the Mohammedan, and the Christian" to
participate in economic exchange in the first place is mutual advantage, not mutual respect. The understandings that underpin exchange
may initially be only a *modus vivendi* for them, not norms the participants accept. But these practices can't even function unless a sufficient number of participants internalize the norms that govern them.
As Hobbes says about covenant, individuals can expect to be accepted
into such practices over time only if they internalize the relevant

norms. When they do, what they internalize is a conception of the equal dignity any individual has within such practices, regardless of religious faith. This gives them a new way of valuing others, as from a perspective all can share regardless of religious commitment. And it gives them a justification for the practice that is more than a *modus vivendi*, namely, that it expresses respect for this very value.

Another example of this phenomenon, or a fictional description of one, that is closer to the case of religious toleration is provided in a fascinating text by the medieval Iberian philosopher, Raymond Lull (1232–1316). Lull's *Book of the Gentile and the Three Wise Men* is a tale of a "gentile, very learned in philosophy," who, with growing concern about his unbelief, engages "three wise men" in mutual dialogue, a Jew, a Christian, and a Saracen, hoping to discover what he should believe about religion.[17] Lull has the three meet a woman, named "Intelligence," who explains to them the method of "demonstrative and necessary reasons" (Lull's own rationalist "Art"). The men agree that, as they can expect no resolution of their religious differences "by means of authorities," they should conduct their discourses by this method. After the three present beliefs on which they agree, there follow three books that respectively present the characteristic doctrines of Judaism, Christianity, and Islam, always within the constraints of mutually accepted standards of reasonable evidence and argument. At the end of this process, the Gentile is about to announce the conclusion he has come to when he is interrupted by the wise men who tell him that they do not want to know:

> This is a question we could discuss among ourselves to see, by force of reason and by means of our intellects, which religion it must be that you will choose. And if, in front of us, you state which religion it is that you prefer, then we would not have such a good subject of discussion nor such satisfaction in discovering the truth.[18]

After the Gentile's departure, they agree to continue meeting, saying: "Do you think we have nothing to gain from what happened to us in the forest? Would you like to meet once a day and . . . discuss according to the manner the Lady of Intelligence showed us . . . ?"[19]

What, however, *do* they have to gain? Although they say their aim is agreement in belief, there is no reason to suggest that this is in the offing. Even if it were, the three would have to view the prospect ambivalently since, for each, it is more likely than not that an agreement point will conflict with their current beliefs on controversial issues. What the three have gained and can continue to gain, whether they end up agreeing or not, is the good of respectful dialogue, a practice in which each expresses (and appreciates) respect for each as an equal. Throughout the process, as they recognize the force of others' reasons and take their arguments seriously, they recognize their equal authority to form their own beliefs and participate in a common discussion. And in being valued in this way by the others, they appreciate their own intrinsic value.

It is possible, therefore, to enter into a practice whose norms require that participants treat others as equals regardless of religious faith, initially to regard those norms as a *modus vivendi,* but to end up accepting the norms and the conception of equal dignity that they enshrine. The three might, for example, initially eschew arguments from authoritative religious text and tradition entirely for strategic reasons. As they enter into the practice and into each others' reasoning, however, they are drawn into implicitly recognizing the authority of these reasons and, through them, the intrinsic authority of the others as rational persons.

IV. CONCLUSION

I have argued that what made religious toleration problematic for early modern Europeans was the idea that the authority of human beings and human political institutions derives from God's superior right of command, that to be a human moral subject is to be *subject to* God's authority. Once, however, we see moral subjecthood as an inherent dignity any person has through the capacity to lead her own life and to enter into collective deliberation about a common life, religious toleration will seem a central feature of political institutions that express respect for this dignity. Only if the public space of political deliberation and action is constructed with rights of participation that are unconditional on religious loyalties can citizens express a respect for others as equals through their political practice.

I began with Hobbes's definitions of war and peace and with the Hobbesian claim that peace requires politics and that the sort of politics it requires is absolutely authoritative sovereignty rooted in a covenant. For Hobbes's contemporaries, however, political sovereignty was grounded in *divine* sovereignty. This made religious difference potentially subversive—not just as a source of political disagreement, but as a challenge to established authority that threatened civil war. If Hobbes is right that peace requires politics, then perhaps a stable peace requires egalitarian politics, one that includes a regime of religious toleration that respects all as equals, regardless of religious belief and practice.[20]

NOTES

1. Thomas Hobbes, *Leviathan, with selected variants from the Latin edition of 1668,* ed. Edwin Curley (Indianapolis: Hackett Pub. Co., 1994), chap. 13, para. 8. Hereafter all references to *Leviathan* will be placed in the text.

2. I am indebted here to David Wootton, who claims that the shift from a conception of subjection to subjectivity explains a fundamental shift in attitudes toward atheism ("'Enemies of All Society': Toleration for Atheists from More to Mill," talk given at the University of Michigan, February 9, 1998).

3. The former is discussed in Will Kymlicka, *Multicultural Citizenship* (Oxford: Clarendon Press, 1996), pp. 156–57, and in Michael Walzer, *On Toleration* (New Haven, Conn. and London: Yale University Press, 1997), pp. 17–18. The latter is discussed in Walzer, *On Toleration*, pp. 14–17.

4. *Oxford English Dictionary*, 2d ed. A keyword search of *awe* in *The Psychology Index* of periodicals published since 1967 reveals only 44 entries, most of which are psychoanalytic in character. (An example: "Awe and Premature Ejaculation: A Case Study.")

See also Edmund Burke on the sublime: "Whatever is fitted in any sort to excite the ideas of pain and danger, that is to say, whatever is in any sort terrible, or is conversant about terrible objects, or operates in a manner analogous to terror, is a source of the *sublime*" ("The Sublime and Beautiful," in *Edmund Burke* [New York: P. F. Collier & Son, Harvard Classics, 1937], p. 35).

5. Samuel Pufendorf, *The Law of Nature and Nations*, trans. C. H. and W. A. Oldfather (Oxford: Clarendon Press, 1934), bk. 1, chap. 6, para. 9, p. 95.

6. I am indebted here to the work of Sarah Buss.

7. Martin Luther, "On Secular Authority" (originally published in 1523), in *Luther and Calvin on Secular Authority*, ed. Harro Höpfl (Cambridge: At the University Press, 1991), p. 6.

8. Martin Luther, "The Bondage of the Will" (originally published in 1525), in *Martin Luther: Selections from His Writings*, ed. John Dillenberger (Garden City, N.Y.: Anchor Books, Doubleday & Co., 1961), p. 196.

9. Suarez followed Aquinas in holding that the content of natural law is settled by our social and rational nature, but he claimed that what makes it an obligating law is that it expresses God's authoritative command (Francisco Suarez, *On Law and God the Lawgiver* [originally published in 1612], in *Moral Philosophy from Montaigne to Kant*, ed. J. B. Schneewind [Cambridge: At the University Press, 1990], pp. 67–87).

10. Thomas Aquinas, *Summa Theologiae* 2.2., quest. 10, in *On Law, Morality, and Politics*, ed. William P. Baumgarth and Richard J. Regan, S.J. (Indianapolis: Hackett Pub. Co., 1988), p. 256.

11. Quoted in Philip Gorski, "Social and Political Preconditions of Religious Toleration in Early Modern Europe: France and the Netherlands Compared," University of Michigan, International Institute, Advanced Study Center Working Paper Series, 1997–98.

12. John Calvin, "On Civil Government," in *Luther and Calvin on Secular Authority*, ed. Höpfl, p. 50.

13. Martin Luther, quoted in Joseph Lecler, S.J., *Toleration and the Reformation* (New York: Association Press, 1960), especially 5.1, pp. 147–64.

14. Muhammad Arkoun, "Toleration, Intolerance, Intolerable: A Comparative Approach of Religious and Modern Reason," University of Michigan, International Institute, Advanced Study Center Working Paper Series, 1997–98, p. 10.

15. I am indebted here to Fawwaz Traboulsi, "Theories and Practices of Religious Tolerance/Intolerance—The Lebanese Experience," University of Michigan, International Institute, Advanced Study Center Working Paper Series, 1997–98.

16. Voltaire, "Lettres philosophiques," *Melanges* (Paris: Pleaide, 1961), pp. 17–18. I am indebted to Elizabeth Anderson for calling my attention to this passage.

17. *Selected Works of Raymond Lull*, ed. and trans. Anthony Bonner (Princeton, N.J.: Princeton University Press, 1985), pp. 110-304. I am much indebted to Cary Nederman, "Medieval Discourse of Tolerance: Demonstration in Interreligious Dialogue," University of Michigan, International Institute, Advanced Study Center Working Paper Series, 1997–98, for bringing this work to my attention and for insightful discussion of it. I am also indebted to Cary Nederman for discussion of my ideas about this work. Hereafter references to this work will be cited as SWRL.

18. SWRL, pp. 300–301.

19. SWRL, p. 303.

20. I am indebted to members of the audience when this essay was presented in the Boston University Institute for Philosophy and Religion on March 4, 1998, and especially to my commentator, Charles Griswold, for very helpful discussion.

Common Ground
and Defensible Difference[1]
JOHN CLAYTON

THE VIGOR WITH which radically conservative religious movements have gained ground around the world—East and West, North and South—caught the liberal intellectual establishment unprepared. Many consoled themselves at first by insisting it was a temporary blip and predicted that the corrective forces of secularization would soon reassert themselves and set things back on course in and beyond the West. However, this has not happened. In the meantime, the liberal community has gone on the offensive, warning with uncharacteristic sensationalism against domestic culture wars or global clashes of civilizations if commonality is not maximized. Rawlsians may have soberly realized that citizens of modern democratic societies share less in common than they had once imagined, but they have not abandoned the strategy of seeking out and expanding the possible patches of overlapping consensus that may survive. This typifies the intuitive response of liberalism, both classical and contemporary, to diversity: privatize difference and cultivate common ground as a means of containing the potentially destructive social effects of cultural, especially religious, diversity.

Who indeed could doubt that staking out and tending common ground is the first thing required to overcome difference and to create a common good? Where there are differences of opinion between persons or states or religions, most of us instinctively look to strategies that maximize common ground. The image of common ground evokes public parks and village greens. It is an image full of warmth and reassurance, exuding a sense of community and well-being. It is an image that can inspire even the likes of former British Prime Minister John Major to eloquence in homage to village cricket, warm beer, and prim spinsters cycling to Evensong.

But the image of common ground has another side, one that has to do with control and power. Access to shared space requires a willingness to conform to rules (usually posted) that regulate hours of access, modes of dress, kinds of activities that are permitted not only by visitors but also by their pets. Such regulations are rarely oppressive, but *are* occasionally idiosyncratic. Access to common ground is never entirely free of regulation; the regulations on display reflect local community standards, and the more nearly one approximates those standards, the less difficulty one will have feeling "at home" in public space.

Common ground is not always unitive; it can be the cause of conflict. Sometimes the greater the share in common ground, the more destructive the conflict. It might be observed, at the risk of seeming overliteral, that no one has more common ground than do the Palestinians and the Israelis. *What they share in common is in fact the basis of their conflict.* Common ground, in short, does not always contribute to peace. Nor, I would add, does radical difference necessarily give cause to worry about imminent culture wars at home or impending clashes of civilizations on the global scene.

Clarification of defensible difference, not identification of "common ground," may be what is required to gain the cooperation of disparate religious interests in achieving pragmatically defined goals that enhance human flourishing. This approach would entail a shift from focusing on reasons as grounds to focusing instead on reasons as motives and on reasons as goals; that is to say, focusing less on the *grounds* of argument and more on the *ends* of argument. That, at least, is the possibility I want to put forward. To get there, however, there is groundwork to be done.

The terms *public* and *private* are notoriously slippery—and not just in England, where public schools are private, nor just in America, where the private lives of politicians are treated as matters of intense public concern. So upside down have public and private become that more Americans can name women with whom the President has been sexually linked than can name members of his cabinet. One does not have to wait for a Gallup poll to be confident that more Americans could discuss in lurid detail the President's private sexual preferences than could intelligently discuss his public policies. Even apart from this episode, however, it has to be allowed that the conceptual boundaries between *public* and *private* are somewhat indeterminate. The private sphere can be extended to cover everything that is not an official function of government, or it can be restricted to what goes on between consenting adults within their own four walls. The public realm can be conceived narrowly, or it can be expanded in liberal democracies to include anything open to all qualified members of the public, such as the market place, the academy, and the "public square."

For the American conscience, however, it is organized religion's possible involvement in matters political that causes greatest suspicion about religion's public role. This suspicion is deeply rooted in our origins as a nation. The Republic and its ideals were forged at a time when the European liberal thinking that so impressed the likes of Jefferson and his generation had served up a minimalist idea of civil government. Citizens were to be left relatively free of interference to pursue their own vision of the good life, providing that pursuit did not impede the ability of other citizens to pursue theirs. In respect to organized religion, this was perceived to have two consequences, both of them embodied eventually in the first amendment to the U.S. Constitution: it is not the business of federal government to privilege parochial religious interests by establishment, but it is the business of government to protect the free exercise of religion from hindrance, be it initiated by those hostile to religion, by other religious groups, or by some agency of government.

Jefferson spoke of the need for a "wall of separation" between the state and the affairs of religion, a phrase over which he took some care. It was, he admitted, seasoned to Southern tastes, and he feared it might be too strong for the more delicate digestion of those living in the North.[2] In retrospect, his intended wall was neither especially high nor particularly substantial. It was more like the back wall of an English terrace house: high enough to keep the neighbor's children and pets out of the flower beds, but low enough not to exclude light or exchanges of local gossip on the weekends. For instance, Jefferson did not think all forms of religion unfit for access to public space; rational religion retained privileged rights of access to the public arena. However modest his wall may have been, it has been raised and reinforced by subsequent custom, legislation, and judicial interpretation, until it is now a formidable barrier that effectively excludes religious access to the public realm. Even though the wall may have been "improved" over time, its foundations remain Jeffersonian. He set the tone of the

American liberal tradition by insisting on the separation of personal belief from civic virtue. In Jefferson's view, it is not of public concern whether a citizen has this religion or that or no religion at all.

Religion in the Jeffersonian project was effectively privatized and made subject to market forces, not to state monopoly. Though it is not actually entailed by Jefferson's position, the extended "wall of separation" threatens to deny private religion access to public space or influence in defining public virtue. The liberal state is fully secular; public reason, secular reason; public virtue, secular virtue. Critics of modernity sometimes point to the privatization of religion as an important aspect of the much-hyped loss of community and fragmentation of cultural values. Accompanying this indictment has gone a call, first from the right and more recently from the left, to reassert religion's right of entry to the public sphere of civic life.

Early architects of classical liberalism anticipated the charge. In a recent article on religion and community in the thought of the Scottish economist Adam Smith, Charles Griswold has examined the initially counterintuitive argument of *The Wealth of Nations* that incorporating religion into civic life *undermines* community by leading to a variety of public vices, including fanaticism and intolerance, while the privatization of religion *builds up* community by encouraging a variety of liberal virtues, including moderation and tolerance.[3] On this account, diversity of religious interests in a society leads not so much to culture wars as to peace and harmony.

How does it do that?

If the civil government withdraws from the religion business, so to speak, and favors no religious persuasion with establishment, then religion—being based on a combination of volatile and irrational factors—can be predicted to fragment into a large number of independent sects. These sects will then compete vigorously for new members, since their very survival depends upon the moral and financial support of their membership. In order to make themselves more attractive to more people, however, the individual sects will tend to moderate their more extreme positions. They will then adopt a less strident and more tolerant attitude toward other groups, an attitude which is highly conducive to community. Ergo, privatization leads to an enhanced sense of community.

Earlier, I noted the hold that the image of "common ground" has on our thinking about ways to avoid the destructive effects of religious difference. It would seem *prima facie* that Adam Smith's appeal to the imagery of the market offers an alternative that values diversity positively without requisite "common ground." First impressions may be misleading, however, so it will be necessary to return to this issue. Before doing so, it may prove useful to see how Jefferson used forces at work in the market place to project the future of religious diversity in America.

The privatization of religion, Jefferson insisted, was an advantage both to the state and to true religion. Establishment leads to the corruption of the state and of religion alike. Exclusion of parochial religious interests from the public arena is necessary both for the integrity of the state and for the prosperity of true religion. Privatization advantages the state, he argues in language reminiscent of Smith, because a diversity of "good enough" religious groups in a society acts to stabilize and to moderate religious excesses. Writing at a time when many States still had legally established churches, Jefferson pointed to the successful experiments in New York and Pennsylvania where, in the absence of legal establishment, religious diversity and public order happily flourished together:

> Religion is well supported; of various kinds, indeed, but all good enough; all sufficient to preserve peace and order: or if a sect arises, whose tenets would subvert morals, good sense has fair play, and reasons and laughs it out of doors, without suffering the state to be troubled with it. They do not hang more malefactors than we do. They are not more disturbed with religious dissensions. On the contrary, their harmony is unparalleled, and can be ascribed to nothing but their unbounded tolerance, because there is no other circumstance in which they differ from every nation on earth. They have made the happy discovery, that the way to silence religious disputes, is to take no notice of them.[4]

That last sentence is telling. In it we glimpse how Jefferson's private opinion on the pointlessness of sectarian religious disputes and the irrationality of parochial religious interests colors his recommendations for public policy in respect to religion. Religion is privatized not to allow a hundred flowers to bloom but to subject the diverse religious sects to the corrective forces of the market place that serve to control fanatical excess and also to instill liberal virtues, such as tolerance and "good sense." Privatization of sectarian religion effectively allowed Jefferson to institute his private religious preferences as public policy. The forces of the market place, not the forces of state, would be used to maximize rationality in religion.

In a society where all religious groups have equal protection under the law and free access to the market place, citizens can be expected to shop around a bit, but they will eventually settle on the "best buy," which in Jefferson's estimate would be the religious option that is highest in rationality. "Reason and free enquiry are the only effectual agents against error. Give a loose to them, they will support the true religion, by bringing every false one to their tribunal, to the test of their investigation."[5] Unregulated market forces would eliminate faulty goods, thus driving rationally defective religions into liquidation. Religious diversity, for Jefferson a given, is viewed as an instrument of its own destruction. Irrational parochial interests give way over time to the superior market leadership of rational religion, which emerges not just as market leader, but as unregulated monopoly. And it does so not by the force of legal establishment but by the power of persuasion, in and through the sort of "free enquiry" idealized in Enlightenment rationality.

This seems rather distant from Adam Smith. For Smith, diversity is not simply tolerated until true religion can eliminate its false competitors; it is actively encouraged. The greater the diversity, the better, on Smith's account. But this is misleading. Encouraging diversity is as strategic for Smith as it is for Jefferson. Both men regarded all sectarian religious groups as fundamentally irrational. The two men differ only in their views of how rational religion overcomes what is patently false and irrational. For Jefferson, it would occur by sects being displaced one by one by rational religion. For Smith, it would occur as gradual modifications to all the sectarian options as part of the overarching process of moderation, until they all finally converge at or near "pure and rational religion."

In both accounts of diversity, difference is an embarrassment, a sign of irrationality, to be overcome by the totalization of reason. Otherness may be publicly tolerated, but it is privately held in utter contempt.

Smith and Jefferson judged the religious sects of their acquaintance to be irrational, in part because their style of argument did not conform to the canons of public rationality idealized in what is widely called by supporters and detractors alike the "Enlightenment project"—a phrase that has all the descriptive credibility of the "Holy Roman Empire." Having myself tried elsewhere to define it, I shall resist the temptation to do so again here.[6] For present purposes, it is sufficient to note that in its terms, we are required in all our deliberations to attain neutrality by divesting ourselves of allegiance to any particular standpoint and to achieve universality by abstracting ourselves from all those communities of interest that may limit our perspective. As sovereign selves we lay sound foundations on which to build with reasoned confidence. This account evokes procedures outlined by Descartes in his *Discourse on Method* and applied in his *Meditations on First Philosophy.*

Descartes is your worst nightmare as a neighbor. No sooner has he bought the house next door than he begins worrying that it may be haunted. Then one day he mutters that roofs have been known to leak and infers from this datum that his roof must be unreliable. The next thing you know, he has the roof off and then begins to dismantle the place floor by floor, room by room, until he has the ground cleared. Not content, he digs on until he hits bedrock. With a worrying air of Gallic self-satisfaction, he then proceeds to lay new foundations and to begin rebuilding his house. You offer to help, but he refuses all assistance.

According to the terms of the Enlightenment project, we must learn to rely on ourselves alone and not on others, present or past, if we are to avoid error. The free use of reason by a sovereign self, unencumbered by all such entanglements, is a sure guide to truth, justice, and virtue. It is also sufficient to discover all that is necessary to know about God, immortality of the soul, and the requirements of the moral law.

Rational religion is supposed to be public religion both in the sense of its being open equally to all and in the sense of its being supported by reasons that are reasons for everyone—that is, it is imagined to conform to classical liberal canons of public rationality. Rational religion was not treated as one sect among other sects, but as the ground common to all religious sects, from which they may deviate to varying degrees, the degree of their deviation being a measure of their irrationality. In practice, however, "rational religion" was little more than the residue that remained after eliminating all the distinguishing doctrines of the diverse Protestant groups that proliferated in parts of Europe and in much of eighteenth-century America. It was able to pass itself off as "universal" only because of the paucity of knowledge about religious traditions that had no share in the narrative traditions of historical Christianity. Other groups could be imagined to share in rational religion of the requisite sort because of the sheer thinness of contact with such groups.

The point is easily made in reference to America circa 1800. Almost 90 percent of the citizens of the U.S. at that time who belonged to a religious community identified themselves with some Protestant group. About 10 percent were Roman Catholics and only 0.5 percent were Jewish.[7] If we focus more narrowly on Jefferson's own state, whose *Statute for Religious Freedom* became the model for the first amendment of the U.S. Constitution, the homogeneity is even more staggering. In the whole of the Commonwealth of Virginia at the turn of the century, there was not a single Roman Catholic church, and the nearest Jewish congregations were in Philadelphia to the north and Charleston to the south. In such circumstances, maximizing common ground may well have been a reasonable and practical strategy for containing the damage that might be done to the public good by the fact of religious diversity. But this is not the sort of religious diversity that occupies us today, whatever the level of magnification used in our enquiries, whether we focus on the local, regional, or global scene.

Contrast the sort of diversity that concerned Jefferson and his generation with the sort of diversity evident today in a city like Boston or in a major research university like Boston University. Contrast it also with the kind of diversity evident today in the very European countries that produced the leading architects of the rational religion embraced by classical liberalism. In Britain today, for instance, there are more Hindus than Jews and more Muslims than Methodists.[8] Nor is Britain in this respect unique among European lands. The precise mix may be different, but the sort of religious diversity experienced in many European countries today is not that different. *What kind of strategy would be effective in respect to this sort of diversity, so that it has a chance of becoming a positive good rather than a detriment to the stability of an open society?*

In recent academic debates about the role of religious differences in threatened culture wars and impending clashes of civilizations, too much attention has been given to destructively conflictual consequences of difference and too little to the positive benefits of diversity or to the complex strategies that religions themselves develop to accommodate difference, whether it exists within a single religious community or among a plurality of religious communities that may have existed for some time alongside one another, cheek to jowl.

Sometimes these strategies are purely local, partial, and inconsistent with a given community's "official" polity and practice. They may nonetheless be effective strategies, which, without external interference, can have long-term local benefit. In 1992, the world's attention was focused on Ayodhya, an inconspicuous village in India, where a mob of Hindu nationalists destroyed the sixteenth-century mosque that in times of Islamic ascendancy had been built over the legendary birth spot of the God Rama. Press coverage of this event and the violence that ensued throughout India was intense and unremitting. Less well covered was the fact that local Hindus and Muslims had long ago reached an accord that allowed a corner of the mosque to be used by Hindus to honor Rama.

Local accommodation is more widespread "on the ground" among religious populations than might be imagined, as is extensive syncretism and a variety of pick-and-choose combinations. A successful Japanese family might follow certain Shinto practices, opt for a Christian wedding for their daughter, but at death find comfort in a Buddhist funeral. It is not unusual for contemporary Christians to experiment with a wide variety of meditative and spiritual practices belonging properly to other paths, legitimated by narrative traditions, grounded in doctrinal schemes, and directed at goals quite different from their own path, narrative, doctrine, and goal, and to conduct such experiments with the expectation of spiritual insight that somehow goes beyond what is otherwise available to them in their own tradition's spiritual practices. In some areas of Nepal, Buddhism and Hinduism are so intermingled in popular belief and practice that a credible difference can no longer be found. If one were to examine the classical polemical texts of Buddhist and Brahmanical philosophers, however, it would be hard to imagine that such syncretism could be possible in principle, much less that it could be sustained in practice. Yet it is.

We academics, notoriously susceptible to the mental hobgoblins identified by Emerson, find it easy to dismiss examples from popular religion as intellectually uninteresting. I protest. I would go on to suggest that such muddling efforts may even contribute more to peace and human flourishing than does professorial hand-wringing over domestic culture wars and global clashes of civilizations. But I will not labor that point here. Instead, I will retreat to academically more comfortable territory and remind us that strategies for accommodating difference occur not just at the popular level. At more reflective levels, spiritual and intellectual elites of religious groups develop means for dealing with difference inside and beyond their boundaries. Some may even be philosophically interesting in their capacity to suggest models of public reason at odds with the dominant paradigm of classical liberalism that continues to inform academic ideals of public reason.

Rather than viewing religions as inherently "irrational" because they fail to conform to the style of tradition-free reasoning idealized in classical liberal or Enlightenment accounts of rationality, it may be better to see religions as *localized rationalities,* that is, as largely coherent instances of group-specific reasoning.

Reasons do matter intensely to religious communities, but what counts as a good reason in what circumstance may be tradition-specific and itself be a matter of controversy within a community. To discern what count as "good reasons" in a given situation requires one to get one's intellectual fingernails dirty: that is, one must root out particular cases for closer scrutiny. To be maximally effective, this digging about will need to be comparative, so one has to root around under more than one tree; otherwise, there is a danger of attaching general import to a single and possibly atypical instance. It is also necessary to shift the focus of attention from rationality in general to the practical operations of reason in specific contexts, contexts in which reasons as ends and reasons as motives will almost certainly be pertinent to identifying the role of reasons as grounds, contexts in which the boundaries between—say—logic, rhetoric, and dialectic are not nearly as well formed as they are in philosophy textbooks.

Attending to the practical operations of reason in differing varieties of traditional religious discourse opens up a complex and fascinating world of local knowledge and local rationality. We can visit that world, but we may not want to live there. Even so, a visit to this exotic world may expose us to previously unimagined possibilities that might enable us to extrapolate fresh ways to theorize the practical operations of reason in the public world of political discourse.

When uncertainties arise or claims are contested in religious communities, complex strategies typically come into play, with differential weightings assigned to authoritative sources (sometimes textual, sometimes oral, sometimes personal), recognized precedents and traditions of interpretation, contemporary experience of narrowly religious or broadly secular kind, and other local circumstances. The kinds of reasoning found in such contexts typically resemble legal argument more closely than the mathematical-experimental reasoning idealized in classical liberal notions of public reason.

The comparison with jurisprudence, however, should not lead us to assume that the operations of reason in religious contexts are always conservative. There are loose and strict constructionists among canon lawyers as well as among constitutional lawyers. As in jurisprudence, however, innovation is frequently disguised as embodying the "spirit" of the tradition, or as a recovery of the "true meaning" of some authoritative text or tradition of interpretation, or as a reassuring means of resolving a seeming conflict between competing authorities. Religious traditions renew themselves and reshape themselves through these complex operations of practical reason. By such operations, they rarely achieve community-wide consensus. But they do sometimes manage thereby to confine the destructive consequences of internal dissonance and in the process redefine the limits of credible difference in the community. They may also transform internal diversity into positive energy that enables communities more effectively to adapt to constantly changing circumstance.

One common mechanism for defining the limits of credible difference inside religious groups has been the controlled conflict allowed by formal disputation. Formal public debate has been a feature of traditional education in a number of groups, including Islam, Christianity, and Indo-Tibetan and Chinese religions. I focus here on Islamic and Indian practice.

In Islamic cultures, *kalam* emerged as a method of arguing but also as a structure for formal disputation in and among the disparate schools of law that centered on the principles developed by eminent jurists (who have traditionally been occupied as much with philological, hermeneutical, and philosophical issues as with narrowly legal ones). Muslims recognized from early days that *shari'a* would require interpretation, since it is not reasonable to expect to find explicit guidance to cover all cases that can arise. In a *hadith* from the formative phase of Islam, there is a remarkable exchange between the Prophet and a companion, Mu'adh, who was about to be made a provincial governor.[9] As governor his duties would include settling disputes and offering legal judgments from time to time. The Prophet asked Mu'adh how he would render judgments. "According to God's Scriptures," was his reply. And if the answer is not found there? Then, he said, "according to the traditions of the Messenger." And if the answer is not found there? "Then I will rely on my reason." The Prophet is reported to have expressed his approval and to have offered a prayer of thanksgiving. The use of reason being encouraged in this *hadith* is not the tradition-free reason of the classical liberal paradigm, but a reason infused with the controlling authority of *shari'a* as given in the Qur'an, the cycle of *ahadith* that surround the life of the Prophet, the learned consensus (*ijma*) of prevailing tradition. It is in short an intricately textured reason.

Even such richly textured reason could not guarantee uniformity of case law in Islam, however, and jurists developed individual approaches to interpreting the obligations of *shari'a* in new circumstances, approaches that may have had considerable local influence but no overall authority. By one count, there were at the beginning of the ninth century over five hundred competing systems of legal interpretation with at least local influence. The winnowing effects of history, however, together with the vagaries of political patronage—and, not to be forgot, the weight of reasoned argument in legal disputation—resulted by the thirteenth century in a narrowing down of these local authorities in orthodox Islam to just three or four generally recognized approaches to the law, ranging from the relatively liberal Hanafi to the traditionalist Hanbali, with two moderate schools (Maliki and Shafi'i) occupying the middle ground. Each school had a coherent and cohesive approach to the law; its decisions embodied their distinctive jurisprudential principles. All four of them came to be recognized by orthodox or Sunni Muslims as legitimate. What they agreed upon came to be accepted as the orthodox consensus or *ijma;* what they disagreed about was still tolerated as conceivable within orthodoxy without threatening its stability. These four schools, in my terms, mark the limits of credible or defensible difference within Sunni Islam. Diversity of legal perspectives in Islam also helps account for its remarkable ability to manage change by adapting itself to new circumstances without losing a sense of identity.

Disputation or *vada* arose in Brahmanical circles in India well before the beginning of the common era, out of the question-and-answer methods of instruction used to elucidate the intricacies of Vedic ritual or to solve metaphysical puzzles in Vedic scripture. Disputation between learned experts may have developed also from ancient Brahmanic methods of resolving legal disputes and from medical practitioners' methods of arriving at an agreed diagnosis or method of treatment. In addition, philosophical dialectic had independent origins outside Brahmanic circles within Jaina and Buddhist groups, each of whom had developed its own distinctive procedures and categories which eventually fed into the mainstream traditions of *vada* disputation.

The Buddhist influence in particular on that wider tradition was considerable. Despite the Buddha's warning against engaging in any doctrinal dispute that could risk schism, Buddhist *pitakas* abound in reports of controversy inside their circles regarding the correctness of rival doctrinal interpretations. Such controversies had over time a certain winnowing effect on Buddhist positions, so that certain schools emerged with widespread credibility, so much so that their existence was attributed to the Buddha's intention to make provision for different levels of spiritual attainment, a tale told by Madhyamikas, who would have placed themselves at the highest level.

Since Buddhist schools differed in their conception of the nature of reality, debates about ontology and cognition presented practical obstacles. How do you run a debate between someone who believes that our perceptions mirror external objects and someone else who is persuaded that every theory about the nature of things collapses by virtue of insurmountable internal contradictions? You could only do so if the latter person were willing *for the sake of the debate* to posit the reality of external objects. You must learn to see things as an elephant sees them, the great Dharmakirti advised, if you want to debate with an elephant. The acquired capacity to think as the opponent thinks is a key to the practical operation of reason in the Indian paradigm of public reason. For the willingness and skillful means to reflect systematically on the other's perspective from within that perspective as if it were one's own perspective not only enabled internal Buddhist debates between the Madhyamikas and the Sautrantikas; it also enabled external debates with non-Buddhists.

Religious groups in long-term contact with other religious groups typically develop discourses for debate across their respective borders. The type of argument that had been used for *intra*traditional debate was also adapted for *inter*traditional use. In Persia and elsewhere, *kalam* provided a framework for public debate among Muslims, Jews, Christians, and other local groups. As a style of argument, *kalam* had much influence within the Jewish and Christian communities, as well as becoming *the* discourse of public debate in the region. The popular success of open debate in cosmopolitan Baghdad alarmed more conservative Muslims from elsewhere. Ibn Sa'di, a tenth-century visitor from Spain went to a public debate at which he found gathered together not only members of disparate Islamic sects, but also non-Muslims of all sorts, including "Magions, materialists, atheists, Jews, and Christians." Upon his return to Spain, ibn Sa'di described what he had witnessed abroad as a calamity (in an evident pun on the word *kalam*) by virtue of the fact that the Muslims present at the debate did not insist on everyone's accepting the authority of the Qur'an as a condition of participation.[10]

A century later, however, the Muslim ruler of Moorish Saragossa, in correspondence with a certain "monk of France" who was inclined to try to trump arguments by quoting the New Testament, reminded him that all religions make such appeals, and argument [*kalam*] is the only means we have of distinguishing possibility from absurdity.[11] I do not know what the *monk* from France replied, but it would not be long before *friars* from France would be touting also in Spain the value of scholastic discourse as a vehicle of disputation between Christians, Muslims, and Jews.

If ibn Sa'di had been concerned that Muslims had not pressed their numerical and political dominance in debates in Baghdad, he would have been equally alarmed at the readiness with which Christians regularly pressed their dominant position of power in the Latin West. Sometimes there was an effort at fairness, sometimes not, and even in those cases where the ruler swore his protection, he was not always in a position to make good his promise. As the distinguished Nahmanides realized before engaging in debate in Barcelona (1263), it was "catch-22." If he did badly and lost, his people would suffer added pressure and humiliation at the hands of the triumphant Christians; if he did well and won, his people might suffer even greater retaliation. Who won? It depends whether you believe the summary of the debate written by the Christians or the one written by Nahmanides, the publication of which led directly to his exile.[12]

From these examples, we see not only that religious communities develop a language for arguing across their confessional boundaries, but also that the asymmetry of political power in Islamic and Christian lands meant that in practice these discourses were in constant danger of being subverted politically as discourses of domination.

In regions where political advantage was more randomly distributed, however, debating traditions led to more interesting results over time. In India, for instance, *vada* became a public discourse for defining defensible difference between competing groups able to survive public scrutiny. To say that political advantage was more randomly distributed does not of course mean that political factors were absent from the Indian debating tradition or that debates were not a means of one local group gaining political advantage over another. This is especially true of court debates, where royal patronage and prejudice was often decisive to the outcome of the disputation. In a wonderful exchange in the *Milindapanja*,[13] King Milinda asks the Buddhist pandit Nagasena if he would debate with him. Nagasena replied that he would debate with the king as scholars debate, but not as kings debate.

How is it that scholars debate? "When scholars debate with one another, your Majesty, there is a winding up, an unraveling; one or other is convicted of error, and mistakes are acknowledged; distinctions and counter-distinctions are drawn; there is also defeat, and yet they do not lose their temper. Thus, your Majesty, do scholars debate."

And how do kings debate? "When kings debate, your Majesty, they state a proposition, and if anyone differs with them, they order his punishment. 'Away with him!' they shout. Thus, your Majesty, do kings debate." In response, King Milinda graciously agreed to debate Nagasena in the idealized manner of scholars.

Representatives of any philosophical perspective—Brahmanic or Buddhist or Jaina or even Carvaka—had free access to the forum of public debate, providing, that is, that they were willing to have their school's claims publicly challenged according to the rules of *vada*. *Contestability*, not *neutrality*, was the price of entry to the public arena in the Indian *vada* tradition. One could enter public space and participate in public reason without pretending to rise above difference or to abstract oneself from one's entanglements with the communities of interest that make us who we are. Unlike classical European liberalism, the Indian debating tradition did not require one to give up one's own grounds in order to participate in public reason: public reason is open to all, but a share in "common ground" is not required. Reasons given in debate do not have to be reasons for everyone, but they must be contestable by anyone with requisite knowledge and an interest in the topic.

In any given debate, there was of course a winner and a loser. And opponents from different *darsanas* typically engaged in debate in order to defeat their opponents and to establish the superiority of their own perspective. Buddhist logicians nonetheless typically insisted that it is unworthy to enter into debate in order to win or defeat an opponent, that one should enter into the dialectic of debate to arrive at the truth. Assuming the conditions of defeat and victory were met, however, there would be a winner and there would be a loser. Egos were at risk—even, one suspects, in the case of Buddhists who theoretically had no ego to be threatened. To be defeated in an important debate involved loss of face and, depending on the wager, maybe more. Some groups, notably the Naiyayikas, had the reputation of being ready to use any means, fair or foul, to win debates.

However important winning was to most of those who engaged in public debate, the long-term effect of the debating tradition was not to arrive at an overall World Cup-winning team or to achieve a general consensus on matters in dispute. Nor was it, as Adam Smith might have expected, for the rough edges of difference to be worn away as once-strong positions became more moderate. The long-term effect was quite the opposite: not to diminish but precisely to specify difference. The lines separating the emerging *darsanas* were firmed up by a gradual sharpening of the points of difference that distinguished them.

Preparation for debate forced each competing *darsana* to reflect systematically on its own position and also on the opponent's, since they would have to defeat the opponent on his or her own grounds. In the process, it became clear that their difference—their *alterity*— was not simply a difference about this or that issue; it was systemic.

Their difference was *darsanic;* it was perspectival. But the *darsanas* that survived this process gained credibility and earned thereby a place in the set of *darsanas.* They were regarded as worthy opponents in debate.

None of the *darsanas* was left unaffected by their extended process of polemic and debate, but each one was affected differently. At one time independent perspectives, Nyaya and Vaisesika moved toward each other until they finally merged, with the combined *darsana* integrating the logical and dialectical skills of the one with the realist ontological commitments of the other. And the Naiyayikas, once nontheistic, became forceful apologists for what might be called somewhat anachronistically "rational religion." At one time subsidiary to Mimamsa, Vedanta came to have a separate existence from what then came to be Purva-Mimamsa. And, as Vedanta became conceptually more variegated within and eventually acquired political advantage without, it assumed an increasingly prominent place in accounts of the *saddarsanas.*

Not all perspectives survived having their basic claims contested in debate. Although evidently regarded at one time as equal in standing to Samkhya and Yoga, the Carvaka may have failed to clear the hurdle of public contestability, surviving not in its own right as a living *darsana,* but only as a stereotyped image in the polemical texts of other *darsanas.* Why then did it continue to be treated as a possible perspective even after it had ceased to be an active presence within Indian philosophy? The Carvaka represented a philosophical position that is not otherwise present among the *darsanic* systems. Only the Carvaka represented materialism in ontology; only they rejected inference as a *pramana;* only they denied the cycle of rebirth and the moral basis of world order. In short, without the Carvaka the construction of philosophical systems would have been left unfinished and the outer limit of credible philosophical reflection would have been left undefined.

This gives us a clue to the way that the set of philosophical *darsanas* achieved definitive shape. Each surviving *darsana* represented a possible point of view, without which the "set" would have been incomplete. Collectively, they possess a kind of coherence based not on their being built on "common ground" but on together constituting the sum total of defensible possibilities that could be conceived within the Indian *imaginaire.* Sa-Skya Pandita, the eminent thirteenth-century Tibetan scholastic philosopher, insisted that the traditional Indian *darsanas* exhaust the possibilities philosophically.[14] A worthy opponent stands in one of the four main Buddhist lineages or belongs to one of the recognized non-Buddhist sects. There are these and no others. Anyone who holds a coherent point of view holds one of these positions, whether or not they realize it. If there is any merit in this remark, then one product of the practice of *vada* could be said to have been a determinate set of recognized *darsanas*. In my language, the process produced a clarification of publicly defensible difference.

Earlier, I suggested that the notion of public reason in classical liberal theory is not able to cope with the kind of radical religious diversity that confronts us today, whether we look at matters more regionally or more globally. Latterly, I have been suggesting that attending to the strategies religious communities themselves have developed to accommodate the other in their midst may offer an alternate way of conceiving public reason—one in which reason lies open to all, to be sure, but does not require abandonment of group-specific reasons as the price of entry to the public arena. In the medieval Indo-Tibetan tradition of public debate between different perspectives, for instance, we encountered a conception of public reason that allowed public debate in which tradition-specific reasons might be offered and which resulted not in general consensus but in the clarification of publicly defensible difference.

I now want to suggest that what we found there is in fact nearer to the actual operations of public reason in modernity than is the idealized account of rationality found in most classical and much recent liberal theory. To make my point, I want to refer to selected aspects of the contemporary global debate about human rights.[15]

Just as academics may have worried too much about religious diversity as a cause of local or global violence and may have attended too little to ways that religious communities might contribute to a better understanding of the positive role of diversity in public reason, so academics may have concentrated too much on the violation of human rights in traditional religious communities and may have looked too little at what traditional religious communities might contribute to a richer understanding of human flourishing than has historically been the case within the modern secular discourse of rights.

One reason why the positive role religions might play in defining and enforcing human rights has tended to be ignored in international discussions on human rights must surely be sought in the popular presumption that the public discourse of rights is universal in scope and ideologically neutral in respect to underlying principles. The private discourses of religious communities are perceived in contrast as parochial or local in scope and as being grounded in group-specific commitments. The moral discourses of the disparate religious communities carry conviction for some people at some time and in some place, but they cannot be expected to carry conviction for all people at all times or in all places. At most, they express the tradition-constituted values of a limited community of interest and thereby fail to achieve the generality of moral discourse required for the recognition and implementation of human rights. For human rights—entitlements all persons are supposed to possess simply by virtue of being persons—would seem by definition to be rights whose authority cannot be contingent upon limiting circumstances, historical or cultural. Human rights are presumed to trump group-specific privileges and duties.

The diverse moral discourses of religious groups more typically spell out duties which are specific to the members of their own communities and which often could not even in principle be reasonably extended as requirements for persons beyond their borders. And legitimation of group-specific duties derives ultimately from some authority that is accepted as authority by that group alone. Such discourses can be said to express group-specific norms, but not universal maxims.

Any talk of "human rights" and "religious values" must, therefore, deal with the dilemma of universal and local in at least these two interrelated aspects: first, how group-specific duties relate to human rights and, second, how human rights are legitimated. In regard to legitimation, the issue is whether human rights claims must always be backed by reasons that can be reasons for everyone, or if they might also be backed by reasons that are accepted as such only by participants in some localized community of interest.

This dilemma faces anyone engaged in discussion of human rights, but it is made more acute by the extravagant claims religious groups often make for their moral code and its unique authority. Of course, all religious codes are in a weak sense unique in that each is the code of one religious community and not another. Yet some religious groups claim for themselves uniqueness in a strong sense: namely, their code exclusively provides a reliable guide to the good life by virtue of its authority as revealed law. Their code is claimed to have universal validity, even if its authority is not acknowledged beyond the community's edge. But when a religious group claims universal validity for their own code, its authority is in practice still restricted to the group that acknowledges its laws as binding. However sweeping the claim on the code's behalf, its authority remains localized to the group for whom it is acknowledged as revealed law. For such religious groups, therefore, the tension persists between the universal entitlement to human rights and more localized group-defined duties and liberties.

The way this tension has been stated assumes that secular rights discourse is in some strong sense universal and objective, whereas the competing moral discourses of determinate religions are local and partisan, being confined to the communities of interest that embrace them. Yet the secular discourse of rights (including human rights) is itself a construction of a specific historical and cultural circumstance, as is the concept of the autonomous self as rights-bearer. And the idea of rights encoded in such discourse is also tied to the place in which it is formed or gains endorsement. Human rights are historical constructions, not natural kinds. For instance, John Locke, a major architect of the modern formation of rights discourse, could without violating his understanding of rights defend in his *Second Treatise of Government* the institution of slavery. A later upholder of the Lockean tradition of human rights may have been ambivalent in his attitude toward the institution of slavery, but Thomas Jefferson cannot have had foremost in mind his own slaves when he extolled in one of the most eloquent documents of his age the inalienable rights of life, liberty, and the pursuit of happiness.

Surely none could claim that Locke's or Jefferson's understanding of rights was "universal," whether in the sense of being an equal entitlement to everyone or in the sense of gaining general endorsement by everyone. Nor could one reasonably think that its underpinning was ideologically neutral. Human slavery may not have been eradicated in the world (indeed, it may be more widespread today than it has been at any time in human history), but it no longer has morally earnest defenders. What has changed since Locke's or

Jefferson's time to make slavery indefensible, however, is not just that a further item or two has been added to the short list of so-called "core rights." What has occurred, more crucially, is a transformation of our vision of what constitutes a human right and of what entitles someone to be a rights-bearer.

Every understanding of "rights" is bound to a time and place. This holds for our own notion of human rights as much as it does for that of Locke or Jefferson. Over time, the concept of rights may develop or be stretched or be altered to fit some new circumstance or it may be finally abandoned as outmoded. But it does not stay fixed. The discourse of human rights is itself temporal and not eternal, local and not universal. And this applies to the Universal Declaration of Human Rights, no less than it does to the American Declaration of Independence or the French *Déclaration des droits de l'homme et du citoyen*, the datedness of which may be more readily evident. The 1948 Universal Declaration was a historic document. It is rightly regarded as a key moment in shaping the postwar world. In the meantime, however, it has become also a historical document. It can now be seen to mirror the concerns of that time and to embody its asymmetry of political power. The understanding of what count as human rights presumed by it has now been altered and stretched and developed by ensuing Charters, Conventions, Declarations, and Protocols. The discourse of rights has continued by this means to construct itself anew. And rival conceptions of human rights compete for wider endorsement within an increasingly global culture of rights.

This feature of the modern discourse of rights ironically brings it nearer to the competing moral discourses of sectarian religious groups which, according to the idealized Enlightenment self-image, the tradition-neutral language of rights was itself supposed to supersede. The dilemma of universal and local seems, therefore, to end in a proliferation of localized norms, vying with one another in the world's market place.

Does this not leave us awash in a sea of relativism? There is another way of explaining what is going on, a way that brings together the argument of this paper. More significant than the perceived threat of relativism in matters moral is the simple fact that the discourse of rights has become in modern times, and preeminently since World War II, the shared public language in which to differentiate the defensible from the indefensible in our behavior toward others. It has effectively become the most widely accepted global currency in which to negotiate differing views about what weighting attaches to competing entitlements due to persons as persons. In this fact, rather than in pseudointellectual shilly-shallying over problems of incommensurability and relativism (problems which are themselves functions of an unimaginative and flat-footed theory of public reason), is to be found the key to undo the deadlock between local and universal in regard to religious values and human rights, religious diversity and public rationality.

This is not to say that there is a consensus about the rights we have or the values that underpin them. Nor is it to ignore the fact that the spread of the language of rights from West to East and from North to South was both enabled and tainted by colonialism, whether political or economic or cultural. The discourse of rights has nonetheless established itself as the language in which competing values are publicly justified and, in the face of opposition, publicly contested. The language of rights provides a public frame within which disparate communities of interest, religious and nonreligious alike, can test the soundness of the other's position and have their own position contested in return. The outcome of the process is unlikely to be moral consensus; but we may reasonably hope for an emerging sense of the credible limits of what is and what is not defensible human behavior toward others.

Such debates do not occur in some neutral space. Nor are they generated by value-free reasoning. There is no place that is not some place in particular, and there are no reasons that are not reasons for someone. Such debates cannot be expected to lead to global consensus on "core rights" or on prioritization in the hierarchy of rights. But they remain strategies that can be pursued within a public discourse of rights. The price of gaining access to that language is not agreement to set aside all attachments and commitments in order to achieve universality and neutrality. The price of entering into that realm of discourse is no more than a willingness to be a reasonable partisan, that is, to abide by the rules of engagement. Testing and being contested—by this means the discourse of rights constructs itself anew and the hierarchy of rights is subjected to public scrutiny. By this means, from different motives and disparate grounds, specific limited goals may be tactically agreed upon by culturally diverse groups who share no common historical narrative and occupy no "common ground" save only the fragile and threatened planet that fate has destined as our shared home.

We must of course learn to be good neighbors. But the New England poet Robert Frost reminded us years ago that neighborliness can also be shown in mending walls that mark off boundaries: *it is not so much common ground as good fences that make good neighbors*. In a similar spirit, I want to suggest that clarifying defensible difference may help build up a sense of community and encourage a variety of liberal virtues, including civility toward the stranger and toleration of otherness. It may also contribute to the recognition of cultural and religious diversity as a positive good.

NOTES

1. Inaugural Lecture as Professor of Religion, Chair of the Department of Religion, and Director of the Graduate Division of Religious and Theological Studies at Boston University.

2. Thomas Jefferson to Levi Lincoln, 1 January 1802.

3. Charles L. Griswold, Jr., "Religion and Community: Adam Smith on the Virtues of Liberty," *Journal of the History of Philosophy* 35, no. 3 (1997): 395–419.

4. Thomas Jefferson, *Notes on the State of Virginia* (1787), Query 17, in *Thomas Jefferson: Writings*, ed. Merrill D. Peterson (New York, 1984), p. 287.

5. Ibid., p. 285.

6. See my Inaugural Lecture as Professor of Religious Studies at the University of Lancaster, "Thomas Jefferson and the Study of Religion" (Lancaster, 1992), p. 7.

7. See Edwin Scott Gaustad, *Historical Atlas of Religion in America* (New York, 1976).

8. See A. H. Halsey, ed., *British Social Trends since 1900* (London, 1988).

9. Cited in Noel J. Coulson, *Conflicts and Tensions in Islamic Jurisprudence* (Chicago, 1969), p. 4.

10. Cited in Moise Ventura, *La philosophie de Saadia Gaon* (Paris, 1934), p. 93. I am grateful to Paul Morris, Victoria University (New Zealand), for having supplied me with this reference.

11. D. M. Dunlop, "A Christian Mission to Muslim Spain in the 11th Century," *Al-andalus* 17 (1952): 273ff.

12. For the Christian and Jewish texts relating to the Barcelona disputation, see Hyam Maccoby, ed., *Judaism on Trial: Jewish-Christian Disputations in the Middle Ages* (London, 1982), pp. 97–150. See also Robert Chazan, *Daggers of Faith: Thirteenth-Century Christian Missionizing and the Jewish Response* (Berkeley, 1989), pp. 71ff.

13. Adapted from *The Questions of King Milinda* 2.1.3., trans. W. Rhys Davids (Delhi, 1969 [1890]), 1:46.

14. David P. Jackson, ed., *The Entrance Gate for the Wise* (WSTB, 17; Vienna, 1987), 2:343ff.

15. The position sketched here is elaborated more fully in John Clayton, "Universal Human Rights and Traditional Religious Values," in *Human Rights and Responsibilities in a Divided World*, ed. Jaroslav Krejci (Prague, 1997), pp. 29–46.

Religious Strife
and the Culture Wars

RONALD F. THIEMANN

THE PAST TWO DECADES have been a time of testing for the American republic. The fabric of our common life has been stretched to the breaking point by a series of divisive social issues like abortion, welfare reform, race relations, and gay/lesbian rights. The disputes over these matters have often been bitter and the adversaries unwilling to seek the compromises that might adjudicate their differences. Our ability to discern a common ground on which to resolve these disputes has been further complicated by the rapid growth in ethnic diversity that occurred during the 1980s and 90s. This pattern of immigration has greatly enriched the cultural diversity of our country, but it has also spawned new fears and prejudices that too often erupt into ethnic and racial violence. At a time when the middle classes sense a decline in their overall standard of living, new immigrants appear to pose a threat to established but still struggling populations, and possibilities for conflict abound. Legislative efforts like Proposition 187 in California, designed to deny benefits to unregistered aliens, and the 1996 Federal Welfare Reform Act, which initially denied benefits to registered and legal immigrants, serve to fan the fire of ethnic distrust. The American republic is experiencing an unprecedented degree of diversity, and the fragile bonds that unify us have come under great strain.

A spate of recent books has bemoaned the divisions that this new diversity has created in American public life. A worry common to all these works is that the current focus on particularity—racial, ethnic, sexual, or cultural—threatens permanently to divide American society into separate cultural or political enclaves, thereby undermining the notions of unity or commonality essential to the identity of the nation. The politics of difference, these authors argue, will finally destroy the sense that all Americans are engaged in a common enterprise. These arguments attack two different but related phenomena: the problem of "multiculturalism" and the challenge of the "culture wars."

THE PROBLEM OF MULTICULTURALISM

In his recent book *The Disuniting of America* the distinguished historian Arthur Schlesinger, Jr., suggests that the new "cult of ethnicity" imperils the "historic idea of a unifying American identity."

> *E pluribus unum.* The United States had a brilliant solution for the inherent fragility of a multiethnic society: the creation of a brand-new national identity, carried forward by individuals who, in forsaking old loyalties and joining to make new lives, melted away ethnic differences. . . . The point of America was not to preserve old cultures, but to forge a new American culture. . . . [But now] instead of a transformative nation with an identity all its own, America in this new light is seen as preservative of diverse alien identities. Instead of a nation composed of individuals making their own unhampered choices, America increasingly sees itself as composed of groups more or less ineradicable in their ethnic character. The multiethnic dogma abandons historic purposes, replacing assimilation by fragmentation, integration by separatism. It belittles *unum* and glorifies *pluribus*.[1]

Schlesinger's concern about the fragmentation of American culture is surely well placed, but his analysis does little to help us out of our current difficulty. By perpetuating the "melting pot" mythology and by characterizing the early history of the United States as one in which "individuals" were free to make "their own unhampered choices," he is simply engaging in bad history. A careful study of American immigration shows that the maintenance of cultural identity has always been essential to the successful integration of immigrant populations into the larger American society. The presence of Irish, German, Polish, and Italian subcultures in American cities clearly facilitated the transition of successive waves of immigrants to these shores during the nineteenth century. The genius of the American experience has not been that immigrant populations were required to abandon their previous identities as "alien," but that the framework of American democracy was sufficiently flexible to allow new citizens to understand themselves as both Irish and American, Polish and American, and so on. In the process of Americanization both identities were transformed. The identities of those European immigrants were decisively modified by the American experience, but at the same time, the definition of what it means to be an American was decisively modified by the phenomenon of European immigration.

The United States became a multiethnic society with a single national identity precisely because our democracy did not make ethnic identity the basis for citizenship. Thus, Schlesinger is surely wrong, and dangerously so, when he quotes with approval the remark of Hector St. John Crevecoeur, "What then is the American, this new man? . . . Here individuals of all nations are melted into a new race of men."[2] The genius of America is that it did not require persons to abandon their ethnic identity as the price for citizenship. Our democracy seeks to shape neither a new uniform American culture nor a new "race of men"; it seeks rather to create a diverse nation whose citizens are dedicated to the fundamental values of democracy: liberty, equality, and mutual respect.

The question facing American democracy today is whether our national identity can embrace the new American pluralism. Can we shape a conception of the *unum* that is in continuity with the past and yet genuinely open to the new realities of the contemporary *plures?* The founders sought to create a democratic polity grounded in particular core values yet sufficiently flexible to respond to the changing social and historical conditions of a growing nation. Enlightenment notions of liberty and equality did not include slaves or women in its purview, yet the struggle to extend the full rights of citizenship to women and persons of African descent expanded those notions beyond their eighteenth-century limitations. Advocates of those rights argued successfully that the full meaning of such ideas could not be realized as long as persons were excluded from citizenship simply by virtue of their gender or race. The full meaning and application of the values of liberty and equality can only be determined as we seek to follow the historical and social trajectory of such ideas. The core values of American democracy are historically and socially situated and are constantly being debated and reinterpreted.

In contrast to many contemporary cultural critics, I want to argue that the politics of the particular are not necessarily a threat to our historic sense of a national identity. Whenever new groups seek to find a place within democratic polity, political debate becomes more strident and sharp-edged, because questions of power and privilege are at stake. The excluded will inevitably challenge the prerogatives of those who hold power, and the established will often develop a defensive posture against such protests. Stridency and passion may be signs of the robustness of democracy rather than indications of its decay. Our national identity is established through the tradition of democratic debate concerning the core values of our polity. If a tradition is, in Alasdair MacIntyre's helpful definition, "an historically extended, socially embodied argument"[3] about the meaning of the values that constitute that tradition, then vigorous and passionate debate should be expected. It is only when the debate undermines the core values of the democratic tradition that our national identity is genuinely threatened.

THE CHALLENGE OF CULTURE WARS

Some will read the argument I have just presented as being hopelessly naive and optimistic. Many commentators have argued that our national core values are indeed at risk in the current debates over issues like abortion and gay/lesbian rights. Most prominent among those cultural critics has been James Davison Hunter, who, in his two recent books *Culture Wars* and *Before the Shooting Begins,* offers a dire analysis of our present condition.

> The central dynamic of the cultural realignment is not merely that different public philosophies create diverse public opinions. These alliances, rather, reflect the *institutionalization and politicization of two fundamentally different cultural systems.* Each side operates from within its own constellations of values, interests, and assumptions. At the center of each are two distinct conceptions of moral authority—two different ways of apprehending reality, of ordering experience, of making moral judgments. Each side of the cultural divide, then, speaks with a different moral vocabulary. Each side operates out of a different

mode of debate and persuasion. Each side represents the tendencies of a separate and competing moral galaxy. They are, indeed, "worlds apart."[4]

In order to illustrate this point Hunter introduces his readers to two combatants for America's soul, two religious Americans deeply divided over a San Francisco ballot proposition that would allow gay couples to register as "domestic partners," thereby granting them hospital visitation and bereavement rights. Chuck McIlhenny is the 43-year-old pastor of a fundamentalist Presbyterian church who led a coalition of evangelical Protestants, Roman Catholics, and black Pentecostals against the domestic partners legislation. "The fight between a biblical morality and the new morality," he asserts, "is crystal-clear in San Francisco. . . . I like to describe San Francisco as the city that leads the way of secular humanism. If you want to see a *godless city*— in its governmental, political, and social dimension—this is it. Homosexuality is just the tip of the iceberg. . . . The homosexual issue is a secondary issue. The real fundamental issue is a secular humanism which rejects Christ and the Scriptures as your basis to society. And the ultimate end is always death—death to a society."[5]

Richmond Young is a 38-year-old gay man, an editor at a large publishing firm. A member of a prominent well-established San Francisco family, he is an adult convert to Catholicism and a vocal supporter of the domestic partners proposal. Homosexuality, he argues, "is not a sin at all. Jesus wasn't interested in what people did in bed but whether people deal with others in a loving and compassionate way. In the end, Christ will judge us on the basis of our actions toward others. . . . The essence of Americanism to me is contained in the words of the Declaration of Independence, particularly the lines that say, 'We hold these truths to be self-evident, that all men are created equal.' . . . I think of gay people as those who stand in the line with many others who are waiting to have their claim on that part of the Declaration of Independence recognized."[6]

Hunter's own analysis of this conflict is grim and to the point:

> In the final analysis, each side of the cultural divide can only talk past the other. . . . This is true because what both sides bring to the public debate is . . . nonnegotiable. . . . What is ultimately at issue are deeply rooted and fundamentally different understandings of being and purpose . . . [i.e.] different conceptions of the

sacred. . . . Communities cannot and will not tolerate the desecration of the sacred. The problem is this: not only does each
side of the cultural divide operate with a different conception
of the sacred, but the mere existence of the one represents a certain desecration of the other.[7]

The conclusion to be drawn is evident. If I consider you and the position you hold to be a desecration of my view of the sacred, then I can
tolerate neither your view nor you as the person who holds it. While
such a conflict may not lead inexorably to acts of violence, the prospects for peaceful coexistence between such cultural combatants
seem dim indeed.

Hunter has, of course, merely provided sociological flesh for
the skeleton of an argument offered more than a decade earlier by
philosopher Alasdair MacIntyre in his widely read book *After Virtue*.
MacIntyre has argued that our moral disagreements over issues like
abortion and homosexuality are so profound that we will never reach
consensus on the most basic ethical and political issues. Since our arguments begin from "rival and incommensurable moral premises," we
are doomed, he suggests, to interminable and irresolvable moral and
political disagreement. In such a situation, politics becomes "civil war
waged by other means,"[8] as force, deception, and manipulation domi-
nate the political atmosphere. If contending parties argue on the basis
of incommensurable premises, then they have no hope of reaching
rational agreement. Consequently neither has any stake in the use of
rational argument as the means of political persuasion. Politics thus
becomes a mere clash of wills, as each party, interest, or faction seeks
to gain the upper hand in the struggle for political control.

Are these cultural critics correct? Are we doomed to either interminable moral disagreement or active, perhaps even violent, cultural conflict? Is religious disagreement, that is, competing notions
of the sacred and of the moral authority that flows from the sacred,
the ultimate source of our culture wars? Must religion lead inevitably
to cultural contention, discord, and warfare? When religion enters our
common public life will it always serve to fragment and divide democratic citizens?

It will come as no surprise to you that I want to answer "no" to
each of these questions. But in order to do so, I must address both the
philosophical and the theological questions inherent in the Hunter/

MacIntyre position. So I will begin with the question of whether our
contemporary moral disagreements are truly grounded in "incommensurable moral premises" and then move by way of conclusion
to the question of whether theology, in particular Christian theology,
contributes more to the problem or the solution of the so-called "culture wars."

A PHILOSOPHICAL CRITIQUE

I place myself among a group of scholars whom I call in my
book *Religion in Public Life: A Dilemma for Democracy*[9] "liberal
revisionists"—people like Jean Elshtain, William Galston, Jeffrey
Stout, Charles Taylor, and Michael Walzer. Moral disagreements, revisionists argue, are often vigorous and occasionally irresolvable in
practice, but such disagreements take place against a broad background of fundamental consensus concerning the goods that ought to
be pursued in a liberal democracy. That consensus is itself revisable
and open to critical questioning, but the elements comprised by it are
never simultaneously and universally called into question. Indeed,
genuine disagreement requires *some* common premises or else the
contending positions would simply "talk past one another" rather than
engage in true conflict.

There is a philosophical and a political point to be made
here, and both are essential to the revisionist position. The claim that
moral premises are "conceptually incommensurable" is an exceedingly strong philosophical assertion. Incommensurability implies that
competing moral premises rest within conceptual frameworks that
differ utterly from one another. But what would be the meaning of
such wholly disparate conceptual schemes? And if there were such
divergent frameworks, how could genuine disagreement take place
between them? As Donald Davidson has shown, true disagreement
requires a background of more basic agreement if we are even to determine the terms of the dispute.[10] If we disagreed about *everything*, that is, if our premises were truly *incommensurable*, then we
would be unable to disagree; we would simply, as I said, "talk past
one another." Jeffrey Stout gives a homely example to illustrate Davidson's point.

If you and I disagree about some proposition, moral or non-
moral, we will at least have enough in common to make sense of

that proposition. We couldn't disagree about it if we couldn't make sense of it. If you push disagreement down too far, it tends to disappear by becoming merely verbal. Suppose you and I disagree about clocks. I say that clocks are vehicles one drives to work, that nearly all clocks nowadays cost many thousands of dollars, and that one needs a license to operate them legally. You hold the more orthodox opinions about clocks. Here is a case where apparent disagreement goes so deep that it becomes merely verbal. We begin by assuming that we're disagreeing about clocks, but it soon becomes clear that we don't share enough beliefs about what we're calling clocks to identify a common subject matter to disagree over.[11]

The philosophical conclusion to be drawn, then, is that genuine moral disagreement requires a substantial background of agreement in order for the dispute to be coherent. That does not mean, however, that we will always be able to identify the moral principles to which we can appeal to resolve such disputes. Moral disagreement may remain practically intractable, even if the premises are not conceptually incommensurable.

A POLITICAL CRITIQUE

The political consequences of this philosophical point are particularly important for the revisionist position. If moral disagreement in our pluralist society is not irresolvable *in principle*, then a basic presupposition of the Hunter/MacIntyre position can be overturned. Even if democratic societies cannot agree on the ultimate *telos* for all human beings, it does not follow that they are unable to generate a limited but still real consensus concerning the common goods such societies should pursue. *Despite* the pluralism of contemporary life, it remains possible that liberal societies can define a range of fundamental values which underlie our shared civic life. Yet *because of* the pluralism of contemporary life, it is necessary to limit the scope of that overlapping consensus. "In other words," Jeffrey Stout writes, "certain features of our society can be seen as justified by a self-limiting consensus on the good—an agreement consisting partly in the realization that it would be a bad thing, that it would make life worse for all of us, to press too hard for agreement on all details in a given vision of the good."[12]

Ultimately there is an important theological concern underlying the philosophical and political points I have just made. Assertions concerning "culture wars" or "incommensurable moral premises" can easily become counsels to despair. If it is true that our deepest moral disagreements are irresolvable, then why should any of us devote ourselves to efforts of peacemaking and reconciliation? I firmly believe that the most important political task for communities of faith today is to witness to hope in a culture that is increasingly cynical about our common human future. Broadside attacks on liberalism (MacIntyre and Hauerwas) or cultural despair about our de-Christianized society (Lindbeck and Bellah) do not function to nurture a sense of hope about God's reconciling action in behalf of the entire cosmos. Indeed, these approaches can have the unintended but devastating consequence of discouraging Christians and other people of faith from engaging in positive political actions in the public realm. But if persons formed in those communities in which the virtues of faith, hope, and love are nurtured fail to manifest those virtues in public life, then the *polis* will indeed be left to those with a shrunken and desiccated view of the possibilities of political community. Then the claim concerning "culture wars" will be not a description of public life but a self-fulfilling prophecy.

If these theoretical points, are, as I believe them to be, correct, then a fundamental practical task remains for the American republic, namely, to develop citizens who are capable of negotiating the difficult waters of pluralism without losing touch with their own distinctive religious and moral commitments. The crucial question remains: Can communities of faith contribute to that task while still remaining true to their own traditions? Or put differently: can a genuine theology of pluralism be developed out of the particular resources of our religious traditions?

A THEOLOGICAL PROPOSAL: FAITH AND PLURALISM

The greatest challenge facing American democracy today is, I believe, to develop "pluralist citizens," people capable of living in a variety of different and sometimes conflicting worlds of meaning, while still maintaining a robust sense of personal and communal identity. Many people fear an encounter with those who are different, because they suspect that these "others" will hold opposing fundamental beliefs about the world and human behavior. If the beliefs of these "others" are in conflict with my own, and I hold my own beliefs to be true, then it seems to follow necessarily that the beliefs of these "others" are an offense to me. And, as James Davison Hunter has pointed out, when I take my own beliefs to define the nature of the sacred, then the beliefs of the "others" are not just false or offensive but sacrilegious.

It is clear that many theologians and practitioners of religion accept the absolutist understanding of truth I have just described. Faith requires, many believe, not only the affirmation of one's own religion's truth but the claim to its absolute superiority. Such claims imply that those who disagree with one's own religious beliefs stand outside of or in opposition to the sacred. Such opposing beliefs are not only false; they are also sacrilegious, that is, an assault on all that I hold sacred. Therefore not only can I not tolerate those beliefs; I cannot tolerate those who hold them. That is why practitioners of other religious beliefs are often characterized as infidels, blasphemers, apostates, or heretics. That is also why the history of religion is filled with so much violence and bloodshed.

Despite the widespread acceptance of religious claims to absoluteness, I want to argue that such claims are neither essential to most religious traditions nor the best interpretation of those traditions' claims to truth. In making this argument I will draw upon the resources of my own faith, Christianity, but I am confident that similar arguments are available in other traditions as well. If people of faith are committed to claims of absoluteness, then they will not be capable of helping to shape faithful disciples who are also good citizens in a diverse society. If, however, there is an alternate, theologically sound view of religious truth, then it may be possible for churches and other communities of faith to serve as "schools of virtue" for pluralistic democracies.

"For here we have no lasting city, but we seek the city which is to come" (Heb.13:14). If pluralism creates a situation in which people have conflicting commitments and divided loyalties, then it should hardly be a novel experience for people of faith. Faith in God demands of religious believers their ultimate loyalty. Indeed, the sin of idolatry is defined as the transfer of the commitment owed solely to God to any other object or person in the world. That one owes ultimate loyalty to

God does not mean, however, that other lesser loyalties cannot lay claim to one's commitment. These other loyalties—to spouse, children, job, or in this case nation—are serious and important, but they should never become the commitments that fully define one's identity. Absolute love of spouse, children, job, or nation can easily become jealous, obsessive, or fanatical. The challenge to the person of faith is to see all the goods of this life as gifts from the hand of a gracious and loving Creator. Loved ones claim deep and abiding loyalties from us, but when a parent or spouse faces death, faith reminds the believer that the beloved is returning to the care of the One from whom all good gifts come. So it is also with the commitment to community or nation; these, too, demand our serious loyalties—occasionally even our loves—but they dare never substitute for the loyalty and love owed to God.

The engagement of the religious citizen with democratic regimes is best captured under the notion of "pilgrim citizenship." Recognizing the penultimate character of the public realm, believers will not seek their final resting place in this sphere of power and persuasion. Nonetheless, people of faith will sometimes find the public realm to be a place of genuine fulfillment and bracing engagement, a place in which their own deepest convictions and beliefs are tested, criticized, confirmed, and reformed. Precisely because a pluralistic society requires conversation and exchange with those who are "different," public space provides a context within which faith seeks understanding in dialogue with persons holding diverse commitments. Conversation makes a crucial contribution to understanding in the public realm because people of faith do not enter that realm with a divinely authorized program of policy prescriptions. Religious persons bring a set of fundamental convictions and orienting principles to public debate, but the application of the resources of faith can only be determined in each particular situation. Religious convictions and principles may provide a basic framework within which policy reflection takes place for the believer, but those resources do not determine choices in the public realm.

People of faith, then, should function in a democratic society as "connected critics,"[13] persons committed to the fundamental ideals of democracy yet able to see the shortcomings of any particular democratic regime. Because connected critics care so deeply about the values inherent in a particular venture, their critique serves to call a community back to its better nature. Because people of faith share the fundamental values of democratic societies, they remain connected to public life even as they engage in criticism; because their commitment to democracy remains penultimate, however, they can appeal to transcendent ideals to critique current practice and to elevate the understanding of democratic values themselves. Two of America's greatest "public theologians," Abraham Lincoln and Martin Luther King, Jr., appealed to religious ideas to criticize the practices of slavery and segregation, and in so doing redefined the very meaning of freedom and equality for American citizens. People of faith—pilgrim citizens and connected critics—can help churches and other communities of faith serve as "schools of virtue" for a pluralistic democracy, places where the critical consciousness of an informed citizenry can be nurtured.

But still, some would ask, doesn't engagement in the give-and-take of pluralist democratic conversation deny the ultimate or absolute character of one's religious commitment? Isn't pluralism in fact the great *threat* to religious commitment today? Hasn't our society drifted into such a state of relativism that no commitment, not even that of faith, makes a final and ultimate claim on people's lives?

If my argument is to be understood, it is essential that pluralism, i.e., the openness to the voices of others, not be confused with moral or ethical relativism, i.e., the belief that there are no definitive standards for belief or action, that moral choice is simply the expression of personal preference. Communities of faith must come to recognize the compatibility between deep and abiding commitment to the truth claims of one's tradition and an openness to and respect for the claims of another tradition. Truth claiming and an acceptance of pluralism are not inconsistent. Nicholas Rescher has stated the issue well:

> Pluralism holds that it is rationally intelligible and acceptable that others can hold positions at variance with one's own. But it does not maintain that a given individual need endorse a plurality of positions—that the fact that others hold a certain position somehow constitutes a reason for doing so oneself. . . . Pluralism is a feature of the collective group; it turns on the fact that different experiences engender different views. But from the standpoint of the individual this cuts no ice. We have no alternative to proceeding as best we can on the basis of what is

available to us. That others agree with us is not proof of correctness; that they disagree, no sign of error.[14]

Moreover, it is important to recognize that my argument in favor of pluralism is motivated not by some desperate concern that religious folk be given a hearing in an increasingly secular world but by my own deepest religious and theological commitments. And with an account of those commitments I want to conclude my defense of a pluralist understanding of religious truth.

"Faith is the assurance of things hoped for, the conviction of things not seen" (Heb. 11:1). For believers religious faith is the most deeply felt and most broadly encompassing conviction a person can have. And yet it would be a profound theological mistake to equate the confidence of faith with apodictic or absolute certainty. For the Christian tradition, faith is our finite, sinful grasping of the saving grace of a transcendent God, offered as a gift through the person and work of Jesus Christ. God's grace reorients the believer's life and inaugurates a lifelong journey of discipleship. That life of discipleship is a process of "faith seeking understanding." Since Christians confess God to be the transcendent mystery who lovingly shares himself with us, our knowledge and grasp of God's mysterious nature will always be partial and inadequate. Consequently, all religious and theological statements must be uttered with a genuine sense of both gratitude and humility.

Moreover, the biblical narratives through which the identity of God is displayed to the reader reach their climax in a remarkable sequence whereby Jesus undergoes death at the hands of the Romans and yet "on the third day" is raised to life by God. At the heart of the Christian Gospel lies the mystery of God's redemptive suffering, whereby God brings life out of death itself. No rational account can justify the belief that life can emerge from the despairing depths of the grave, and yet that affirmation constitutes the core of the Christian Gospel. There is no inevitability that those who read the Gospel texts will accept the belief that Jesus, the crucified, now lives, but those who do commit themselves to a life of faith and discipleship. This mysterious movement from unbelief to faith lies beyond the competence of reason to grasp. Whether God's promise of new life is reliable, whether the path of discipleship leads to its promised end, we cannot know with certainty now, for "we see through a glass darkly."

Still, believers follow on in hope and the power of the Spirit, awaiting that day when we may "see face to face." For now we have only faith, the demands of discipleship, and the beckoning presence of the One who bids us come and follow. And for some, that is enough.

The God whom Christians confess and worship is thus a God of transcendent mystery, redemptive suffering, and sustaining hope. Christian discipleship is shaped by the theological virtues of faith, hope, and love. At the same time Christians recognize with gratitude and humility the surprising and unexpected character of the Christian Gospel. If God's unsurpassing love is found in a community of sinners and outcasts and epitomized by the symbol of a criminal's death, then Christians can hardly be surprised if the voices of God's promptings are to be found in the insights of those who are fellow travelers on the journey of discipleship, particularly those who are different from ourselves. Grounded in the confidence of faith, the sustenance of hope, and the renewing power of love Christians seek to make their way, like all others, in a world that both confirms and undermines their deepest convictions. Precisely because they must always live in more than one world of meaning, people of faith have insights to offer those who struggle to maintain commitment in the midst of the confusing diversity of a pluralistic world. If people of faith can learn to share those insights in a manner that contributes to our nation's common good, then religion might indeed help to form committed disciples who are also pluralist citizens. And that would be a gift to all persons within our fragile but beloved democracy.

NOTES

1. Arthur M. Schlesinger, *The Disuniting of America: Reflections on a Multicultural Society* (New York: W.W. Norton & Co., 1992), pp. 13, 17.
2. Ibid., p. 138.
3. Alasdair MacIntyre, *After Virtue* (Notre Dame, Ind.: University of Notre Dame Press, 1981), p. 207.
4. James Davison Hunter, *Culture Wars* (New York: Basic Books, 1991), p. 131.
5. Ibid., pp. 7–8.
6. Ibid., pp. 11–12.
7. Ibid., p. 131.
8. MacIntyre, *After Virtue*, p. 236.

9. Ronald F. Thiemann, *Religion in Public Life: A Dilemma for Democracy* (Washington, D.C.: A Twentieth Century Fund Book/Georgetown University Press, 1996).

10. Donald Davidson, "On the Very Idea of a Conceptual Scheme," in *Inquiries into Truth and Interpretation* (Oxford University Press, 1984), pp. 183–98.

11. Jeffrey Stout, *Ethics After Babel* (Boston: Beacon Press, 1988), pp. 19–20.

12. Ibid., p. 212.

13. I gratefully borrow this phrase from Michael Walzer, *Interpretation and Social Change* (Cambridge: Harvard University Press, 1987).

14. Nicholas Rescher, *Pluralism: Against the Demand for Consensus* (Oxford: Clarendon Press, 1993), p. 89.

PART III

World Religions and Peace

Gandhi: The Fusion of Religion and Politics

JOHN HICK

WE SHOULD BEGIN with Gandhi himself because, in contrast to many significant thinkers, it is impossible to separate his thought from his life. Indeed once, when asked what his message was, he replied that his life was his message.[1] This was not a boast, but something that those who had to do with him already knew. He tried to persuade others to accept his basic insights only after he had first lived them out in a career which was, throughout his adulthood, a continuous series of what he called experiments with Truth.

So the tremendous impact which Gandhi made upon so many people, challenging them to change their outlook and in quite a number of cases to change the course of their lives, came from the fact that what he taught was morally compelling and that he was visibly living it out, often at great cost to himself and finally at the cost of his life. He once said, "The act will speak unerringly,"[2] and it was undoubtedly his acts that made his words believable, drawing others into practical commitment. They had either to respond to the challenge of nonviolent persuasion in action or dismiss him as an impractical dreamer, or a deluded fanatic, or a political schemer.

The myth-making tendency of the human mind has long affected the public image of Gandhi. Some Western enthusiasts have uncritically glorified his memory, filtering out his human weaknesses; and the popular picture of him among devotees in India has attained mythic proportions, so that he is counted by many among the divine *avatars* or incarnations. On the other hand, he is still sufficiently recent for the man himself to be visible behind these clouds of adoration. There are people still living who knew him and, further, his may be the most minutely documented life that has ever been lived.

Gandhi himself would have nothing to do with his own idealization. He rejected the title of *Mahatma* which, he said, had often
deeply pained him and had never pleased him.[3] He said, "I myself do
not feel like a saint in any shape or form."[4] In the earlier days his followers called him *Bhai* (brother), and as he grew older they referred
to him as *Bapu* (father), and *Gandhiji*. He was acutely, sometimes
painfully, conscious of his own faults. He blamed himself for many
misjudgments and mistakes, including the major one that he called his
"Himalayan blunder"[5]—his call to the people in 1919 to practice mass
satyagraha before they were ready for it.

There were, then, problematic sides to Gandhiji's character. On
the one hand, he was a magnetic personality, with no inner barriers
between himself and others, radiating love and full of humor, a person whom it must have been immensely exciting and inspiring to be
with. He had a remarkable serenity in the midst of intense activity,
approaching the ideal of which he spoke when he said of the truly
religious life, "I have not a shadow of doubt that this blessed state of
inward joy and freedom from anxiety should last in the midst of the
greatest trials conceivable."[6] And as Margaret Chatterjee reports, "All
who were close to Gandhi have testified to his irresistible sense of fun,
his bubbling spirits which seemed to well up from an inner spring in
the face of all adversity"[7]—though it is also true that at the end of his
life he was filled with deep sorrow and despair at the disastrous parti-
tion of India and at the failure of both politicians and populace to act
out his teaching of nonviolence and mutual love. Louis Fischer, who
spent a good deal of time with him, says that "Gandhi accepted people
as they were. Aware of his own defects, how could he expect perfection in others?"[8] "Life at Sabarmati Ashram [Fischer says] and, after
1932, at Sevagram in central India, was serene, simple, joyous, and
unconstrained. Nobody stood in awe of him. Until he was too old, he
sat in the scullery every morning with the ashramites peeling potatoes;
he did his share of other chores as well."[9] At the same time he insisted
on certain standards of behavior—cleanliness, punctuality, participation in the physical work of the ashram, including at least half an hour
of spinning every day. However, "with all his strictness about the personal conduct of his co-workers . . . he was completely tolerant toward
their thinking."[10]

Gandhi was indeed a living paradox, attractive yet dominating,
and we ought to be aware of both sides of his character. His moral in-

sights were so strong and uncompromising that he imposed them upon his followers by the sheer force of his conviction. Such was his overwhelming charisma that he could be a dictator within his immediate circle. Some, probably thinking of saintliness as inherently detached from politics, see Gandhi's political skill as incompatible with his reputation for saintliness. But why should not a saint be highly competent in practical affairs? What to some was sly cunning was to others Gandhi's ability so often to outwit those—whether the British rulers or rival Indian leaders—who were trying to outwit him.

In the case of great figures of the distant past, any flaws are now hidden by the idealizing devotion of many generations. But it is precisely because Gandhi is close enough to us for us to know so much about him, including his real human weaknesses, blunders, and eccentricities, that his spiritual greatness stands out so convincingly. Both his human limitations and his remarkable capacity for spiritual growth are evident in the way in which he developed through the years. He was not born a mahatma but became one through his response to circumstances. The shy youth in Porbandar grew through his encounter with the West as a law student in London, and then developed rapidly in response to racial discrimination in South Africa into an assured and formidable nonviolent activist. His ideas gradually became clearer and more compelling, and as the acknowledged leader of the movement for Indian independence he was a charismatic personality who impressed everyone who met him and who directly and indirectly influenced millions. And despite all his failings he still emerges as one of the truly great human beings of the modern world.

Within his rocklike conviction Gandhi's approach to life was always one of openness to new experiences and new encounters and readiness to grow into a different and fuller understanding. To quote Judith Brown, "He saw himself as always waiting for inner guidance, to which he tried to open himself by prayer, a disciplined life, and increasing detachment not only from possessions but also from excessive care about the results of his earthly actions. He claimed to be perpetually experimenting with *satyagraha*, examining the possibilities of 'truth force' as new situations arose. He was, right to the end, supremely a pilgrim spirit."[11] And speaking of the last phase she adds, "The later 1930s saw the aging Gandhi still an optimist—about human nature, himself and Indian public life. But he was coming to terms with the passing years painfully and not without struggle, his hope often temporally darkened by events as clouds blot out the sun but cannot finally remove it. . . . His profound spiritual vision of life as a pilgrimage generated in him a mental and emotional agility which responded to change as an opportunity to be welcomed rather than resisted with fear."[12] We can say that he embodied his own ideal of the optimist: "The optimist lives delighting in thoughts of love and charity and, since there is none whom he looks upon as his enemy, he moves without fear."[13]

Gandhi was not a theoretical thinker; his practical utterances were nearly always made *ad hoc* in particular situations and were open to revision in the future. Thus he freely discarded statements of his own when they no longer applied or when he had come to see things differently. He said frankly, "My aim is not to be consistent with my previous statements on a given question, but to be consistent with truth as it may present itself to me at a given moment."[14] Further, he was a strongly intuitive thinker whose insights welled up with imperative force from the "inner voice" of his unconscious mind. These intuitions came shining in their own light as the impact of Truth, utterly devoid of doubt or ambiguity. Hence their power not only in his own life but also in the lives of so many whom he influenced. But Gandhi was well aware that there can be evil as well as good intuitions, and this is why he insisted so strongly on the purification of the self by discipline, vows, and a renunciation of wealth and possessions. "A pure heart," he said, "can find and see the truth."[15] It was because he knew that he was sincerely striving for *moksha,* for unity with the Divine, that he believed that what he called Truth sometimes illuminated his mind through this "inner voice."

Lest his reliance on intuition should suggest that Gandhi was vague or muddle-headed, he clearly had a high quality of intelligence, as well as an unwavering respect for facts, and considerable forensic skill. He had been called to the bar in London and had practiced for many years as a successful barrister in South Africa. And whenever he approached the authorities, whether on behalf of some local group or of India as a whole, with a case for redress or reform or independence, he always did so on the basis of careful research. For example, in 1916 Gandhi was asked to help the indigo plantation workers of Champaran in Bihar, who were being grossly exploited, often by absentee landlords. He took up their cause and was soon arrested and imprisoned for refusing to obey a judicial order excluding him from the district. The news spread rapidly and large numbers gathered in his support. But instead of inciting a riot Gandhi had his followers help to calm and control the crowds. "In this way [the authorities] were put at ease, and instead of harassing me they gladly availed themselves of my and my co-workers' co-operation in regulating the crowds. But it was an ocular demonstration of the fact that their authority was shaken. The people had for the moment lost all fear of punishment and yielded obedience to the power of love which their new friend exercised."[16] When the magistrate wisely released him Gandhi set up a center to which thousands of peasants came to record their evidence, which was carefully checked and collated. On this basis he wrote an exact and damning report, as a result of which an official enquiry was held and reparation was at last made to the peasants. "The *tinkathia* system [under which the peasants were forced to devote three-twentieths of their land to indigo] which had been in existence for about a century was thus abolished, and with it the planters' *raj* came to an end."[17] This was the first major victory of Gandhi's method of rational and nonviolent persuasion, and it made his new type of leadership known throughout India.

It is time now to look at Gandhi's famous statement that Truth is God. He did not mean primarily truth in the sense that comes most naturally to the Western mind, namely, true propositions. He says explicitly that he meant it in the Indian religious sense of *satya,* which means, in a variety of English phrases, "being," "reality," "that which alone truly is," "the ultimate." At the beginning of *From Yera-vada Mandir* Gandhi wrote, "The word *Satya* (Truth) is derived from *Sat,* which means 'being.' Nothing is or exists in reality except Truth. That is why the term *Sat* or Truth is perhaps the most important name of God."[18] God is not, then, a Person but is beyond the personal/impersonal distinction as the ultimate reality underlying everything. Gandhi's frequent habit of speaking of this reality in personal terms, as guiding, protecting, commanding, is also characteristic of much Indian thought, in which Vishnu, Shiva, Rama, Sita, and innumerable other gods are all thought of as partial manifestations of the formless (or ineffable) ultimate, referred to as Brahman. But because we are persons we generally need to personify that reality. As Gandhi said, "As we cannot do without a ruler or a general, such names as 'King of Kings' or 'The Almighty' are and will remain generally current."[19] But Truth "is That which alone is, which constitutes the stuff of which all things are made, which subsists by virtue of its own power, which is not supported by anything else but supports everything that exists. Truth alone is eternal, everything else is momentary. It need not assume shape or form."[20]

Critics tend to think of the successful leader of the Indian independence movement who, as was natural in India, used religion as a means to that end. Everything that he said, however, shows that he was primarily a seeker after God, Truth, the Ultimate, and a politician only because this led him into the service of his fellows and so into conflict with all forms of injustice. For Gandhi there was in practice no division between religion and politics, for true religion expresses itself politically, and the only way to achieve lasting political change is through the inner transformation of masses of individuals. But the great aim of his life was, in his own words, to "see God face to face"[21]—though seeing God face to face "is not to be taken literally . . . God is formless."[22] The place where he "saw" God was in responding to the needs of the poor, the downtrodden, the marginalized, the outcastes. He says of his time at Champaran, "It is no exaggeration, but the literal truth, to say that in this meeting with the peasants I was face to face with God, Ahimsa and Truth."[23] For in the Truth that he encountered there was no distinction between one's own salvation and that of others. And so he could say that his great aim, which he believed should be everyone's aim, was to attain *moksha*. When a foreign visitor asked him why he was spending his life on behalf of India's poverty-stricken villagers he said, "I am here to serve no one else but myself, to find my own self-realization through the service of these village folk. Man's ultimate aim is the realization of God, and all his activities, social, political, religious, have to be guided by the ultimate aim of the vision of God. The immediate service of all human beings becomes a necessary part of the endeavour simply because the only way to find God is to see Him in His creation and to be one with it. This can only be done by service to all."[24]

In his ashrams the day began and ended with prayer, readings (mainly from the *Gita*), hymns (including some Christian hymns), and often a short talk by Gandhi. But worship for him also took the form of spinning, or sweeping the floor, or cleaning the latrines, or nursing the sick, or attacking some specific injustice, or planning some aspect of the campaign for independence. It is also very important to understand that for Gandhiji *swaraj*, freedom, meant not simply, or even primarily, political independence, but a transformation of both individuals and society from selfishness to true community. In his manifesto *Hind Swaraj* Gandhi lays down as the first principle, "Real home-rule is self-rule or self-control,"[25] which can alone bring about permanent change. But self-rule required that people could first see and feel the value of mutual help. And so during the Champaran campaign Gandhi's coworkers were also busy setting up schools in six villages in the district and at the same time teaching the people methods of cleanliness and good sanitation.

I have already mentioned that Gandhi was not a systematic thinker, not a philosopher or theologian, but one for whom action came first with theory following behind. When in his letters and dialogues some general principle or philosophical concept was under discussion he quickly brought the conversation round to its practical implications. But at the same time his life and thought unfolded within the context of an inherited Hindu worldview. In religiously pluralistic India Gandhi had been influenced from his youth by Jain teachings. In his *Autobiography* Gandhi often speaks of God as directing and guiding him, yet like most educated Hindus he believed that whilst God could be imaged and worshipped in personal terms, God was nevertheless ultimately beyond the scope of all human ideas. He said, "I do not forbid the use of images in prayer. I only prefer the worship of the Formless."[26] Again, "God is no dispenser of rewards and punishments, nor is He an active agent. . . . At no time and in no circumstances [do] we need a kinglike God";[27] and yet again, "If God is not a personal being for me like my earthly father, He is infinitely more."[28] As he said on another occasion, "There is an indefinable mysterious Power that pervades everything. I feel It, though I do not see It."[29]

But although a devoted Hindu, Gandhi was strongly opposed to many aspects of traditional Hindu culture, such as animal sacrifices in the temples,[30] child marriages,[31] and untouchability. "Untouchability," he said, "is a soul-destroying sin. Caste is a social evil."[32] For whilst he generally acknowledged the traditional caste division of labor he did not see it as religiously based, and he increasingly criticized its harmful aspects. Indeed in his practice he overturned them. In his ashrams people of all castes, colors, nationalities, and religions ate and worked together, with everyone, including Gandhi and his family, joining equally in the manual labor traditionally allocated to the *sudras*, and such dirty jobs as latrine cleaning traditionally done only by the outcastes. He regarded untouchability as a "useless and wicked superstition,"[33] and was revolted by its defense in terms of the doctrine of karma.[34] He said that in his eyes there was no difference between a Brahmin and an outcaste;[35] and he defended marriages between people of different castes.[36] He refused to wear the sacred thread of a caste Hindu because "if the *Sudras* may not wear it, I argued, what right have the other *varnas* [castes] to do so?"[37] And whilst he supported the traditional Hindu reverence for the cow, "cow protection, in my opinion, included cattle-breeding, improvement of the stock, humane treatment of bullocks, formation of model dairies, etc."[38] In short, then, Gandhi's moral insights had far greater authority for him than established traditions, and in his maturity he had no hesitation in sweeping away long accepted ideas and practices that he regarded as harmful excrescences on the body of Hinduism.

Gandhi did however cleave to certain basic Hindu beliefs which were the source of his practical intuitions. In setting these out in order I am taking separately ideas that belong together as aspects of a single integrated body of belief. But nevertheless it may be helpful to us to focus on them one by one.

The first is that each of us in our deepest nature is identical with the universal *atman*, which in the depth of our being is common to us all, although divided in this life into innumerable different bodies and consciousnesses. Gandhi said that "the chief value of Hinduism lies in holding the actual belief that *all* life (not only human beings, but all sentient beings) are one, i.e. all life coming from the One universal source, call it God, or Allah, or Parameshwara."[39] Accordingly, he wrote, "I subscribe to the belief or the philosophy that all life in its essence is one, and that the humans are working consciously or unconsciously towards the realization of that identity."[40] Again, he said, "I believe in *advaita,* I believe in the essential unity of man and for that matter of all that lives."[41] His focus was not upon the Advaita Vedanta philosophy as such—he never allowed himself to become enmeshed in technical philosophical debates—but on its concrete significance. "What though we have many bodies?" he asked. "We have but one soul."[42] Again, "Souls seem to be many; but underneath the seeming variety, there is an essential oneness."[43] Accordingly, "to be true to such religion one has to lose oneself in continuous and continuing service of all life."[44] The political implication for Gandhi of the

unity of life was both that no one can be totally alien and irredeem-
ably an enemy, and that "one's true self-interest consists in the good of
all."[45] And so "I, for one, bear no ill-will against the British or against
any people or individual. All living creatures are of the same substance as all drops of water in the ocean are the same in substance.
I believe that all of us, individual souls, living in this ocean of spirit,
are the same with one another with the closest bond among ourselves.
A drop that separates soon dries up and any soul that believes itself
separate from others is likewise destroyed."[46]

The second closely related belief underlying Gandhi's work is
that there is a divine element in each of us. As he learned from the
Bhagavad Gita, "I [Vishnu] am the *atman* dwelling in the heart of all
beings."[47] In more universal terms, "The Power that pervades the universe is also present in the human heart."[48] This means in practice that
in all situations of conflict there is something in the opponent that can
be appealed to—not only a common humanity but, in the famous
Quaker phrase (and Gandhi felt great affinity with the Quakers), "that
of God in every man." "I have a glimpse of God," he said, "even in my
opponents."[49] So, once again, no one can be utterly and finally an
enemy because no one is without that divine spark within them.
"People may consider themselves to be our enemies," Gandhi said,
"but we should reject any such claim."[50]

He was however well aware that appearances are often against
such an outlook. Referring to Nazism and "the bloody butchery that
European aggressors have unloosed," he wrote:

> In the face of this, how can one speak seriously of the divine
> spirit incarnate in man? Because these acts of terror and murder
> offend the conscience of man; because man knows that they
> represent evil; because in the inner depths of his heart and of
> his mind, he deplores them. And because, moreover, when he
> does not go astray, misled by false teachings or corrupted by false
> leaders, man has within his breast an impulse for good and a
> compassion that is the spark of divinity. . . .[51]

A third, again integrally related, aspect of Gandhi's faith is
ahimsa, nonkilling, and more generally nonviolence. This is an ancient Hindu, but more particularly Jain, principle. It obviously co-
heres with the beliefs that all life is ultimately one and that there is a
divine element in every person. For it follows that in injuring others

we are injuring the whole of which we are part, and injuring the ultimate Truth or Reality which we call God.

Ahimsa is the point at which Gandhi's philosophy becomes political and has a continuing significance for the whole world. *Ahimsa* means in practice that in the midst of injustice the right way to deal with oppressors—whether the South African government in its treatment of the "coolies" or the British *raj* dominating and exploiting the people of India—is not violent revolt but an appeal to the best within them by rational argument and by disobedience to unjust laws even when this involves suffering violence and imprisonment. Willingness to suffer for the sake of justice, appealing as it does to the common humanity of both oppressor and oppressed, is the moral power for which Gandhi coined the word *satyagraha,* the power of Truth. He believed that a policy of nonaggression in the face of aggression, of calm reason in response to blind emotion, of appeal to basic fairness and justice, together with a readiness if necessary to suffer for this, is more productive in the long run than meeting violence with violence. He was convinced that there is always something in the other, however deeply buried, that will eventually, given enough time, respond. For "nonviolence is the law of our species as violence is the law of the brute. The spirit lies dormant in the brute and he knows no law but that of physical might. The dignity of man requires obedience to a higher law—to the strength of the spirit."[52]

But in order for this to happen the *satyagrahi* must have the courage to face the oppressor without fear. Without such courage, which Gandhi seemed able to evoke in many of his followers, genuine nonviolent action is impossible. "Nonviolence," he said, "is a weapon of the strong. With the weak it might easily be hypocrisy."[53] But a *satyagrahi* can be nonviolent precisely because he or she does not fear the oppressor. "Fear and love," Gandhi said, "are contradictory terms. . . . My daily experience, as of those who are working with me, is that every problem would lend itself to solution if we are determined to make the law of truth and non-violence the law of life."[54]

However, he was not opposed to the use of force in all circumstances. For example, he was seriously physically assaulted in South Africa in 1908, and when his eldest son later asked what he ought to have done if he had been there, Gandhi replied that in that situation he should have used physical force to rescue his father.[55] He accepted that violence was necessary in restraining violent criminals; and he said, "I would support the formation of a militia under *swaraj* [self-rule]."[56] "In life," he said, "it is impossible to eschew violence completely. The question is, where is one to draw the line?"[57] But in general, "nonviolence is infinitely superior to violence."[58]

In the colonial India in which Gandhi most notably applied his principles he had to carry the masses with him. And so a great deal of his time was spent in "consciousness raising" by public speaking, often to great crowds throughout the country, by a constant stream of newspaper and journal articles, and by interviews with individuals and groups from both India and abroad. He knew that the ideal of total nonviolence, which involves loving one's enemy, was not going to be attained by the masses in any foreseeable future. He declared, "For me the law of complete Love is the law of my being. Each time I fail, my effort shall be all the more determined for my failure. But I am *not* preaching this final law through the Congress or the Khalifat organization. I know my own limitations only too well. I know that any such attempt is foredoomed to failure."[59] But although perfect *ahimsa* was an ideal rather than a present reality, something approaching it, namely nonviolent noncooperation with the foreign ruler, was possible and would eventually bring about the nation's freedom. He said, "I know that to 90 per cent of Indians, nonviolence means [civil disobedience] and nothing else."[60] Again, "what the Congress and the Khalifat organizations have accepted is but a fragment of the implications of that law [*ahimsa*]. [But] given true workers, the limited measure of its application can be realized in respect of vast masses of people within a short time."[61] He was able to convince a critical mass of his fellow countrymen and countrywomen that a hundred thousand Englishmen could only rule three hundred million Indians so long as the Indians weakly submitted to their rule. But if they had the courage to withdraw their cooperation, and nonviolently disobey unjust laws—such as the salt tax—the British *raj* would be helpless and the imperial rulers would see that their position was both morally and politically untenable. They could not put millions in jail, and although there might be further outbursts of violence, like the terrible Amritsar massacre in 1919, the world would react against this and in the end the imperial power would be defeated and would have to depart. Gandhi said, "Once the British Government are sure that they can no longer hold India, all the difficulties that are now being put forth on their behalf will vanish like darkness before dawn."[62] And this is what finally happened. After the 1939–45 war a new British government came to power and made the momentous decision to grant Indian independence as quickly as possible. It was evident that the demand and expectation for this were growing to the point at which only brute force would be able to check it, and this in an India in which the whole administrative machinery had been gravely weakened during the war. In 1946 the Viceroy, General Archibald Wavell, reported to London: "Our time in India is limited and our power to control events almost gone."[63] Further, members of the new government, including the prime minister, Clement Attlee, had over the years been convinced of the justice of the demand for Indian independence. The dominant intellect of the Labour party, Stafford Cripps, was a friend of Gandhi and Nehru, as were several other members of the Attlee government. The last Viceroy, Lord Mountbatten, who was sent out to bring independence about, admired Gandhi and regarded Nehru as a worthy prime minister of a free India.

Throughout the long struggle for independence it was Gandhi who provided the inspiration, the moral authority, and the immense unifying symbolic power. But in the detailed negotiations during the final phase it was mainly Pandit Jahwarhalal Nehru and Sardar Vallabhbhai Patel who molded the settlement on the Congress side—Nehru the brilliant, sophisticated, charismatic disciple of Gandhi, chosen by him as Congress President at this critical juncture, and Patel the shrewd, tough, forceful, uncompromising political operator. And so the *raj* ended as Gandhi had always said it would, with the British voluntarily handing over power and leaving in friendship—despite the strong opposition at home by old-style imperialists led by Winston Churchill. Instead of going in bitterness and enmity, the British went with great pomp and ceremony, leaving an India which proudly continued to be part of the Commonwealth. It seems very unlikely that history would have taken this course but for Gandhi's influence over the previous thirty years—somewhat as it seems very unlikely that apartheid in South Africa would have ended so peacefully but for the personal influence of Nelson Mandela.

We can now try to formulate the main lessons of Gandhi's life and thought for ourselves at the threshold of the twenty-first century. Gandhi himself believed that the truth of nonviolence would only have its main impact many years after his own death. And it is a mistake to think of Gandhi only in the context of the movement for Indian independence, inseparable though his memory is from that. His great aim was not political independence as such, but rather the transformation of Indian society. True *swaraj* meant freedom from greed, ignorance, prejudice; and most of Gandhiji's time was spent in trying to educate and elevate the masses, dealing with basic questions of cleanliness, sanitation, and diet, combating disease, and fostering mutual help and true community. As Judith Brown writes, "He visualized a total renewal of society from its roots upwards, so that it would grow into a true nation, characterized by harmony and sympathy instead of strife and suspicion, in which castes, communities, and both sexes would be equal, complementary and interdependent."[64] Thus Gandhi's vision went much further than the immediate political aims that he shared with his colleagues in the Indian National Congress. What elements of this larger long-term project are relevant today?

First is the Gandhian approach to conflict resolution, based on a belief in the fundamental nature of the human person—not, however, belief in human nature as it has generally manifested itself throughout history, but in its further potentialities, which can be evoked by goodwill, self-giving love, and sacrificial willingness to suffer for the good of all. As Lamont Hempel puts it, "Gandhi's crowning achievement may have been his ability to inspire *homo humanus* out of *homo sapiens.*"[65] But this was in a number of individuals, not in society as a whole. Many individuals continue to be inspired by Gandhi's teaching and example, but neither India nor any other nation has based its policies on Gandhian principles. It is particularly tragic that his own country has so signally failed to live up to his ideals. Immense inequalities of wealth continue. The category of outcaste (although officially abolished in the Indian Constitution) continues in practice, so that today the *dalits* (the downtrodden) still have to struggle for their basic human rights. The rise of the Hindu supremacist movement led to the mass violence of the destruction of the Ayodia mosque, and now to the wanton testing of nuclear weapons, thus destabilizing the peace of the entire region. All this would have made Gandhi weep.

Does this make his teaching irrelevant today? It remains relevant in the way in which the teaching of enlightened religious leaders in every century is continuously relevant: it stands over us as an ideal that continually challenges us and that proves itself when, all too rarely, it is acted upon. It is challenging because it involves an unwavering commitment to fairness, truthfulness, open and honest dealing, willingness to see the other's point of view, readiness to compromise, readiness even to suffer. In the familiar—but in practice disregarded—words of Jesus, it requires us to love our enemies and to turn the other cheek rather than retaliate. Gandhi received the same insight from the Hindu precept, "The truly noble know all men as one, and return with gladness good for evil done," which he says became his guiding principle.[66] Such a response refuses to enter the downward cycle of mutual recrimination, hatred, and violence. The lesson of history is not that this has been tried and failed, but that the failure has been in not trying it. When tried in India, even to the limited extent that Gandhi was able to get his compatriots to adopt it, it succeeded; and we have seen its relevance again in the work of Martin Luther King in the United States, and in the spirit of reconciliation created in the new South Africa by Nelson Mandela.

But *ahimsa* as practical politics is a long-term strategy. It took time and patience and ceaseless effort and example to evoke the limited realization that nonviolent action in India, even simply as a tactic, is more effective than violent revolt. It is thus pointless to ask how Gandhi would have fared in, for example, Nazi Germany. He would no doubt have been quickly eliminated. The more useful question is what would have happened if someone like him had been at work in Germany for the previous twenty years.

Another contemporary implication of Gandhi's thought concerns ecology and the preservation of the earth and the life on it. Here Gandhi was far ahead of his time, anticipating the widespread Green movement of today. To quote James Gould, "Gandhi has emphasised opposite values to those of the consumer society: the reduction of individual wants, the return to direct production of foodstuffs and clothing, and self-sufficiency rather than growing dependency. As the limits of growth and the inherent scarcity of resources broke upon the world in the 1960s, the Gandhian idea of restraint suddenly made sense."[67] E. F. Schumacher, author of the influential *Small Is Beautiful*, regarded Gandhi as the great pioneer in insisting that the rampant growth of capitalist industrialism is incompatible with a sustainable world ecosystem. He said, "Gandhi had always known, and rich countries are now reluctantly beginning to realise, that their affluence was based on stripping the world. The USA with 5.6 percent of the world population was consuming up to 40 percent of the world's resources, most of them nonrenewable. Such a lifestyle could not spread to the whole of mankind. In fact, the truth is now dawning that the world could not really afford the USA, let alone the USA plus Europe plus Japan plus other highly industrialised countries. Enough is now known about the basic facts of spaceship Earth to realise that its first class passengers were making demands which could not be sustained very much longer without destroying the spaceship."[68] Gandhi saw this in terms of his native India, which was then still a developing country in which people in hundreds of thousands of villages lived in extreme poverty. In 1928, referring to these villages, Gandhi wrote that "under British rule, millions of children are starving for want of nourishing food and they are shivering in winter for want of sufficient clothing."[69] And so instead of building up modern industries with labor-saving machinery in the cities, thus drawing villagers into the urban slums, he urged basic employment for all. He wanted "production by the masses rather than mass production." Every policy should be judged by its effects on the multitude of ordinary citizens. For example, cottage industries, such as spinning, required very little equipment and should be encouraged and supported throughout the vast rural areas. But the opposite has happened. When asked whether Gandhi has turned out to be right, Schumacher "pointed out that the number of rich, even very rich, people in India had increased as had the number of desperately poor people. He added that the situation in India reflected the situation of the world as a whole and Gandhi would undoubtedly consider this a sign of grievous failure."[70] But in the matter of aid to impoverished peoples Gandhi was at least a generation ahead of his time. In 1929 he wrote, "The grinding poverty and starvation with which our country is afflicted is such that it drives more and more men every year into the ranks of the beggars, whose desperate struggle for bread renders them insensible to all feelings of decency and self-respect. And our philanthropists, instead of providing work for them and insisting on their working for bread, give them alms."[71] That aid should be given in such a way as to free the recipients to help themselves is now a widely accepted principle in international aid circles.

Gandhi's "feminism" is also of interest today in shifting the focus from the transformation of women to the transformation of men. On the negative side, Gandhi never wholly broke free from the assumptions of the ancient patriarchal culture of India. In this context his concern for the position of women in society was ahead of his time but behind that of the feminist movement as this has developed since, mainly in the West. Gandhi had been impressed when in England by the courage and dedication of the suffragettes, although he did not approve their militancy. And when women responded to his call in South Africa and India, showing themselves as willing as the men to face violent police action and jail, Gandhi saw that they had a unique contribution to make.

To quote Ranjit Kumar Roy, early on "Gandhi realised that the success of this *Satyagraha* had been due to the new moral force that women's entry brought into the movement. Indeed the presence of women had generated public support and mobilized the 'apathetic and the marginally interested' to join the movement. Gandhi was quick to understand that women could become the 'leader in the *Satyagraha* which does not require the learning that books give but does require the stout heart that comes from suffering and faith.'"[72] Further, because true liberation was always much more for Gandhi than political independence, but meant more fundamentally the humane transformation of society, he "believed that by taking part in the nationalist struggle, women of India could break out of their long imposed seclusion."[73] His conception of the kind of gender revolution that is needed strikes a chord today. The wholehearted adoption of *ahimsa* can be seen as releasing the feminine aspect of the male, making for a gentler and less aggressive masculinity. Sushila Gidwani puts the point challengingly in this way: "Gandhian feminism aims at changing men to become qualitatively feminine while the modern feminism aims at changing women to become qualitatively masculine."[74] This indictment is certainly not true of all Western feminists, but Gidwani does point to Gandhi's revolutionary change in the conception of ideal masculinity.

Another major aspect of Gandhi's thought with implications for today is one that was not novel in the East—it was familiar from the Vedas and from the work of such great ecumenical spirits as Kabir, Nanak, the Sufis of Islam, the Buddhist Asoka, and many more—but that is highly controversial within Christianity, though somewhat less so today than in Gandhi's time. This is his understanding of the relation between the great world faiths. "The time has now passed," he said, "when the followers of one religion can stand and say, ours is the only true religion and all others are false."[75]

In his youth Gandhi lived within a very ecumenical community. His family were Vaishnavites, but would freely visit Shaivite temples, and they had Jain, Muslim, and Parsi friends and neighbors. Gandhi was particularly influenced by a Jain, Raychandbhai, who introduced him to the idea of the many-sidedness of reality *(anekantavada)*, that many different views may all be valid. This includes religious views. Gandhi shared the ancient Hindu assumption that "religions are different roads converging at the same point. What does it matter that we take different roads so long as we reach the same goal? I believe in the fundamental truth of all great religions of the world. I believe they are all God given and I believe they were necessary to the people to whom they were revealed."[76] He regarded it as pointless, because impossible, to grade the great world faiths in relation to each other. "No one faith is perfect. All faiths are equally dear to their respective votaries. What is wanted, therefore, is a living friendly contact among the followers of the great religions of the world and not a clash among them in the fruitless attempt on the part of each community to show the superiority of its own faith over the rest. . . . Hindus, Mussalmans, Christians, Parsis, Jews are convenient labels. But when I tear them down, I do not know which is which. We are all children of the same God."[77] However, his "doctrine of the Equality of Religions"[78] did not move towards a single global religion, but enjoins us all to become better expressions of our own faith, being enriched in the process by influences from other faiths.

These, then, are ways in which Gandhi's thinking was ahead of his own time and relevant to our time: the challenge to nonviolence in dealing with opponents, nonconfrontational politics, ecology and what has been called "Buddhist economics," feminism, and the relation between religions. And underlying all this, as an available source of inspiration for each new generation, is Gandhi's indomitable faith in the possibility of a radically better human future if only we will learn to trust the power of fearless nonviolent openness to others and to the deeper humanity, and indeed deity, within all. To most people this seems impossible. But Gandhi's great legacy to us is that his life has definitively shown that it is possible, however rarely, in the world as it is.

NOTES

1. Judith Brown, *Gandhi: Prisoner of Hope* (New Haven & London: Yale University Press, 1989), p. 80.

2. Margaret Chatterjee, *Gandhi's Religious Thought* (London: Macmillan & University of Notre Dame Press, 1983), p. 73.

3. Mohandas K. Gandhi, *The Selected Works of Mahatma Gandhi*, 6 vols. (Ahmedabad: Navajivan Publishing House, 1969), 1: xviii–xix.

4. Mohandas K. Gandhi, *Young India*, 20 January 1927.

5. Gandhi, *Selected Works*, 2:702.

6. Raghavan Iyer, *The Moral and Political Writings of Mahatma Gandhi*, 3 vols. (Oxford & New York: Clarendon Press, 1986), 2:38.

7. Chatterjee, *Gandhi's Religious Thought*, p. 108.

8. Louis Fischer, *The Life of Mahatma Gandhi* (New York & London: Harper & Row, 1950), pp. 213–14.

9. Ibid., p. 213.

10. Ibid.

11. Brown, *Gandhi*, p. 80.

12. Ibid, pp. 312–13.

13. Gandhi, *Navajivan*, 23 October 1921.

14. Brown, *Gandhi*, p. 283.

15. Iyer, *Moral and Political Writings of Gandhi*, 2:195.

16. Gandhi, *Selected Works*, 2:614.

17. Ibid., 2:634.

18. Ibid., 4:213.

19. Ibid.

20. Iyer, *Moral and Political Writings of Gandhi*, 2:576.

21. Gandhi, *Selected Works*, 1:xix.

22. Iyer, *Moral and Political Writings of Gandhi*, 1:587.

23. Gandhi, *Selected Works*, 2:615–16.

24. Gandhi, *Harijan*, 29 August 1936.

25. Gandhi, *Selected Works*, 3:201.

26. Chatterjee, *Gandhi's Religious Thought*, p. 111.

27. Gandhi, *Selected Works*, 5:342–43.

28. Gandhi, *Harijan*, 16 February 1924.

29. Gandhi, *Young India*, 11 October 1928.

30. Gandhi, *Selected Works*, 4:251.

31. Ibid., 5:445.

32. Ibid., 5:444.

33. Brown, *Gandhi*, p. 58.

34. Gandhi, *Selected Works*, 5:404–5.

35. Gandhi, *Indian Opinion*, 20 May 1905.

36. Brown, *Gandhi*, p. 290.

37. Gandhi, *Selected Works*, 2:585–86.

38. Ibid., 2:636.

39. Iyer, *Moral and Political Writings of Gandhi*, 1:515.

40. Chatterjee, *Gandhi's Religious Thought*, p. 106.
41. Gandhi, *Navajivan*, 15 February 1925.
42. Gandhi, *Young India*, 4 December 1924.
43. Iyer, *Moral and Political Writings of Gandhi*, 1:451.
44. Ibid., 1:461.
45. Ibid., 2:122.
46. Gandhi, *Indian Opinion*, 29 April 1914.
47. Gandhi, *Selected Works*, 4:305.
48. Ibid., 5:380.
49. Iyer, *Moral and Political Writings of Gandhi*, 1:438.
50. Ibid., 1:530.
51. Gandhi, *Modern Review*, October 1941.
52. Iyer, *Moral and Political Writings of Gandhi*, 2:299.
53. Ibid., 1:294.
54. Ibid.
55. Ibid., 2:298.
56. Ibid., 2:391.
57. Ibid., 2:257.
58. Ibid.
59. Gandhi, *Young India*, 9 March 1922.
60. Iyer, *Moral and Political Writings of Gandhi*, 2:363.
61. Gandhi, *Young India*, 9 March 1922.
62. Gandhi, *Harijan*, 16 March 1940.
63. Patrick French, *Liberty or Death: India's Journey to Independence and Division* (New York & London: HarperCollins, 1997), p. 245.
64. Brown, *Gandhi*, p. 213.
65. Lamont Hempel, "Overview: The Elusive Legacy," in *Gandhi's Significance for Today*, ed. John Hick and Lamont Hempel (London: Macmillan, and New York: State University of New York Press, 1989), p. 5.
66. Gandhi, *Autobiography*, chap. 10.
67. Hempel, "Overview," in *Gandhi's Significance for Today*, ed. Hick and Hempel, p. 12.
68. Surur Hoda, "Schumacher on Gandhi," in *Gandhi and the Contemporary World*, ed. Antony Copley and George Paxton (Chennai: Indo-British Historical Society, 1997), p. 141.
69. Iyer, *Moral and Political Writings of Gandhi*, 1:506.
70. Hoda, "Schumacher on Gandhi," in *Gandhi and the Contemporary World*, ed. Copley and Paxton, p. 140.
71. Gandhi, *Selected Works*, 2:647.
72. Ranjit Kumar Roy, "Gandhi on Women: Their Role in the World of Politics," in *Gandhi and the Contemporary World*, ed. Copley and Paxton, p. 224.

73. Ibid., p. 226.

74. Sushila Gidwani, "Gandhian Feminism," in *Gandhi's Significance for Today,* ed. Hick and Hempel, p. 233.

75. Mohandas Gandhi, *Indian Opinion,* 26 August 1905.

76. Norman Scotney, "Gandhi's Lifeline-Belief: Towards Religious Pluralism," in *Gandhi and the Contemporary World,* ed. Copley and Paxton, p. 239.

77. Gandhi, pp. 23, 31.

78. Iyer, *Moral and Political Writings of Gandhi,* 1:545.

Can We Keep Peace with Nature?

STEPHANIE KAZA

FLICKERING LIGHTS, crack snap of branches flailing into the night, ice everywhere. Ten-inch icicles drip from the car. Sidewalks slicken with a solid coat of obsidian smooth ice. Gravel and salt are no use; the freezing rain covers the limp gestures of safety with yet more ice. Grass blades swell to thumb-size stubs; ice spears poke in all directions from hay bales and windblown shrubs. The trees take it the hardest—weak crowns tipping over under the load and then, CRACK! giving up to gravity. Crack! Crack! Crack! like gunfire; the sound of the ice storm is like gunfire.

In early January, 1998, northern Vermont, New Hampshire, New York, and southern Quebec went through the most significant ice storm on record for the region. Warm tropical air from the south surged unusually far north, causing an unprecedented thaw. The moisture-laden front pushed over the top of the cold arctic shield, melting the snowpack in the mountains. In the St. Lawrence and Lake Champlain valleys, as well as in New Hampshire and Maine, the warm rain fell through cold air and created chaos. For five days the stationary front encased the region in an ice fog. When the sun finally broke through, the storm had taken a major toll on the landscape. Sugarbushes, pine forests, tree plantations, urban plantings all suffered serious losses. It was the rare tree that was still intact.

The ice storm raised serious questions about keeping peace with nature. It is one thing to consider keeping peace with gentle meadows and sovereign redwood forests. It is quite another to consider peaceful relations with extensive weather events. We are perhaps capable of peaceful relations with the natural world under stable conditions, although there is much evidence to contradict this. But when these conditions deteriorate, as during a major ice storm, do we have the psychological reserves to handle such extreme stress? Watching

Montreal struggle to return electrical power to over a million residents has been sobering. The heavy ice took down major transmission towers and countless wires snagged by collapsing trees. Crews from all over the continent worked around the clock for four weeks to clear branches and reconnect torn lines. One wonders: if events of extreme magnitude like this happen in too many places at once or too quickly in sequence, can we keep up, let alone keep *peace?* With global climate change predictions now coming true, will we be too busy scrambling to preserve our own homes and communities to be concerned about any other lives?

Many have brought their minds to bear on human-nature relations—from Thoreau to Muir, from Rachel Carson to Gary Snyder. Many have debated whether humans are separate and/or above nature or not, and if so, on what basis? Some have painstakingly documented human impact on wetlands, forests, deserts, and prairies. Only just recently have the world's major religious traditions joined the conversation about how people can live peacefully and sustainably on this overtaxed planet.

As part of that conversation, I will explore some ways in which Buddhist traditions might keep peace with nature. Buddhism has taken many cultural forms over the 2500 years since the Buddha lived. Texts and teachings from Buddhists in India, Sri Lanka, Thailand, Burma, Vietnam, Korea, Japan, China, Tibet are all available today in English translation. These represent a great flowering of Buddhist understanding, sometimes simplified into the Theravada, Mahayana, and Vajrayana schools of thought and practice. Today Buddhist scholars and practitioners in the West are writing their own sutra commentaries and practice manuals. For my purposes here I will draw on overview materials rather than original texts, since I am primarily concerned with the emerging literature in "Buddhism and Ecology." I am less interested in looking at the contradictions between traditions and more concerned with finding useful springboards for developing a "green" Buddhism which can engage the planetary environmental crisis and generate better peacekeeping in the future. Here I will review the seeds of this possibility which are sprouting in a number of different places and traditions.

Nature, like Buddhism, can be a problematic term. I considered using the word *environment* to avoid the difficulties of *nature,* but as poet and essayist Wendell Berry points out, "no settled family or community has ever called its home place an 'environment'. . . . The real names of the environment are the names of rivers and river valleys; creeks, ridges, and mountains; towns and cities; lakes, woodlands, lanes, roads, creatures, and people."[1] So back to the problematic word *nature*.

Three aspects characterize nature in most Buddhist traditions. The first derives directly from the fundamental Buddhist law of codependent origination, *paticca-samutpadda* (in Pali). According to this law, all phenomena (that is, all of nature) arise from a complex set of causes and conditions, each set unique to the specific situations of arising. Thus, the well-known simple but penetrating Pali verse:

> This being, that becomes;
> from the arising of this, that arises;
> this not being, that becomes not;
> from the ceasing of this, that ceases.[2]

Ecological understanding of natural systems fits very well within the Buddhist description of interdependence. Nature, then, is primarily relational, dependent on many causes and conditions in diverse spatial and historical arrays.

The second aspect of nature is that it is nondualistic, all-inclusive. There is nothing which is *not* of nature, horrible or benign, and humans are most definitely part of nature, not separate from it in some other world. Like most organisms, people view some aspects of nature as more useful, pleasant, or preferable than others. And, like most organisms, they do what they can to form strong relations with these aspects. But in the bigger view, all aspects and beings are in fact at play in the all-inclusive realm of nature. Sunspots, PCBs, viruses, El Niño—all are part of the interdependent web.

The third aspect is paradoxical but critical. From a Buddhist view, all phenomena of nature are impermanent; nothing is absolute. What all beings share in common is that they arise and they pass away—mountains, mayflies, snowflakes—no matter how long or how dramatic the nature of each existence, it still fades from view sooner or later. Thus in Buddhism there are no absolute gods outlasting other beings. Yet there is still the sense of continuity of being—*ch'i* in Chinese, *ki* in Japanese—awkwardly translated as "matter energy," "material force," or "vital power." *Ch'i* represents the "unfolding of continuous creativity," not out of nothing, as in a Western Judeo-Christian view, but through ongoing transformations of what already exists.[3] Nature is this vital force in full many-splendored revelation. So even though all individual phenomena are impermanent, each gives rise to others in perpetual motion, thus establishing a world in continual transformation. This contrasts sharply with the traditional Western worldview of nature as more or less static, a relatively unchanging background for human activities.

The term *peace*, like *nature*, is riddled with romantic idealization, projection, and doublespeak. Contemporary Buddhist leaders Thich Nhat Hanh and His Holiness the Dalai Lama describe peace as something you do, a spiritual practice. For Thich Nhat Hanh, "peace is every step." Each calm, mindful breath or step is a step generating peace and awareness. For the Dalai Lama, peace comes from the practice of kindness and compassion. As he says, "although it is difficult to attempt to bring about peace through internal transformation, this is the only way to achieve lasting world peace."[4] Those following the bodhisattva way are encouraged to practice equanimity or patience, one of the six *paramitas* or practices of perfection. Peace, from a Buddhist perspective, is a state of mind which can envision and manifest peaceful relations with others. Internal and external peace are seen as mutually regenerating and cocreative.

Buddhist practice emphasizes the principle of nonharming or *ahimsa,* and this acts as a force for generating peace. Nonviolence, as this is sometimes translated, means more than the absence of violence, including violent thought. It means acting positively towards constructing peace. To quote from the opening stanzas of the Dhammapada, "For hate is not conquered by hate: hate is conquered by love. This is a law eternal."[5] With a Buddhist perspective on nature, one aims to practice peace or loving nonharming with a wide embrace. Thus peacekeeping includes ending the violence towards plants and animals, rivers and oceans that is so widespread across the planet. Thai teacher Buddhadhasa suggests that peace means being true friends to all beings and to one's self. Certainly there is no shortage of opportunities for peacemaking in this end-of-the-century escalation of the war against nature.

Does Buddhism have anything to offer to this challenging and quite serious question: can we keep peace with nature? As I have worked on this topic, I find the question haunting me like a koan—

a puzzle too penetrating to solve with simplified intellectual under-standing. It calls for real world contact with the suffering of nature today: the glaring heat on the ravaged land of industrial clearcuts, the garish chemical soup of polluted waters, the sprawling megacities gagging on traffic and smog. Here in these places of life-threaten-ing deterioration, the question becomes more real, more disturbing, more difficult to answer honestly. As a gesture towards some depth of reflection, I have organized my response according to the Buddhist tetralemma or fourfold logic used by Nagarjuna and others. First, I'll argue NO, pointing out good reasons we cannot keep peace with nature, even as Buddhists. Second, I'll argue YES, Buddhist philoso-phies and practices do exist that demonstrate it is possible to keep peace with nature. Then, to confirm the complexity, I will also explore the other two options: BOTH yes and no, and NEITHER yes nor no.

NO PEACE WITH NATURE

In the small but growing wave of enthusiasm for an environ-mental Buddhism, British scholar Ian Harris has taken on the task of critiquing the methods and claims of green Buddhist writers. He points out that there is no unified tradition of environmental thought or practice across the historically and culturally disparate Buddhisms of India, China, and Japan. Further, there are a number of different words and concepts for *nature,* some much closer than others to the already complex Western meaning of the word. Harris feels mod-ern green Buddhist enthusiasts blur important distinctions from the diverse Buddhist lineages, thereby violating an enduring tradition of critical thinking. From his point of view, this sloppiness can only undermine the selective arguments made by naive seekers. In some cases, he suggests, Western and/or nationalistic thinking has so per-vaded Eastern behavior that it is hard to find the Buddhism behind Thai or Japanese exploitation of the natural world.[6]

Certainly Buddhism is not a nature religion *per se;* it is not orga-nized primarily around human relations with nature nor does it advo-cate "worshipping" the sun or moon or particular animals or plants. In fact, the examples cited in the emerging green Buddhist literature suggest a fairly limited history of environmental engagement. Where monastic temples served to protect surrounding lands, it was often for economic or agricultural purposes. In many traditions, the isolated rural lands were seen as an aid to spiritual transformation. In Japanese Buddhist culture, it has been suggested that spiritual engagement is primarily with nature in symbolic form—for example, the highly refined Japanese tea garden or elegant flower displays. Can this kind of engagement with representational nature inspire lifestyle change or does it actually serve to cover hypocritical denial of the more pressing urgencies of pollution and population control?

Still other writers have proposed philosophical and sociopolitical critiques of Buddhism, which, at face value, would indicate little hope for peacekeeping from this quarter. Filipino Reuben Habito, a Zen priest and a former Catholic social organizer, feels that Buddhist religious teachings place too much emphasis on personal liberation and not enough on social or structural change.[7] This can lead to a passive attitude toward the environment, except where it aids in enlightenment. Alan Sponberg believes green-leaning Buddhists have become too enamored of interdependence without equal commitment to the more challenging developmental tasks of training and transformation. In his view, eco-Buddhists might get the concept but not gain the spiritual strength to implement it.[8] In both critiques it is apparently easier to teach and transmit the principles for individual enlightenment than to develop effective social organizing tools. Another problem lies in attributing all conditions to acts of karma. If Buddhists believe physical disability or infertility is a result of misdeeds in a former life, they may not bother to look for endocrine disrupters or pesticide residues in the local drinking water.

In Japan, the sensitive aesthetic appreciation for nature seems completely removed from the social denial of the costs and dangers of nuclear energy and the heavy logging destruction wrought by Japanese corporations in Malaysia. When Stephen Kellert administered a comparative survey of Japanese and American attitudes toward nature, he found the Japanese actually less concerned about the environment than Americans and less interested in recreational engagement with wild nature.[9] In Thailand, activist Sulak Sivaraksa has charged that Buddhism as a state religion is too corrupt, too busy maintaining its power and influence to support eco-resistance movements such as the forest monks.[10] In fact, the Thai Buddhist hierarchy has thwarted the efforts of a number of village monks to protect their local forests. Tibetans unfortunately are so busy doing all they can to survive in exile under radically different ecological conditions that they can hardly be active environmental peacekeepers in India, let alone Tibet. Meanwhile, the ecological stability of the high Himalayan plateau is now seriously under siege by Chinese logging, agriculture, and uranium waste dumping.

How about green Buddhism in the U.S.? Here I would advance the critique that the relatively new wave of Buddhism is too preoccupied with training teachers and building centers to take on any serious environmental issues. The American habit of individualism spills over into American Buddhist centers, where members often come for personal spiritual gain rather than to support a community, let alone participate in social action. In some Zen centers vigils, protests, and even restoration projects are actually frowned on as a distraction to meditation practice.

Can Buddhists help keep peace with nature? The evidence for answering NO is real. There is no unified movement here or long tradition across cultures of actively caring for nature. There are problems in implementing Buddhist philosophy in a real world setting outside the hermitage hut of the dedicated seeker. But this is only one of four viewpoints. A number of other sources point to a hopeful YES.

YES, PEACE WITH NATURE

When Bill Devall and George Sessions published the first book on deep ecology in 1985, they included a short piece by American Zen priest Robert Aitken on "Gandhi, Dogen, and Deep Ecology."[11] This followed on the heels of poet Gary Snyder's earth-celebrating stanzas, filled throughout with references to Zen.[12] The 1970s and 1980s saw a virtual explosion of Buddhist literature and practice groups in America, and to many it seemed obvious that Buddhism had more to offer the ecologically concerned spiritual seeker than Christianity. Unfortunately, the legacy of Christianity in North America is not particularly positive. There are reasons for the enduring stereotype that Western religions objectify nature and assert dominion over it. For one, there is the wake of indigenous genocide following missionary contact with its soul-saving eradication of native languages, ceremonies, spiritual taboos, and region-specific cultures. For another, there is the biblical command, "Thou shalt have dominion over the land," and the consequent earth-shaking impacts of colonization. Linear grids on the curving landscape, territorial disputes, gold, gray whales, and giant redwoods—all seen as free for the claim-staking. Third, there is the clear separation between spirit and body, between heaven and earth, promoted in Christian texts and worship. The body and the earth are seen as inferior, transitory, changeable, and unreliable—in short, to be used but not cherished, since the main goal was beyond this life. Those who turned to Buddhism for ecospirituality could be sure the new tradition did not carry at least this karmic baggage. Even if their view of Buddhism was incomplete or a romantic projection, at least it offered some breathing room for the imagination, to *hope* that peaceful relations with nature could exist in *some* spiritual tradition.

When Buddhism began to flower in America in the 1960s and 70s, it ran head on into the environmental movement. Environmentalism already carried a certain overtone of spirituality characterized by Bronislaw Szerszynski as "feral" religion, where choices and rituals in everyday life come to reflect eco-spiritual perspectives. He points to monastic forms of Thoreauvian renunciation, sectarian groups of spiritually-motivated eco-warriors, and lesser degrees of involvement through churchly piety (membership) and lifestyle practices (recycling, etc.).[13] In the same vein, Bron Taylor has described Earth First! as a new religious group united around earth-based values, worldviews, rituals, and community.[14] Of course there is already a long history of serious ethical reflection on environmental relations between people and nature from such great minds as Henry David Thoreau, Ralph Waldo Emerson, John Muir, Aldo Leopold, and Rachel Carson, to name a few. For Buddhism developing in America the odds seemed loaded that it would pick up a green tinge.

Two influences support a move in this direction: philosophical congruities with environmentalism and an emerging interest in Buddhist environmental activism. A number of thoughtful teachers and scholars have drawn attention to fundamental tenets of Buddhism that support an ecological worldview. Robert Aitken in Hawaii and John Daido Loori in New York have drawn on Zen texts such as Dogen's "Mountains and Waters" sutra, and practices such as the precepts and *paramitas;* Vietnamese Zen teacher Thich Nhat Hanh has focused on interdependence and mindfulness as the way to enlightened practice. His Holiness the Dalai Lama has taken a strong stand linking Buddhism to environmental protection in Tibet and elsewhere. In the United States green Buddhists-to-be have also found great inspiration in the creative writing of Gary Snyder and teacher-activist Joanna Macy.[15]

So what does Buddhism offer philosophically to support an ecological worldview? I would suggest that the two most accessible principles for Buddhists and non-Buddhists looking for an alternative are: 1) interdependence and 2) liberation in awareness. Interdependence affirms the relational perspectives of ecology and systems thinking. The jewel net of Indra, a metaphor for interdependence, poetically describes the complex and only partially knowable web of life with every being a multifaceted jewel in a multidimensional netted web, each reflecting all the others. Interdependence or mutual co-arising includes not only the *actions* of the many beings, but their *thoughts* as well. The intention and attitude of the actor becomes a critical part of what actually happens. Environmental ethics, paradigm shifts, ecophilosophies are then important work for the environmental activist. As Gary Snyder suggests, "it can mean every word heard is heard to its deepest echo."[16] Keeping peace with nature from a Buddhist perspective thus includes generating peacekeeping thoughts towards nature. This focus may provide the leverage point needed to turn the tide of destruction undermining life for us all.

Liberation through awakening or consciousness-raising is the method for accomplishing this turn. This affirms the persistent efforts of environmentally concerned people to educate others about the state of the earth. The practice of awareness or mindfulness fosters appreciation for nature and a reflective and peaceful attitude; it can also reveal hidden assumptions about privilege, comfort, consumption, and inadvertent abuse of nature. In a speed-crazed society focused almost entirely on economic progress, there is little time or incentive for these slower awareness practices. For those trying to resist or question the runaway pace of millennial madness, sitting down and stopping can be just the right medicine.

What other Buddhist principles are lifted up to support peaceful relations with nature? In the Mahayana tradition, much weight is placed on the Bodhisattva path, where one takes a vow to return again and again to relieve the suffering of all sentient beings—surely the environmentalist's life work! In the Theravada tradition, the metta sutta of loving kindness is extended to all beings, wishing that they be free from harm and blessed by mental and physical well-being. Of the

Four Noble Truths, the fourth describes the Eightfold Path of liberation from suffering; among the eight spokes of action are Right Action,
Right Speech, Right Livelihood. Each of these offers a locus for practicing peace with nature in a concrete way while simultaneously
cultivating spiritual stability and insight. In upholding the precepts
of Right Morality, one is encouraged to exercise restraint and moderation, to simplify one's needs and desires so as to reduce suffering
for others. These guidelines support a Thoreauvian withdrawal from
consumer addictions, a requirement for reducing the vast wakes of
ecological impacts behind each product.

Central to Buddhist practice across traditions is an attitude of
compassion, or open-heartedness to the suffering of others. The principle of *ahimsa* or nonharming mentioned earlier derives naturally
from a true experience of compassion. When one sees oneself as part
of a mutually causal web, it becomes clear that there is no such thing
as a private autonomous self, independent of all others. Thus one becomes accountable for all of one's actions, since they affect others in
varying degrees. Environmental ethics based on these Buddhist principles would be firm with those who spread toxics and carcinogenic
chemicals throughout the food web. In American society where reason is valued over emotion and ethics are often utilitarian, the Buddhist cultivation of open-hearted response to nature is a welcome
relief. *This* world now cries for our attention, not some promised land
after death. In many ways, Buddhism offers a much needed antidote
for the depleting projects of Western industrialism. Because the scope
and scale of environmental destruction is so all-embracing and quite
overwhelming, those brave enough to venture forth toward healing
and peace need the stability and equilibrium of a sound spiritual practice which Buddhism may well provide.

So where are the examples of eco-Buddhist activism today? Is
this territory all theory and no action? Or can we see some models of
peacekeeping in action? Let me suggest three aspects which make up
a whole effort: 1) holding actions of resistance, 2) creating new vi-
sions, and 3) changing cultural structures. In these examples, activists
are often practicing Buddhism with a small *b*, as Sulak Sivaraksa
says—that is, Buddhism that supports virtuous action in whatever
context, rather than proselytizing for itself.[17] Perhaps the best example
of resistance comes from the "ecology monks" in Thailand. Buddhist
monks in rural villages serve the local community by providing family

and religious ceremonies and opportunities for merit-making, such as planting trees. Villagers, in return, offer food to the monks on their morning alms walks. Where village forests are threatened by logging or development, some monks have taken the side of the forest. They lead the villagers in tree ordination ceremonies, in which the yellow cloth of monkhood is wrapped around a prominent tree to charge it with protecting all the others. A number of monks have also engaged in restoration and rural development projects to support village life and reduce urban migration. In some cases, the monks' work is regarded as obstructionist to Thai economic growth; more than one monk has been asked to disrobe for his environmental work. Thai forest protection efforts have inspired similar tree ceremonies in the U.S. where Zen leaders have ordained important oaks and redwoods. Some of the strongest Buddhist resistance actions in the U.S. are around protection of the Headwaters old growth redwood groves in northern California where Buddhist deep ecologist Bill Devall and others are resisting the accelerated clearcutting by Maxxam corporation.[18]

Green vision efforts abound. An offshoot of the International Network of Engaged Buddhists and the Buddhist Peace Fellowship, self-titled the "Think Sangha," is undertaking a series of reflection papers on Buddhism and consumerism. The Boston Research Center for the Twenty-First Century has drawn attention to the Earth Charter people's vision by publishing a booklet of Buddhist views on the charter's proposed principles. His Holiness the Dalai Lama in his Nobel Peace Prize acceptance speech proposed a Five-Point Peace Plan for Tibet in which the entire province (or nation-state, depending on your perspective) would be declared an ecological reserve. Rita Gross, Buddhist feminist scholar, has laid out a Buddhist framework for considering global population issues. I have recently completed a counterpart Buddhist perspective on consumption issues. In her Deep Ecology workshops, Joanna Macy draws on Buddhist principles to combat the paralyzing states of grief, despair, and fear that prevent people from acting on behalf of the environment.[19]

As for models of cultural change, these are still in progress and often meet with resistance in their own quarters. Two Buddhist centers in rural northern California, Green Gulch Zen Center and Spirit Rock, already demonstrate a great commitment to the environment through vegetarian dining, land and water stewardship efforts, an organic farm and garden (at Green Gulch), and ceremonies which include the natural world. People who visit can see ecological action as part of a Buddhist way of life.[20] A group of young people at Green Gulch who call themselves "eco-sattvas" meet regularly to plan restoration projects which become part of the work practice.[21] Gary Snyder, esteemed elder among eco-Buddhists, has cooperated with others in his local region to establish the Yuba River Institute. John Daido Loori's monastery in the Catskills of New York, Mount Tremper, features frequent "Mountains and Rivers" retreats based on the center's commitment to environmental conservation on the land. Applying the same principles in an urban setting, Tetsugen Bernie Glassman has developed a set of green small businesses which employ local street people, sending products to socially responsible companies such as Ben and Jerry's.

YES, all of these people seem to be saying, YES, it seems possible to bring Buddhist principles of peacekeeping to bear in situations of environmental degradation. YES, Buddhism has something to offer in creating a green vision for the future. Even if the challenges seem endless, the need is great and those who aspire to the Bodhisattva vows must respond. It is not a matter of being reasonable so much as being spiritual in effective ways. I know for me such ecological work is core to my understanding of the Buddhist vows.

Now, perhaps I should stop right here with a hopeful vision: Buddhism will lead the way and the planet will be saved. However, a fuller treatment of this difficult question is more realistic, and this requires consideration of the more likely outcome: "BOTH yes and no" will happen, and also "NEITHER yes nor no" will happen. I turn now to the remaining two positions of the Buddhist fourfold logic for this question.

BOTH YES AND NO

Both yes and no: this piece of the answer addresses human fallibility and imperfection. Despite the highest aspirations for a life of enlightened bodhisattvic action, most of us will fall short of the ideal. The ideal, in fact, is a made-up projection of what is possible; from a Buddhist perspective, this tends to ignite our yearning and take us away from the immediate reality before us. Reality, as it turns out, is far more complex, synergistic, and unpredictable than any visionary ideal. The conversation over YES vs. NO takes up a lot of time and energy, often distracting people from directly addressing the issues.

So what does "both yes and no" look like? How does it fill out the universe of possibility only partially described by NO or YES alone? First, it is spotty, partial, incomplete. Some Buddhist centers will take up environmental practice and make it a central part of their work and meditation; some will focus on other social action projects— hospice, prison work, gay liberation; still others will struggle with internal politics and remain divided over the degree of environmental engagement. This will frustrate the front line of in-house activists, some of whom will give up and apply their efforts elsewhere. Likewise, some countries or regions will make greater progress toward environmental stability than others. In California and the Pacific Northwest where there are more Buddhists and Buddhist centers as well as a very active environmental community, green Buddhist projects may be more successful than elsewhere. Thailand's number of ecology monks may swell, while Burma monks are imprisoned for even assembling to meet. And in each situation where a group or institution has made great strides forward, the positive progress may be interrupted by a change of leadership or priorities.

Second, Buddhist (and non-Buddhist) peacekeeping with nature will be full of contradiction. There will be some morally thoughtful behavior followed by other unconscious behavior. A green Buddhist might commit to vegetarianism to reduce participation in animal suffering, but still commute an hour to work each day, thereby spewing 80 pounds of carbon dioxide emissions into the atmosphere.[22] A Buddhist center might opt to buy produce at the best price available rather than develop a local organic garden. Even the most informed green Buddhists will be stuck with some environment-degrading habits that seem unavoidable—petroleum products, computers, road salt. The response will waver between awareness and denial. Sometimes it is just too painful to consider all the facts at once.

Third, the vacillating combination of yes and no will inevitably be inadequate to the task. It will not be *fast* enough to meet the accelerating pace of global environmental deterioration. We know already, for example, that existing CFCs in the atmosphere will continue to deplete ozone even if they are entirely eliminated on the ground. The scope of efforts will also likely not be *broad* enough; there aren't enough Buddhists or environmentalists to go around! Thus we retreat to a triage approach, first suggested by Daniel Jantzen in discussing the ecological plight of Central America. Triage means trying to save the most savable areas or species and letting the near-dead go. The only trouble with this battlefield approach is that the "dead" don't just decompose; they release toxins into the surrounding aquifers and farmlands and spread the chain of death even farther. The scale of effort required here is enormous; Lester Brown of the World Watch Institute says nothing short of a revolution in the next ten years can significantly halt the widespread assault on the environment.[23]

Fourth, we can expect shifting priorities around the tension between individual and structural change efforts. In one sense, it is much easier to make personal lifestyle changes, at least in the U.S. where choice is still a major privilege. This is not necessarily an option in Tibet, Poland, or Siberia. But sweeping change can only happen at the structural level—green taxes on resource extraction, for example, or incentives for solar energy development. Buddhists may be particularly helpful in questioning consumerism, especially on the individual level where moderation and restraint are conducive to spiritual practice. Structural change will call for a different degree of community organizing—are green Buddhists willing to take on the challenge? Actually there already are a number of practicing American Buddhists in important nonprofit organizations such as Natural Resources Defense Council, Rainforest Action Network, and Center for a New American Dream. But Buddhist activists, like all activists, can burn out on pressing for structural change and overlook the personal challenges of Buddhist liberation practice. It's a quandary. For every person concerned about these issues, the tension will never be completely resolved.

Fifth, "yes and no" means working with uncertainty. There will never be any assurance that it is all going to turn out "all right," no matter how the situation stands at any moment. This is very unnerving; we all most naturally want to survive and have a safe and peaceful life. But under the current conditions, there are no guarantees. Does this mean giving up on hope? Yes, a Buddhist would say; one's efforts cannot depend on something as abstract or intangible as hope. Instead they must be grounded in the stability of one's own commitment. In the Soto Zen tradition I practice, lay ordained students vow to practice the three pure precepts and ten grave precepts. On Earth Day 1990, several of us affiliated with Green Gulch Zen Center wrote an environmental version of these precepts to strengthen the breadth of our commitment.[24] Three in particular stand out, although one could develop environmental commentaries on all ten.

The first, "No Killing," challenges practitioners to confront food choices (the killing of animals for meat, for example, or the killing of soil for industrial agriculture), forestry practices (clearcutting, herbicide spraying), endangered species, air and water pollution—the list goes on. The fifth precept is traditionally phrased as "no taking drugs or alcohol"; we reframed this to "we vow to not harm self or others through poisonous thought or substance." This raises ethical questions about pesticides, nuclear radiation, and chlorination which are not easy to answer. The tenth precept, "not to defame the Three Treasures," means environmental practice is everywhere. Of the three treasures, the Buddha can be seen to include animal and plant teachers with their own evolutionary wisdom, the Dharma then encompasses the teachings of all beings as truths to learn from, and the Sangha is the wider ecological practice community. Taking care not to harm any part of these three treasures is a lifetime challenge of minimizing personal and social impact on the environment.

Thus at the heart of "Both Yes and No" can be a vow of spiritual practice commitment which holds one steady even in the face of uncertainty, fallibility, contradiction, and inadequacy. Some days of peacekeeping efforts will be filled with life-affirming progress; others, such as the day President Clinton signed the salvage logging rider, will be bleak, indeed. Accepting the complicated dimensions of "both yes and no" is an aid to deepening spiritual commitment on behalf of the planet.

NEITHER YES NOR NO

But what about this last of the four answers to our difficult koan? "Neither yes nor no" is the negative space behind all the others, the undefined realm, the source of unknown events, any of which could spur cultural change beyond our wildest imagination. Certainly, in spite of all the NO critiques, much will go forward anyway. And even with all the YES examples and concepts, many green ideas and projects will never manifest. What are some of the things that might arise to address this set of causes and condition we now find ourselves in? Let me suggest at least four types of factors at work in the unknowable interdependent web.

Many have said it will take a major catastrophe to wake people up to the state of the environment. Break-off of the Antarctic ice shelf, widespread plankton die-off, inundation of coastal cities—these would be alarming signs of systems overload and synergistic escalation of human impact. Each of these extreme events would be "Big Wake-Up Calls," time to pay serious attention to what's happening; the fate of much life on earth is at stake. Extreme events can act as catalysts for mobilizing social action and cultural change. In addition to weather-related events, we might also see major famine or food supply crises or a virulent new plague. Major crop loss has also been predicted and already there is evidence of that in Africa and North Korea. Unfortunately such catastrophes generate tremendous suffering; we would wish for less extreme teachings perhaps. Yet these powerful events can generate powerful insight, illuminating the systems-level suffering throughout the interdependent web.

On the other hand, we may see inspirational leadership in unexpected places. A great religious leader such as the Dalai Lama has the capacity to inspire thousands to follow his example or vision. What if the eco-sattvas in California motivate thousands of young people to join the forest defenders out of spiritual compassion? As a teacher, I know I can't predict which seeds of understanding will ripen when in which students. So much depends on the right fit of conditions. In 1968, when Gary Snyder first wrote "The Smokey the Bear Sutra," could he have guessed how far his words would travel?[25]

Perhaps hardest to imagine are world-changing structural shifts, on the order of the collapse of the Soviet Republic or the dismantling of the Berlin wall. These could, of course, have positive *or* negative effects on the environment. Globalization through international trade agreements is already taking a toll on indigenous cultures, endangered species, and resource-rich habitats. What if women nuns' ordination in Thailand was approved? This would allow women to join forces with the ecology monks and double the resistance efforts. In India there has been some movement towards village-managed forests coops, but what if local control meant local exploitation of nationally valued lands (as proposed in Utah)? A single policy change, such as San Francisco's elimination of pesticides in favor of Integrated Pest Management, could contribute significantly to reducing human health hazards.

Of course, I can't begin to name all the possible unknown factors, but one area to watch closely is ecospiritual activism. Will there be more rabbis leading Tu B'Shevat seders in threatened forests? Will the evangelical Christian lobby extend their sphere of influence beyond the Endangered Species Act? Will the indigenous peoples' alliances come to bring more weight in ethical reparations to the lands? I think Buddhists could work effectively with all these groups; perhaps they will in surprising and innovative ways.

This last piece of the puzzle may actually be the most significant of the four. Keeping peace with nature means keeping open to the possibility that things could take a surprising turn—for better or for worse. Obsessing on either the best hope or the worst fear can block access to other options. Including "neither yes nor no" means practicing with "don't-know mind," allowing the other members of the system to contribute to the peacemaking. What if, for example, the trees and birds and fishes were represented at public hearings, as they are at North American Bioregional Congress sessions? Within this "don't-know mind," we can't anticipate how people will draw on their existing skills, knowledge, and creativity to respond to the current and evolving state of the world.

Of the four positions—no, yes, both yes and no, neither yes nor no—which will prevail? How will it go? Can we keep peace with nature? The answer partially depends on the way we think about the questions. One's care for one's family, childhood home, professional training, religious beliefs, friends—personal and social liberation from suffering calls on *all* of these—a fierce attention, no flinching, total commitment. I myself lean toward the positive signs, but that is as much as anything because the pain of it all is almost too much to bear sometimes. I believe most people would *prefer* to find peaceful relations with nature. But still the koan haunts me—what will it actually take to accomplish this?

Here is one response from bold thinker and companion along the way, poet Gary Snyder:

For the Children

The rising hills, the slopes,
of statistics
lie before us.
The steep climb of everything, going up,
up, as we all
go down.

In the next century
or the one beyond that,
they say,
are valleys, pastures,
we can meet there in peace
if we make it.

To climb these coming crests
one word to you, to
you and your children:

stay together
learn the flowers
go light [26]

NOTES

    1. Wendell Berry, "Conservation is Good Work," in *Sex, Economy, Freedom, and Community* (New York: Pantheon Books, 1996), p. 35.
    2. Quoted and discussed in my article, "Towards a Buddhist Environmental Ethic," *Buddhism at the Crossroads* (Fall 1990):22–25.
    3. Tu Wei-ming, "The Continuity of Being: Chinese Views of Nature," in *Nature in Asian Traditions of Thought*, ed. J. Baird Callicott and Roger T. Ames (Albany, N.Y.: State University of New York Press, 1989), pp. 67–78.
    4. His Holiness the Dalai Lama, *A Policy of Kindness*, ed. Sidney Piburn (Ithaca, N.Y.: Snow Lion Publications, 1990), p. 57.
    5. *The Dhammapada*, trans. Juan Mascaro (London: Penguin Books, 1973).
    6. Ian Harris, "Buddhism and the Discourse of Environmental Concern: Some Methodological Problems Considered," in *Buddhism and Ecol-*

ogy: The Interconnectedness of Dharma and Deeds, ed. Mary Evelyn Tucker and Duncan Ryuken Williams (Cambridge: Harvard University Press, 1997), pp. 397–402.

7. Reuben L. F. Habito, "Mountains and Rivers and the Great Earth: Zen and Ecology," in Tucker and Williams, *Buddhism and Ecology,* pp. 165–76.

8. Alan Sponberg, "Green Buddhism and the Hierarchy of Compassion," in Tucker and Williams, *Buddhism and Ecology,* pp. 351–76.

9. Stephen R. Kellert, "Concepts of Nature East and West," in *Reinventing Nature: Responses to Postmodern Deconstruction,* ed. Michael E. Soulé and Gary Lease (Washington, D.C.: Island Press, 1995), pp. 103–21.

10. Sulak Sivaraksa, "Integrating Head and Heart: Indigenous Alternatives to Modernism," in *Entering the Realm of Reality: Towards Dhammic Societies,* ed. Jonathan Watts, Alan Senauke, and Santikaro Bikkhu (Bangkok: Suksit Siam, 1997), pp. 52–87.

11. Robert Aitken, "Gandhi, Dogen, and Deep Ecology," in *Deep Ecology: Living as if Nature Mattered,* ed. Bill Devall and George Sessions (Salt Lake City: Gibbs M. Smith Books, 1985), pp. 232–35.

12. See, for example, Gary Snyder, *Myths and Texts* (New York: New Directions, 1978; originally 1960); and *Turtle Island* (New York: New Directions, 1969).

13. Bronislaw Szerszynski, "The Varieties of Eco-Piety," *Worldviews, Environment, Culture, and Religion* 1, no. 1 (1997): 37–56.

14. Bron Taylor, "Earth First!'s Religious Radicalism," in *Ecological Prospects: Aesthetic, Scientific, and Religious Perspectives,* ed. Christopher Chapple (Albany, N.Y.: State University of New York Press, 1994).

15. See Robert Aitken, *The Mind of Clover* (San Francisco: North Point Press, 1984); Thich Nhat Hanh, *The Miracle of Mindfulness* (Boston: Beacon Press, 1976); Thich Nhat Hanh, *Being Peace* (Berkeley: Parallax Press, 1987); His Holiness the Dalai Lama, "The Nobel Peace Prize Lecture," and "The Ethical Approach to Environmental Protection," in Piburn, *Policy of Kindness,* pp. 15–27 and 118–28; Gary Snyder, *The Practice of the Wild* (San Francisco: North Point Press, 1990); Joanna Macy, *Despair and Personal Power in the Nuclear Age* (Philadelphia: New Society Pubs., 1983); Joanna Macy, *World as Lover, World as Self* (Berkeley: Parallax Press, 1991).

16. Snyder, *Practice of the Wild,* p. 180.

17. Sulak Sivaraksa, "Buddhism with a Small *b,*" in *Seeds of Peace* (Berkeley: Parallax Press, 1992), pp. 62–72.

18. See my interview with Bill Devall, "Belly Full of Salmon," in *Turning Wheel* (Fall 1993): 30–31.

19. See Amy Morgante, ed., *Buddhist Perspectives on the Earth Charter* (Cambridge: Boston Research Center for the 21st Century, 1997); The

184 World Religions and Peace

Dalai Lama, "Nobel Peace Prize Lecture"; Rita Gross, "Buddhist Resources for Issues of Population, Consumption, and the Environment," in Tucker and Williams, *Buddhism and Ecology*, pp. 291–312; Stephanie Kaza, "Overcoming the Grip of Consumerism" (prepared for the 1998 International Buddhist-Christian Studies meeting, Indianapolis, Ind.); Joanna Macy, *Despair and Personal Power in the Nuclear Age* (Philadelphia: New Society Pubs., 1983).

20. Stephanie Kaza, "Buddhist Response to the Land: Ecological Practice at Two West Coast Retreat Centers," in Tucker and Williams, *Buddhism and Ecology*, pp. 219–48.

21. Eco-sattva, "Universal Chainsaw, Universal Forest," *Turning Wheel*, Winter 1998, pp. 31–33.

22. See John C. Ryan, *Over Our Heads: A Local Look at Global Climate Change* (Seattle: Northwest Environment Watch, 1997), p. 55, for how to calculate the amount of carbon dioxide produced per miles traveled.

23. Lester Brown, "Launching the Environmental Revolution," *State of the World Report 1992* (New York: W.W. Norton, 1992), pp. 174–90.

24. See Wendy Johnson and Stephanie Kaza, "Earth Day at Green Gulch," *Turning Wheel*, Summer 1990, pp. 30–33.

25. Gary Snyder, "The Smokey the Bear Sutra," in *A Place in Space* (Washington, D.C.: Counterpoint Press, 1995), pp. 25–31.

26. Gary Snyder, *Turtle Island* (New York: New Directions, 1969), p. 86.

Religions and the Culture of Peace

RAIMON PANIKKAR

RELIGIONS CAN NO longer live in the ivory tower or muddy walls of their closed organizations. I have been struggling with the agonizing question of religion's relation to peace for the past forty years, not only theoretically but also practically, not exclusively on philosophico-theological grounds but also personally, being myself a Catholic priest, a Hindu believer in my dharma, an initiated Buddhist, and a staunch secular person.

For the sake of clarity, I shall describe the meaning I ascribe to the two operative words of my title. The word *religion* encompasses, in my opinion, a threefold aspect: *religiousness* or the human dimension concerning ultimacy, wherever we may believe this ultimacy to lie; *religiosity* or the social institution (not necessarily an organization) in which the religious dimension of human life is embodied; and *religionism* or the more or less closed system of ultimate beliefs pertaining to one particular collectivity.

The three aspects should be distinguished but they are not separable. For our purposes I shall use the word mainly as connoting an "organized relinking with the sacred," but without forgetting that religion is transcendental to any of its expressions.

By *peace* I understand neither the mere absence of war nor solely the inner contentment of the individual. I take it to mean "the human participation in the harmony of the rhythm of reality."[1] "Peace is in the inner harmony which dwells in truth," wrote R. Tagore in 1924.[2] For our purposes I shall use the word as connoting a nondualistic relationship between political harmony among nations and personal fulfillment of the individual.

After an overall look at the past in order to gain some perspective, I shall describe the present as an *intermezzo* to prepare the ground for my third and main part.

I. THE LESSON FROM THE PAST

Taking into account the historical experience of humanity in its last six thousand years, I may venture a bold statement: the religions of the world have kairologically (not chronologically) passed through three periods:

Monism. Religion is undifferentiated from the rest of human activities and inseparable from human identity. If I belong to the tribe x or the nation y my religion will be x or y. Wars and conflicts carry a religious element and often a justification. To live humanly is a religious act.

Dualism. The second period begins by disentangling religion from the rest of human life. Religion is simply one element in life, and the most important ingredient of religion may be the intellectual. Religion becomes identified with doctrine.

Nihilism. If the first period proved unsatisfactory, the second one, at the present stage of our consciousness, proves equally unconvincing to an increasing number of people who keep religion, if at all, as a luxury for private comfort or as an irrelevant harmless souvenir. The nihilist response is to throw it all away and simply deny the religious dimension of human beings.

My hypothesis is that the three attitudes do justice neither to human nature nor to the very nature of religion.

II. INTERMEZZO

In the turmoil of the present day we find a threefold reaction.

Fundamentalism. We should regain the original insights of religion and fight the loss of tradition, of the sacred, and, ultimately, of humanness. We should have the courage to confess the Truth without compromise. Revelation, God, or Justice is on our side.

Reductionism. Religion should have learned by now to be humble, recognizing that it has to be just a private affair and not be mixed up in human affairs, for the guidance of which we have our reason and our moral sense.

Rejection. Religion has to be dropped as a superfluous remnant of the past, and eventually fought against when it flares up in dangerous revivals.

My submission is that these three attitudes represent the three modern temptations, but that they do justice neither to the true nature of religion nor to the human condition.

III. THE PRESENT TASK

Three facts seem to be undeniable. First, wars are on the increase in the modern world. The increase is in the number of wars, in the number of combatants (we have an army of circa 30 million soldiers), and in the number of victims (some 2,500 daily deaths since the last World War, of which over 60 percent are civilians). The numbers, since 1991, increase day by day. This situation is already an indictment of the present civilization, and should concern all of us.

Second, the very nature of war has undergone a mutation prepared over a century ago and consummated in the Second World War. War consists no longer in battles between armies, but in destruction of peoples, human habitats, and earthly grounds. It is no longer a horrible but yet a ritual act. It is simply destruction.

Finally, religions have contributed precious little to the keeping of peace. Religions have promoted strife and division among peoples and individuals, notwithstanding many other positive services of religions.

How can religions contribute to the culture of peace? I would like to answer this momentous question with one single word, which I borrow from one particular tradition, but which has equivalents in other religions and could be applied to all of them: *metanoia*.

Two general comments should precede my triple interpretation of *metanoia*. They encompass the three meanings and refer to the atmosphere in which *metanoia* (transformation) is meaningful.

The traditional word for my first comment is *humility*. The contribution of religions to peace would defeat its purpose if we were to imagine that human peace, and even religious peace, entails the victory of one religion (obviously our religion) over others, or at least the victory of a diffused form of religiosity or a very general religionism over all other forms. Victory never leads to peace. And this is simply an empirical statement confirmed by human history. No crusade of the God-fearing people against the force of evil has ever brought peace to the human race.

The corollary of this is that mere condescension, mere strategic tolerance, will not do. We need something more. We need conversion: *metanoia*.

My second comment is that *metanoia* is not a sadistic or masochistic accusation against religion or religious people. A common indictment against religions amounts to saying that they have failed. We often hear that they have not succeeded in delivering the goods. But this sentence betrays a mercantilistic spirit. Let me explain.

Those who argue that religions have not brought remedy to the ills of the world are assuming that religions should have been the panacea for humanity. To be sure, religious doctrines have often seemed to make this claim. And certainly a doctrine which is impotent to yield results not only proves itself inefficient but also shows that there is something missing in that doctrine—unless we devitalize doctrines and reduce them to irrelevant notions spinning in the air, accepting a total divorce between theory and practice, and thus reducing theory to an exercise in futility when not in alienation.

Yes, religions have failed. *If* you follow the *dharma, if* you love Christ, obey Muhammad, or the Torah, listen to the *daimôn,* or the Spirits, or your conscience, the earth will be a paradise. But what is that *if?* Why does hardly anybody take seriously that *if?* This leads me to a main thesis of my argument: *the need for a thorough transformation of religions* for the incoming millennium. This transformation is what I call *metanoia.*

After six thousand years of such failures we are no longer convinced by the two standard answers: one existential, the other essential. The *existential* answer consists in accepting the failures of the past while not recognizing the mirage of the future. It points to a new sect, a new religion, a new prophet: "Now, the Christians are going to overcome the deficiencies of Judaism; now, the Buddhists are finally eliminating the baroque exuberance of the Hindu religion; now, the Sikhs, the Muslims, the Baha'is, the humanists, the Marxists, and so on, are going to realize the perfect society," and, to quote the Hebrew Bible, now "the lion and the lamb are going to pasture together"— forgetting that to be a vegetarian is not paradise for the lion.

There is no doubt that such reforms have often been very positive, and that this type of proliferation may be a healthy sign of human vitality. It may show the need of adapting old religions to new conditions and be a stimulus for the ancient systems to renew themselves.

Yet there is no doubt either that after a while all such promises have been shattered and our situation has not substantially improved. "This is the war which will end all wars!" "This is the religion which will establish universal brotherhood!" After six thousand years there is a sad feeling of *déjà vu*. Religions have failed.

The *essential* answer tells us that such is the human condition. All humans are sinners; there is *avydyâ;* Gilgamesh was defeated; we are living in *kali yuga;* the original blessing has been withdrawn; *homo homini lupus;* and so on.

But all religions ask themselves this question, and promise a remedy to the human condition: if you practice *mahâmudra, agapê,* meditation, justice, *dharma;* if you obey the revelation, follow the injunctions of the guru, etc., you shall be realized, redeemed, peaceful, saint, jîvanmukta, and so forth. But the small *if* creeps in insidiously again. Apparently grace, revelation, the *sruti,* the Qur'an, or whatever, is not enough. It seems as if all religions were noncommittal concerning the *if* and were skipping the problem. If grace is really the only thing that matters, and it is sovereignly free, then all the rest is not only superfluous, but harmful, since it gives us false expectations and nurtures the pride of religious people.

Here is my plea for *metanoia.* Conversion has to apply to religions themselves, to religion itself, as an ongoing process. A fundamental and often neglected role of religions is to cope with failure—their own failures to begin with and human failures in general. Perhaps they should concentrate less on *nirvana, mukti,* realization, salvation, heaven, and the like—that is, on success—and instead, in a more humble way, direct their efforts toward healing human wounds, soothing the historical scars of humanity; in a word, toward the culture of peace more than to the preaching of salvation. There is a certain wisdom in some African religions which are not so much concerned with the Supreme God and instead direct their attention to the lesser Gods who create the trouble or offer the remedies.

Religions have failed because this is their *karma,* their nature. In fact, they constantly remind us of the law of the cross, the *naishkarmya karma,* the renunciation of the fruits, the disinterested action, the death to oneself, the love of God for God's sake, and so on. Religions are not the human panacea. They are, as are humans themselves, itinerant, provisional, and imperfect. They show the moon on the pond, not the moon in the sky, to adapt a recurrent Buddhist metaphor. They reflect the divine, may point to transcendence, to the Absolute, but they are not the real moon. They are only the reflection on the waters of the human condition. They do not offer the solution; they help us to see the moon on the pond by advising us to keep the water clear and quiet. That's all. The *if* remains. They offer the ever-renewed hope to go on living, striving, discovering, and not giving up the authentic human condition. They are not the answer; they are constant reminders of the very question: the human mystery, the un-fathomable reality of Life. And some of the answers they give fail to convince many; we may even find them wrong. They are not above this world, although they witness to us that this very world is more—not less—than a merely spatio-temporal reality.

For this they need to descend from their respective Olympus to the *kshetra,* to the *samsara,* the arena of the strains and stresses of human life—in a word, to the field of the city, the *polis,* politics. We are still heirs of the great dualistic divide between the secular and the religious, between the cultivation of the soul (monasteries, ashrams, *viharas*) and the cultivation of the soil (farmers, traders, laypeople).

This dichotomy has been lethal for both, the so-called religious sphere and the alleged only temporal activity. Contemplation has be-come barren, and the creative work of the layperson has degenerated into dehumanizing labor.

The synthesis cannot be made by juxtaposition, an eclectic mix-ture, or by absorbing everything into a religious domain. The work of the *nying-ma* monk, the *ora et labora* of Saint Benedict, the *sam-sara is nirvana* of Nagarjuna, the *in contemplatione activus* of Ignacio de Loyola, are some examples of such a synthesis.

I am not advocating that we make the world into a monastery or engage monasteries in social work. The transformation has to go deeper.

To come to our point: the concern for peace is not an accidental religious issue. Political peace is a question of life or death. Do we want a more serious religious issue? The role of religions is not ful-filled through chaplains to the armies. Religions have to become living forces to disarm the armies, and convince the nations that humans are endowed, not with paws to fight, but with intelligence and words to discuss, debate, dialogue. The decline of rhetoric—in its proper and traditional sense—is directly proportional to the increase in warfare. Instead of speaking to each other we break relations and fight.

Let me proceed to the three meanings of *metanoia*.

1. The first meaning is *repentance*. Due to the influence of the Hebrew Bible, the Greek word of the Gospels and Christian scriptures was sometimes translated as *penance*—which is not altogether wrong. If we repent we shall feel remorse and make the necessary satisfaction, penance.

At any rate this repentance has to be the first obligation of all living religions today. I will single out two major fields: repentance of both the abuses and the uses of religion.

a) There is no doubt that all religions, without exception I dare say, have committed abuses. If I believe myself to be right and conclude from this that the other is wrong and harmful, the temptation of contempt, crusades, persecutions, exploitations, and wars against the "infidels" becomes almost irresistible. Most religions have justified inquisitions, tortures, *jihads,* condemnations, and elimination of the other, under different names and with the most stupendously fallacious arguments. How can a *mleccha,* a *goi,* even understand the lofty tenets of our sublime *dharma,* of our divine covenant?

The direct consequence of this repentance, the penance if we want, is to ask forgiveness. It is cathartic to confess our own abuses. What have Hindus done to the Jainas, Buddhists to the Taoists, Christians to the Muslims, Jews to the pagans, Communists to the unenlightened, capitalists to the poor—and we could just as easily reverse these clauses and have all types of permutations up to terrorism. We have to ask forgiveness now, even for actions of the past. It is not a valid excuse to say that in many cases this was done a long time ago and that we have forgotten about it. This would only increase our guilt. We have so easily forgotten the misdeeds of our ancestors because for us they were apparently not such big mistakes. But the victims have not forgotten—say, what the Spaniards did five hundred years ago on the western shores of the Atlantic.

I am not saying that Hindus should accuse the Muslims or Jews the Christians. I am saying that Hindus should accuse themselves, so the Jews, not the other way around. To be brief, I may quote from a recent paper of the saintly Âcârya Bede Griffiths, a Benedictine sannyasin living for over forty years in an Indian ashram: "The record of the Inquisition in the matter of imprisonment, torture, and burning heretics can only be compared with that of Hitler and Stalin in modern times. . . . Could not the Roman Church make a public statement of its rejection of all such methods of which it has been guilty in the past?"[3] Could we not humbly ask forgiveness of humanity at large and the victims in particular? And this example should apply to all religions.

b) This repentance should cover not only the abuses, but also the superficial uses of religion. We should repent of the trivial watering down of the sublime teachings and examples of founders and saints and of having reduced religion to a diluted ideology for assuaging the pricks of conscience, generally of the powerful. I am not criticizing popular religion; on the contrary, I am chastising the superficiality of lived religions and of religious organizations in particular.

I may put it in a more academic and positive way. Is it not true that under one excuse or another we have neglected the depths and basic intuitions of our respective religious traditions and succumbed to religious consumerism and religious banalities? I am not saying that every human being is already a mystic or a saint. I am defending the view that the primal task of religion is to help us become aware of the unfathomable depths of our own being and of life in general, to make us conscious of who we are. I am not making things complicated. On the contrary, I am affirming that the fundamental things of life are precisely the most elemental ones. In a word, religions should again and again be converted into cultivating the precious and simple gift which has been entrusted to them, letting all other accidentals fall by the wayside. Religions are not clubs for entertainment.

2. The second meaning of *metanoia* is *change of mentality*. This change of mind is imperative in our times. If religions are not to be mere antique bastions of a deceased past, if they are not to become obsolete ideologies or museum pieces, or just the specialty of a selected few, they have to undergo a radical change of mind. There is no time now for mere reforms or good intentions, for merely regretting the past and promising that now we are going to do better, being again deceived by the mirage of the future. We need a radical conversion. Let us not forget that the common sense of the people shows a drifting away from established religions, except for the fundamentalist reactions mentioned before.[4] To say it in popular language: we need to put our own house in order before saying anything about peace in the world.

I shall mention only two points: change of mind both *vis-à-vis other religions* and *vis-à-vis the very meaning of religion itself.*

a) With different degrees of tolerance religions have, by and large, considered the outsider as a pagan, infidel, *goi, mleccha, kafir,* barbarian, undeveloped, primitive, and what not.

Along with historical and political reasons, there is a hermeneutical flaw which we clearly detect in our times of cross-cultural movements. By and large we have interpreted other religions with our own categories which are foreign to the other religions. We have misinterpreted the other. We have used often unconsciously, and thus unavoidably, a double standard: one from within to understand ourselves, and another from without to understand the other. And thus we have not reached the self-understanding of the other. In a word, we have interpreted the other as other, while the other does not see itself as other but as self.

The first task here consists in *dispelling misunderstandings.* And these are endemic, even among scholars. We go on calling many African religions polytheist only because we apply a Semitic idea of theism, ignoring that the so-called polytheists never have believed that they worship a plurality of the *theoi* of the theistic *theos.* We call nonbelievers those who do not believe the God of the cluster of religions prevalent today. Many a Muslim theologian calls the Christian a tritheist, and Christian scholars call Jainism and Buddhism atheistic, and Confucianism a philosophy, extrapolating illegitimately their own understandings of the Absolute and of philosophy. Most Hindu books on Christianity are generally appalling, and most Christian books on Hinduism insulting, and all the more when they are written in goodwill and sympathy. The Marxist idea of religion is a caricature of the worst specimen of European Christianity of over a century ago; and I could multiply the examples. In short, we have a distorted idea of the other; we do not follow what I have termed the golden rule of hermeneutics, which says that no interpretation is correct if the interpreted does not recognize itself in the interpretation.

This is my second point: *to understand the other.* But this is not an easy task. Without expanding here my thesis that understanding amounts to being convinced, I may only say that unless I somewhat share in the self-understanding of the other I will not understand the other. Unless I believe somewhat in the truth of what the other believes, I will not understand the truth that the other believes but will make a caricature of the other's beliefs. Only truth is intelligible. If I do not take something to be true I will not truly understand it. This has led me also to propose the *pisteuma* in religious phenomenology over against the *noema* of an exclusively rational philosophy. Entrenched in our respective religious fortresses we are unable to understand the other, that is, to stand-under the spell of the thing so understood. This is why without love no really personal understanding is possible.

This leads us to a third step: the necessary *dialogical dialogue* for understanding both our religion and the religion of the neighbor. This type of dialogue is not a device to get the others on our side, to win them over. It is a genuine religious activity, and an essential requisite for peace. In point of fact any breach of peace begins with the breaking of dialogue.

Without religious peace it is unrealistic to think of peace on earth; also on the political level. Only with a religious peace shall we arrive at a mutual fecundation of the different religious traditions of the world, not to become one single religion, but to be mutually enriched and stimulated. We all need such an external challenge in order to perfect our inner self.

Let me suggest some examples of such a fecundation. They are nothing but a reawakening of the inner riches of the respective traditions, which need the challenge from the outside.

It is from the incentive of Asian religions that Christianity may rediscover and perfect its own mystical core. It is from the influence of Christianity that Hinduism may find in its own tradition an urge for a greater social concern; it is from the Jaina impulse to nonviolence that many a religion may reinterpret in a more effective way the general injunction of nonkilling; it is from the example of the primordial religions that the so-pompously-called "great" religions may begin to rediscover and reinterpret the deep and constitutive link of the human being with Nature. Or, giving more doctrinal examples: love your neighbor as yourself does not mean love the other as another self, but as your own self. Follow your *svadharma* does not imply that you should not be concerned with the *dharma* of the neighbor. Do not desire *nirvana* does not need to entail sheer passivity or killing the human aspiration towards perfection. *Karma* does not need to deny human freedom, nor does predestination for that matter mean fatalism. *Islam* does not mean blind surrender, nor is original sin an excuse for accepting sinful structures, nor does eschatology need to mean putting all the cards on the final acts of humans or of history, nor does praying to God exclude praying to Nature, nor does the reign of God in politics amount to a defense of theocracy, and so on. We should learn from one another—I mentioned humility at the beginning.

b) The change of mind applies not only to our vision of the others. It applies also to a fundamental conversion of the very notion of religion itself. All too often many religions have been so worried with the supernatural, the atemporal, the *paramârtha,* that they have neglected the natural, the temporal, the *vyavahâra.* The result has been to make religion irrelevant for temporal life, and politics a mere strategy for choosing the best means to maintain uncritically the status quo. When the world at large is undergoing a radical change, religions cannot be insensitive to such a mutation. They can no longer live in ghettoes or apartheids. Today's healthy separation between church and state does not mean a dichotomy between religion and life. But for this, religions have to acknowledge the urgency of a genuine *metanoia,* a real transformation of the very notion of religion.

The transformation I am envisaging goes deeper than a mere reform, and deeper also than the mutual fecundation and stimulation described above. It is a passage from religion to religiousness, which in the Christian tradition I have termed a passage from Christianity to Christianness.

I consider the technocratic complex of today's prevalent and dominating cosmology nefarious for the human race, beginning with the epistemological fallacy of modern science which has made us believe that the main concern and task of human intelligence is measuring and drawing so-called logical conclusions. And yet, not all is wrong with techno-science; thus, a substitution by another totalitarian ideology would be equally unsatisfactory. As Tagore put it, "True goodness is not the negation of badness, it is the mastery of it."[5]

The most positive lasting effect of what we may call the European "Enlightenment" is the slowly permeating conviction of the everlasting value of *secularity,* that is, of the definitive—and not just provisional, or worse, illusory or diabolic—character of the *saeculum. Saeculum* is the spatio-temporal and thus material dimension of reality, which has often been translated as "world." By and large, modern religions (prophetic and mystical exceptions confirming the general rule) have neglected, to say the least, the cultivation of the world, the secular dimension of human life and of reality as a whole.

To come to our point: peace is not only the peace of the soul, the bliss of heaven, or the eschatological happy end to all things. Peace is also a political reality, a secular concept; it has a socio-economic aspect, and so on. Religions cannot disconnect this aspect from the everlasting peace they, until now, were mainly concerned with. They have to contribute to secular peace not out of condescension or because of the urgency of the situation, but because this question is also an essential religious concern.

Earlier I used the term *sacred secularity,* but I could equally have said *secular sacredness,* not to reduce the task of religions to a mere adjectival activity. What I mean is this: The sacred, with whatever name we may express it, is a constitutive dimension of reality and an essential character of the human being. Humans are *homo religiosus,* runs a consecrated phrase. Secularism, as distinct from secularity, is antinatural and antihuman: it denies transcendence and becomes an ideology which pretends to organize life by means of rationally planned structures. A mere socio-economic peace is not only impossible; it would not be peace at all. Human life is sacred, and so is society, and so is the world, the *saeculum,* and reality.

Transcendence cannot, does not, exist alone—that is, without immanence; but transcendence is that dimension of freedom and infinity which is inherent in any being. Transcendence being not only ungraspable, but also infinite, makes possible an immense variety of religious experiences and interpretations. I am not reducing religions to a single and vague religiosity. The different religious traditions of the world have here a place and a task. I am going to return to it, but, first, we have to spell out a little more this transformation, namely, *metanoia,* of religion.

To put it bluntly: religions do not have a monopoly on religion. And this applies not only to any religion, but to the ensemble of the so-called religions, all put together. Who draws the dividing line between systems of belief which, although not called religions, inspire and lead people to consecrate their lives to them, and some forms of established and recognized religions to which people often pay only lip service? Humanism, Marxism, nationalism, scientism, or even hedonism may be as much religions as the better established forms of religion. I have to add immediately that to say religion does not automatically mean a good thing. Fascism, Nazism, and even racism can be lived as religions, albeit diabolical or false. Another thesis which I cannot develop here is that the very notion of religion is constitutively ambivalent. Where there is heaven there is also hell. It is wrong on the part of religions to accept credit for the good side of the human being

and not take responsibility for the bad side of the human being. In this
sense the dialogue of religions and the involvement of religions in the
world is not reduced to the lofty side of human activity. We are all engaged in the same human adventure.

We have, for too long, identified religion with the established re-
ligiosities of religious bodies. These latter are rather political bodies,
and rightly so, which have been disengaged from the main political
body of society, creating in this way the dichotomy from which we
suffer. But religion cannot be reduced to organized religion, nor is a
living organism of religious nature identical with a more or less well-
established organization. An organism has a living soul and an inner
hierarchical order. An organization has a constitution, a board of directors, and needs a police, often called policy. There is more to reality
than what we can control, and this leads us to our third meaning.

3. The third meaning of *metanoia* stands for *overcoming the
mental.* If the first etymological sense of the word is *meta-noein,*
"after-thinking," "afterthoughts" that make us repent and change our
previous mind, the *meta-nous* may also suggest transcending the
mind, going beyond the mental—not reducing humanness to a mere
res cogitans, to quote the father of modern Western philosophy. We
are more than mere reason—certainly not less—as the Jaina *kevalin,*
the Buddhist bodhisattva, the Hindu yogi, and the mystics of most traditions will remind us. Since the "Enlightenment," modern human
beings are reduced to thinking machines, and thought mainly lessened
to calculations and drawing conclusions. All the rest is looked down
upon as merely accidental to human life.

There are three aspects of this meaning of *metanoia.*

a) The philosophical aspect.

With their unconfessed, often unconscious, complex of inferi-
ority vis-à-vis scientific modernity, most religions have repressed the
mystical dimension of the human being, or, paying tribute to the same
modernity, have reserved it for a selected and specialized elite, the so-
called mystics, thus accepting a truncated anthropology as if humankind were just an animal endowed with some material and a few intellectual needs. And the reactions to the opposite extreme of some
religious fundamentalist movements of today are also instances of the
same complex.

Overcoming the mental does not necessarily imply belief in ontological transcendence, acceptance of psychologically paranormal states of consciousness, or religious supernaturalism. It means to ascertain the anthropological urge for more and better, the human openness to the unknown, and the awareness that we are un-finished, that is, in-finite, beings; that human nature is not a perfect, finished, finite thing. Animals suffer and may be unhappy. In humans there is an awareness of the Mystery—awareness that there may be something unintelligible and thus also awareness of the possibility of an unfulfilled life, however we may interpret or repress this sentiment. There is a mystical kernel in every human being, a sense of mystery, and a symbolic awareness which is not identical with intelligibility. But this third eye, third dimension, mystical experience, sense of the unknowable, realization of *sûnyatâ*, *vidyâ*, *anubhava*, or whatever name we may call it, is not separable from the intellect and the senses; it is not a specialty; it cannot be isolated; it has to function in symbiosis with the rest of all our human faculties. Religions, which have been traditionally the reminders of such a sphere of the real, should undertake the task of reincorporating this dimension in ordinary human life, not by juxtaposition or domination of one dimension over the other, but in a nondualistic way.

Only then shall we overcome the constant temptation of religions to absolutize their tenets. I would put it like this: in the distinction between means and ends, religions should relativize the means and deabsolutize the ends.

The relativization of the means amounts to saying that all the wonderful means that religious traditions have excogitated or believed they have received by divine revelation are related to the particular individuals for whom the means are means; thus they are related to concrete situations. Relativism, which stands in contradiction with itself, is not relativity, which is what I defend. The five pillars of Islam, the Christian sacraments, the bodhisattva vows, the dharmic precepts, the injunctions of the Torah, and the like, are wonderful, excellent, and valid means to reach the end of life, but no particular ritual or set of means can claim exclusivity and absoluteness.

Similarly concerning the ends: the end of human life can be expressed only in a myth, not in a doctrine. The doctrine describes the moon we see reflected on the pond. The myth tells us that there is a moon in the sky. Within a given and accepted myth I may say heaven, *mukti, nirvana,* beatific vision, annihilation, contribution to the future, justice, happy life, or whatever. And from our particular doctrinal contexts we may criticize other texts within the same context, but we should not unduly extrapolate a text outside its context. The real end of life can only be expressed mythically, and myths are not susceptible to any possible hermeneutic because they are the horizons which make any hermeneutic possible.

This double task of discovering the relativity of means and ends is only plausible if we do not stifle the mystical dimension of humanity, if we do not deny the reality of the ineffable and have undergone the experience of our human contingency.

b. The contemplative aspect.

To transcend the mind does not mean to fall into irrationalism or to indulge in anarchy. It entails becoming aware of what we may call the mystery, the unknown, the infinite, the divinity, or the like. It implies that we discover, surmise, accept, experience, believe, reckon with, or simply make room for what we call the sacred. I have made a spirited defense of secularity, but I qualified it by adding *sacred* secularity. I shall not linger in describing the sacred. I shall only make a comment which I consider paramount.

Whatever word we may prefer according to different tastes, cultures, and religions, one thing is common to this most essential role of religions: this is the ultimate meaning of *metanoia.*

It is not an important book which will save the world, not a profound idea either which will bring peace to the world. If humans are the problem, humans are also the solution—but not a reductionist notion of the human, not reason alone, not mere sentiment, not a wonderful praxis nor a flawless theory, but the fullness of all our being. This fullness entails what we may call the cosmic and the divine. Humanity is not alone, not an island, not even a continent. We need the sky. Humanity is a *mesocosmos,* the converging point of all spheres of reality. We need therefore the human incarnation, the human person (which we sometimes wrongly call the human factor), the total personification, in some of us at least, in the saint, if this is the word we choose.

This is a delicate subject. It is almost a taboo in certain circles, and often also in religious circles: to speak about the existential factor,

the personal dimension, the total engagement, the consecration to
stand for what we say, and to believe in what we do. Without this
commitment, not to a party line, not to a particular religion or to religion, but to that Reality which we call by so many different names;
without that harmony in our being, between what we say, think, and
act, all our efforts are exercises in futility.

I may quote from a triple source, and I could cite the same experience from other traditions. A Jewish psalm (45:5), in its Greek and
Latin version (44.4), later changed in modern translation, unites intrinsically truth, gentleness, and justice.[6] It stresses the mediator role
of that *prautês* which the Latin renders as *mansuetudo,* and which
probably is the positive word for *ahimsa,* nonviolence (the German
Sanft-mut being perhaps an approximate translation). In a word, there
is no truth without justice and no justice without truth, but the pair is
totally ineffective without the essential mediator role of the subjective
and personal factor of friendliness, *Gelassenheit,* piety (in the classical
sense). It is the same word of the Gospels: "Blessed are the nonviolent"; "Learn from me that I am *praüs* (gently firm, friendly, strong,
nonviolently enduring, *gelassen, saftmütig*), said Jesus. I quote now
the present Dalai Lama (in a published interview in the *India International Centre Quarterly*). After citing a Tibetan saying that "many
illnesses can be cured by one medicine: love and compassion," he
adds that "their practice in public life is typically thought of as impractical, even naive." His Holiness unambiguously affirms: "This is
tragic." And he goes on to state: "Whether a conflict lies in the field of
politics, business, or religion, an altruistic approach is frequently the
sole means of solving it. Often, the very concepts we employ to medi-
ate a dispute are themselves the cause of the problem." And we use
those concepts because we try to protect ourselves in sheer objectivity,
making dehumanizing claims to truth or shielding ourselves in an
equally objectified and impersonal justice which is not human. If religions renounce their most precious gift, which is their call to perfection, sanctification, realization, happiness, salvation, divinization,
fulfillment, or the like—if they renounce the ideal of sanctity, what
are they worth?

I am not saying that a disconnected—or worse, an unenlightened—sanctity is the solution. I am affirming that sanctity is a powerful and indispensable factor. Contemplation is more than theory, and
more than praxis. It is the personal and active incarnation of the ideal

in the individual: the contribution of religions to the culture of peace. And those who are minimally engaged in such a task know by bitter, but equally purifying, experience how difficult it is! Peace is not a thing, not an object, not a substance, not a ready-made solution; peace is always dynamic, always imperfect, on the way, elusive, provisional—but real, effective, powerful, attractive, and inspiring.

c. The metapolitical aspect.

We are reminded of the needed fearlessness for any fruitful action in the world. But a fearless attitude is not a matter of will power. It is the automatic fruit of purity of heart. And in fact, most religious traditions insist that this purity is the first condition for right action and a fruitful life.

I consider three practical aspects as essentially religious. They are religious problems and religions should have the courage to address these burning issues as religious issues and not only political or social problems. We should learn an important lesson from history. Most religions and religious reforms began as revolutionary and upsetting movements. Should I recall the life of the Prophet? The beginning of the Baha'i religion? The spread of Buddhism in China? Luther? Marx? But soon they not only became docile to the status quo; they became subsidiary to it.

Religions appear sectarian, not only in the eyes of the world in general but in the minds of religionists in particular. The proof is the way in which religious education is taught. Hardly anybody objects to the teachings of modern science. Voices are sometimes raised against a certain bias in teaching philosophy or history, but, by and large, they are also accepted as universal subject matters belonging to the education of the human person. Artistic education, even if neglected, does not raise objections regarding its universal character. Not so with religion. If we want to have something apparently universal, we have to turn to moral education, which severed from religion remains without foundation. If religious people themselves have a sectarian view of their own religion, although crudely justified by defending that theirs is the best, the true, or even the absolute religion, we cannot expect a lasting contribution to the culture of peace.

I am not propounding a diluted and amorphous form of religion. I am proposing the awareness of the transcendental relationship of every religion with religiousness, just as any human being has a transcendental relationship with being human and cannot claim that the only, or even the best, form of humanity is to be male, white, rich, educated, Chinese-speaking, or whatever. Each one of us is unique and, thus, possesses an incomparable way of realizing the *humanum*. But in order to be effectively aware of the uniqueness of anything we have to enter into a personal and loving relationship with that particular being. It is for this reason that I sustain academically that true "comparative religion" is not possible.

How could we teach Islam, Judaism, or any religion, expounding the full and enthusiastic view of that religion, without hurting the others and excluding them altogether from the particular description? How can a mother extol the exploits, goodness, and intelligence of her own children without devaluing others? What of the dialogical dialogue? Could the different religious authorities of the planet not come together and devise policies, textbooks, and studies in this direction? Do they not realize the scandal and lack of credibility that religious education represents in the world today?

But we do not have authentic religious education. Instead we have instruction about one particular religion. The religious institutions have uncritically accepted the current antihumanistic view of education—that is, the preparation of the masses to become useful nuts and bolts of the technocratic megamachinery. Real education is for the human being, and authentic religious education is something more than information about a religious ideology. This is more than the insight that in order to know my religion I have to know the religion of my neighbor. It is also the experience that religious education is more than information, and more than providing the faithful with the skills to reach *nirvana,* go to paradise, become the perfect noble person, or the like. I have to know well my part if I want to sing in a choir or play in a symphony.

To teach religion is both to show how to sing in one voice or play one instrument and also to educate the taste to enjoy the entire choir, the complete symphony. This does not suffocate our respective melodies but enhances the beauty of the whole. We should neither confuse the voices nor reduce all of them to our tune. This is pluralism.

Religious education is certainly also the teaching of religion. It is much more than this, but it is also this: teaching religiousness.

The essentials of the religious teachings could be summed up in three ideas: the relinking of oneself with the rest of human beings, with our neighbors, with the community, with our true self; the relinking of humankind with Nature, with all things, with the environment, including machines; the relinking of humanity with the Divine, with Mystery, the Sacred, the Numinous, the Absolute, Transcendence.

Each time, the language should be the most general possible (in order to make sense to different people) and the most concrete possible in order to dwell in the particular linguistic sphere of the respective traditions. A Christian will therefore speak of Christ present in everybody, of the sacredness of creation, and of the Trinity. A Hindu will therefore speak of karma as universal solidarity, of our being part of the entire cosmic process, and of all existence pervaded by the Divine, and so on.

Today all the most important problems for humanity are religious in nature. The technological problem is not a question of engineering, and much less of human engineering. It is an ultimate human problem. And the same could be said regarding armaments, economics, justice, human rights, and so on. All of these issues concern the very dignity of the person and the future of humankind, like the ecological question. All of them overstep national sovereignties and merely political measures. The answer lies not in increasing food, having more powerful arms than the "enemy," finding more effective antipollutants, or setting more money in circulation. They require the literal solving of the problems, the dissolving of them, the *radical* approach by which the fruits will no longer be poisonous because the roots are healthy. These problems of humanity today, precisely because they touch ultimate issues, are religious questions.

NOTES

1. Raimon Panikkar, "Epistula de Pace," Response to *Philosophia pacis, Homenaje a Raimon Panikkar* (Madrid: Símbolo editorial, 1989).

2. Rabindranath Tagore, *Lectures and Addresses* (Delhi: Macmillan, 1980), p. 17.

3. Bede Griffiths, in a paper written in Shantivanam, April 1991. Meanwhile, Father Bede passed away in 1993, at the age of 86.

4. I recently performed a baptism in a parish church of Badalona (near Barcelona). Of the 40,000 people of the parish, not more than 200 attend services more or less regularly. One half of one percent of the population in "Catholic Spain"!

5. Rabindranath Tagore, *Creative Unity*, p. 123.

6. "propter veritatem et mansuetudinem et iustitiam."

Author Index

Aitken, Robert, 171, 172
Arendt, Hannah, 4, 32, 34, 37
Ash, Timothy Garton, 44

Bellah, Robert, 136
Benedict, Saint, 190
Berry, Wendell, 166
Brown, Judith, 147, 157
Buddhadasa, 168

Cahoone, Lawrence, 34–35
Calvin, John, 94, 96
Camus, Albert, 60
Carson, Rachel, 166, 172
Carter, Stephen, 2, 6
Chatterjee, Margaret, 146
Clayton, John, 7, 13, 104–27
Crevecoeur, Hector St. John, 130

Dalai Lama, 168, 172, 180, 200
Daly, Cardinal Cahal, 37–39
Darwall, Stephen, 7, 13, 85–103
Davidson, Donald, 9, 134
Descartes, René, 110
Devall, Bill, 171, 175

Elshtain, Jean Bethke, 3, 4, 5,
    12–13, 32–47, 134
Emerson, Ralph Waldo, 172
Erasmus, Desiderius, 94

Fischer, Louis, 146
Friedlander, Albert, 21–22
Frost, Robert, 126

Galston, William, 134
Gandhi, Mohandas, 9, 70, 145–64
Gould, James, 158
Griffiths, Bede, 191–92
Griswold, Charles, 107

Habito, Reuben, 170
Harris, Ian, 11, 169
Hauerwas, Stanley, 136
Hick, John, 9–10, 11, 13, 145–64
Hobbes, 85–86, 93, 99, 101–2
Hunter, James Davison, 131–34,
    135, 137

Ignacio de Loyola, 190

Jefferson, Thomas, 106–9, 123–24
Jones, L. Gregory, 33

Kaza, Stephanie, 9, 10–11, 13,
    165–84
Kellert, Stephen, 170

Leopold, Aldo, 172
Lindbeck, George, 136
Locke, John, 94, 123–24
Loori, John Daido, 172, 175
Lull, Raymond, 7, 100–101
Luther, Martin, 94, 201

MacIntyre, Alasdair, 96, 131,
    133–34, 135, 136
Macy, Joanna, 173, 175
Mill, John Stuart, 98

Mitscherlich, Alexander, 23
Mitscherlich, Margarete, 23
Moltmann, Jürgen, 3–4, 5, 12–13, 17–31
Muir, John, 166, 172

Nagarjuna, 169, 190
Nhat Hanh, Thich, 168, 172
Niebuhr, Reinhold, 2–3, 6, 11, 13

Panikkar, Raimon, 9, 11–12, 13, 185–204
Parekh, Bhikhu, 6, 13, 63–84
Pufendorf, Samuel, 90, 94

Rawls, John, 75, 86
Rescher, Nicholas, 139
Rouner, Leroy S., 1–13
Roy, Ranjit Kumar, 160

Schlesinger, Arthur, Jr., 8, 129
Schumacher, E. F., 158–59
Sessions, George, 171

Sivaraksa, Sulak, 170, 174
Smith, Adam, 107–8, 109, 119
Snyder, Gary, 166, 171, 173, 175, 180, 181–82
Sponberg, Alan, 170
Stout, Jeffrey, 134, 135
Suarez, Francisco, 94
Szerszynski, Bronislaw, 172

Tagore, Rabindranath, 185
Taylor, Bron, 172
Taylor, Charles, 134
Thiemann, Ronald, 8–9, 13, 128–42
Thomas Aquinas, 76, 93, 94
Thoreau, Henry David, 166, 172

Villa-Vicencio, Charles, 42–43
Voltaire, 99

Walzer, Michael, 134
Washington, George, 1
Wiesel, Elie, 3, 5, 11, 12–13, 48–60

Subject Index

abortion, 71, 75–76, 128, 133
ahimsa, 9, 150, 153–55, 158, 160, 168, 200
animals, 16, 64, 168, 169, 177, 179, 198
awe, 90–91

Baha'i, 188, 201
Boston University, 51, 111
Brahmanic thought, 116, 118
Buddhism, 6, 11, 12, 112, 116, 118, 119–21, 161, 166–84, 185, 188, 189–90, 191, 197, 198, 201

Carvaka, 118, 120
castes, 151–52
Christianity, 9, 18–19, 20, 26–27, 28–29, 33, 68, 81, 100, 114, 134, 137, 140–41, 160, 168, 171, 193, 194, 195, 198
Christians, 3, 6, 68, 75, 86, 99–100, 112, 117–18, 136, 161, 181, 188, 203
colonialism, 125, 155
Communism, 5, 24–27, 29, 50, 51–53, 68, 69, 191
compassion, 60, 74, 153, 168, 200
conservatism, 74, 104
Constitution, United States, 105
culture wars, 104–5, 107, 111, 113, 128–42
Czechoslovakia, 27, 40–41

democracies, 9, 17, 24, 28, 43, 45–46, 104, 130, 131, 134, 136, 138, 140–41
despair, 48, 51, 57, 58, 60

ecology, 9, 10–11, 158–59, 161, 166–84, 203

feminism, 10, 35–36, 159–60, 161
forgiveness, 4, 17, 28–29, 32–47, 191
freedom, 7, 19, 59, 139, 150–51, 155, 157

gay/lesbian rights, 128, 131–33, 177
Germany, 3, 10, 17–27, 29, 40–41, 50, 53, 77
God, 1, 6, 7, 35, 48, 49, 51–52, 53–56, 59, 60, 65, 67, 81, 82, 86, 87, 90, 93–96, 101, 110, 136, 137–38, 140–41, 149, 150, 152, 154, 161, 186, 187, 189, 194
Great Britain, 3, 6, 8, 18, 37–39, 67, 77, 86, 104
Green Gulch Zen Center, 175–76, 179
Green movement, 67, 158

Hasidism, 50, 54–55, 56, 60
Hinduism, 6, 9, 12, 111, 112, 151–53, 161, 185, 188, 191, 193, 194, 197, 203
Holocaust, 13, 21, 36, 53, 55, 57, 59

hope, 5–6, 13, 29, 48–60, 136, 141
human rights, 4, 17, 18, 27–28, 43, 65, 67, 70, 121–25, 203
humility, 187, 192

India, 10, 166, 169, 171, 180–81
interdependence, 167, 173, 180
Islam, 6, 81–82, 100, 114–15, 160, 198, 202
Israel, 21, 29, 50, 54, 55, 59, 105

Jainism, 9, 116, 118, 151, 153, 161, 191, 193, 194, 197
Japan, 166, 169–70
Jews, 18–22, 37, 40, 52, 53–56, 57–58, 59–60, 86, 89, 96, 99–100, 117, 181, 191
John Paul II (pope), 33, 39
joy, 48, 55
Judaism, 100, 168, 188, 202
justice, 4, 29–30, 36, 42, 44–45, 65, 67, 68, 70, 186, 189, 199, 200, 203

King, Martin Luther, Jr., 75, 139

liberalism, 2, 6, 13, 63–64, 66, 67, 69, 70, 72, 73–75, 76, 79, 98, 104–11, 113–14, 119, 126, 136
Lincoln, Abraham, 139
love, 3, 9, 12, 42, 57, 65, 76, 136, 141, 146, 148, 149, 154, 155, 157, 158, 168, 194

Mandela, Nelson, 50, 156, 158
market place, 68, 99, 106, 108–9
Marxism, 74, 188, 193, 196
Mimamsa, 120
Mishna, 49–50
moksha, 148
morality, 1, 3, 49, 71–72, 80, 87, 131–36, 174
Muhammad, 82, 115, 201
multiculturalism, 129
Muslims, 89, 99–100, 111, 112, 114–15, 117–18, 161, 191, 193

natural law, 76
nature, 165–84, 194, 203
Nazism, 19–22, 37, 41, 50, 69, 153, 196
nonviolence, 9, 146–47, 149, 153–55, 156, 158, 161, 168, 200
Northern Ireland, 37–39, 51

Palestinians, 105
Pandora, 60
pluralism, 6, 130, 135–37, 139–40, 202
Poland, 22, 27, 29, 39, 50, 53, 178
prayer, 19, 24, 59–60
privatization, 107–8
Protestants, 6, 8, 20, 22, 37–39, 86, 94–96, 110–11, 132

Quakers, 153
Qur'an, 82, 115, 117

reason, 11, 63–64, 100–101, 107, 109–11, 113–14, 119, 121, 125
reconciliation, 17–31, 32–47, 136
relativism, 124, 139, 198
religious toleration, 6–7, 86–89, 93–102
respect, 8, 9, 64, 71, 73, 74, 79, 81, 83, 89–93, 99, 101, 130
Roman Catholicism, 12, 22, 37–39, 68, 71, 75–77, 86, 94–96, 111, 132, 185, 191–92

Samkhya, 120
satyagraha, 146, 147, 154, 160
secular concerns, 12, 63–66, 74, 77, 79–80, 185, 190, 195–96, 199
secularization, 7, 13, 67, 104, 107
Shinto, 112
Sikhs, 188
Sisyphus, 60
slavery, 36, 123–24, 130
South Africa, 4, 42–46
swaraj, 150–51, 155, 157

Talmud, 48, 49, 56
Thailand, 166, 168, 169, 174–75, 177
Tibet, 170–71, 175, 178
Torah, 5, 55, 198
truth, 1, 12, 19, 23, 26, 29, 30, 33, 42–43, 50, 51, 69, 100, 139, 145, 147, 148, 149–50, 154, 193, 200
Tutu, Archbishop Desmond, 44, 45

United States, 1, 6, 8–9, 128–30, 136, 171, 175, 178

vada, 116, 118, 121
Vedanta, 9, 120, 152
violence, 18, 33, 36, 43, 97, 154–55, 157–58
virtue, 107

Yoga, 120